From my seat as a mediator, I have seen litigation win cases at the cost of ongoing conflict and burned-out lawyers. Family Lawyer as Peacemaker *offers an alternative to the adversarial norm by redefining what zealous advocacy can mean as collaboration toward resolution. Woody Mosten, Lara Traum, and top peacemakers are leading systemic change through healthier conversations, a change that is transforming how many of us work with families in conflict.*

Matthew Carroll
Mediator, Adjunct Faculty, Northwestern University and Aurora University,
President, Indiana Association of Mediators

Family Lawyer as Peacemaker *offers a road map for lawyers to help parties be constructive problem solvers. This fabulous book overflows with practical advice to guide lawyers to shape a rewarding and fulfilling career as a peacemaking problem solvers.*

William J. Howe, III
Former Partner Gevurtz Menache, Portland, OR

Family Lawyer as Peacemaker *offers a transformative vision for legal practice—guiding both families and professionals through conflict with empathy, collaboration, healing, and justice. Drawing on real-world experience, innovative strategies, and timeless values, Forrest S. Mosten and Lara Traum show how lawyers and other professionals can become catalysts for lasting peace, at home and beyond.*

Anthony D. Storm, CFLS
Storm Palyan LLP, President Beverly Hills Bar Association (2025–2026)
Century City, CA

Family law disputes—deeply personal and often painful—especially need the wisdom and hope that peacemaking offers. Woody Mosten has devoted his entire career to advancing this mission, and this powerful book with Lara Traum shows how lawyers can support healing. It both validates the deep personal commitment of those who already serve as peacemakers and inspires others to follow their lead.

John Lande
Isidor Loeb Professor Emeritus, University of Missouri School of Law
Columbia, MO

This book masterfully guides lawyers on a transformative journey, first inward to cultivate the self-awareness and mindset of a peacemaker, then outward to restructure their services and master the practical tools of dialogue and conflict prevention. This is the essential guide for any lawyer ready to practice with greater integrity, compassion, and purpose.

Susan Guthrie
Family Law Attorney, mediator and author of "The Practice Playbook Book Series,"
Chair of the ABA Section of Dispute Resolution
Chicago, IL

Many peacemakers do their work in rarefied environments with diplomats and heads of state and the like. But families might be just as or even more tricky parties to conflicts—and more often than not, no one emerges a "winner." A skilled mediator, negotiator or, more formally, peacemaker can be a godsend in the highly emotional context of a pitched family battle. This is a book that can guide and inspire the aspiring peacemaker because at the end of the day peace starts at home.

Abigail E. Disney, filmmaker, writer, philanthropist, and activist
New York City

AF898108

Family Lawyer as Peacemaker *demonstrates that peacemaking is a vital component of family law practice. Woody Mosten, Lara Traum, and their contributors illustrate how our work can guide families towards peaceful processes and outcomes.*

Shawn Weber
CLS-F, Lead Mediator and Trainer at Weber Dispute Resolution

Family Lawyer as Peacemaker *reimagines the lawyer's role not as warrior, but as healer, guide, and peacemaker. Every family law professional—whether attorney, mediator, mental health professional, or policymaker—should read this book. It will change not only how you practice, but why you practice.*

Patricia Van Haren

While "lawyer" and "peacemaker" may sound like an unlikely pairing, Forrest Mosten and Lara Traum show how the two can—and must—go hand in hand. This book offers a compelling vision of lawyers as guides who help families navigate conflict with clarity, compassion, and purpose. Blending personal stories, practical tools, and case strategies with systemic insights, it provides an invaluable roadmap for professionals committed to transforming family law into a peace-centered practice.

Nancy Ross, LCSW, BCD

A treasure trove of wisdom, innovative peacemaking expertise, and helpful practice building tools from family law peacemaker luminaries, this book is a must-read for every family lawyer, mental health practitioner, and financial professional who helps families navigating some of life's most turbulent waters.

Dr. Carol Hughes
Psychotherapist, co-author of *Home Will Never Be the Same Again: A Guide for Adult Children of Gray Divorce*
Laguna Niguel, CA

In collaborative practice and the wider peacemaking movement, much of our energy rightly goes into building and working within a like-minded professional community. In this inspiring collection, Woody and Lara bring together thought-provoking and insightful contributions that empower each individual practitioner—wherever they are in the world and whatever their role—to be impactful peacemakers. A resource to return to time and again!

Selina-jane Trigg, Lawyer
Christchurch, New Zealand

This book is a thorough and extensive work to help practicing attorneys shift their understanding of "doing law." It describes how to move from an adversarial"win for your client" mindset to a more compassionate, humane relationship with clients on both sides. It addresses the individual practitioner as well as a corresponding retooling of the entire judicial system. It provides a superior vehicle for helping attorneys to find a much more fulfilling and meaningful way to do their professional lives.

The Rev. Dr. John W. Heister
Founding President, New York State Council on Divorce Mediation
Rochester, NY

Drawing on wisdom from the leading voices in mediation and collaborative law, this book offers both inspiration and a practical roadmap for lawyers ready to expand their role beyond advocacy into true peacemaking. Whether you are a seasoned practitioner or just beginning your journey, this book will change the way you see your work and the impact it can have on families and communities.

Robyn Weinstein
Director, Cardozo Mediation Clinic
Associate Director, Kukin Program for Conflict Resolution

Family Lawyer as Peacemaker

Forrest S. Mosten and Lara Traum

AMERICAN BAR ASSOCIATION
Family Law Section

Cover design by Sara Wadford/ABA Design

Printed in the United States of America.

30 29 28 27 26   5 4 3 2 1

ISBN 978-1-63905-714-6

Dedications

This book is dedicated to my grandchildren for whom I wish peace and happiness as they encounter our uncertain world. Love forever, Grandpa.

~Woody

For my grandparents, great-grandparents, and all the ancestors who walked through uncertain worlds and still found courage to create, to dream, and to carry the light within. This book is born of their strength.

~Lara

Contents

The following appendixes can be found at www.americanbar.org.

Acknowledgments

We wish to recognize those whose work inspired this book and whose help in our efforts has been invaluable.

Professor Louis M. Brown (1909–1996) Father of preventive law who invented the field and was mentor and friend to Woody Mosten for over 35 years.

David Hoffman A pioneer in internal family systems, implicit bias, mediation, collaborative law, and peacemaking with his groundbreaking book *Bringing Peace into the Room* (co-authored with Daniel Bowling (1943–2024)).

Dr. Constance Ahrons (1937–2021) She destigmatized divorce through her research and books, *The Good Divorce* and *We Are Still Family.*

Professor Lela Love Modeled peacemaking and contributed to the field through her book *Stories Mediators Tell* and was an invaluable mentor to Lara Traum.

Professor Robert K. Collins Teaches functional empathy in practice, proactively focusing on empowering divorcing families through logic and humor.

Michael Lang Building on the work of Donald A. Schön's, *The Reflective Practitioner*, his book *The Making of a Mediator* and interventions of reflective practice changed our field.

Rabbi Jeff Marx His inspiration as a teacher and belief in proactive requests for forgiveness led to the Peacemaker Pledge.

Maestro Matthew Lazar Brings peace and truth through music and choral conducting, modeling balance and harmony with countless voices in the room.

Kevin Scudder (1960–2023), Brian Galbraith, and Adam Cordover Led the peacemaker movement for collaborative professionals at the International Academy of Collaborative Professionals.

Professor David Binder (1934–2020) Lead author of *Lawyer as Counselor* (with Paul Bergman and Paul Boland) and mentor to Forrest Mosten throughout his career.

Jeffrey Salyards, Lori Nelson, Frieda Gordon, and Barbara Kahn Stark and **ABA Family Section Publication Board** Their unfailing support since 1994 have been responsible for the authors home for our writing at the ABA.

Dr. Jody Mosten Life partner, Rasputin, Beacon for Forrest Mosten.

Alla Roytberg Mother, Best Friend, Work Partner, and Co-Everything for Lara Traum.

We wish to acknowledge each of our guest authors, whose insightful contributions have elevated this book and helped establish it as a foundational text in our field: David Hoffman, Patrick Kalscheur, Laurie Israel, Archana Medhekar, and Nancy Cameron.

We offer special acknowledgment to our longtime writing partner, Judge Elizabeth Potter Scully, whose brilliant chapter we hope will be used worldwide to help educate family judicial officers as peacemakers. Liz is a gifted writer whose contributions consistently enrich our work. Her infectious sense of humor and boundless generosity make every collaboration a true joy.

Introduction

All of us started as traditional family lawyers. We primarily represented people going through divorce. We learned about their parenting and finances. We interviewed them, drafted agreements and court documents. We appeared in court, sometimes initiated by us—sometimes by the other party. We truly cared about our clients . . . but knew little or nothing about peacemaking. We all can confidently say that we learned more about family peacemaking by writing this book than we ever did in practice.

Here are our individual histories regarding peacemaking, which will hopefully be of some help as you take your next steps as a family peacemaker.

Forrest S. Mosten

I launched into mediation in 1979 after starting my career as a founding partner for a private legal clinic, Jacoby and Meyers, teaching law students as Director of Clinical Education at Mercer School of Law in Macon, Georgia, and serving as Assistant Regional Director for Consumer Protection of the Federal Trade Commission in Los Angeles.

I opened a storefront office near the LA airport with the dream of being a family mediator. Promoting family peace had little to do with my practice. Focusing on the harm of adversarial lawyers and what litigation does to divorcing families, plus how clients could save money, were my motivating factors to make mediation my day job.

In fact, I was mediating with this limited vision for approximately 12 years before I realized that building peace within the family was truly the value added of mediation. My road to this insight was attendance at mediation conferences dominated by the work of mediators with backgrounds as mental health professionals (Bernie Mayer), teachers (John Haynes), and business/city planning (Lawrence Susskind). Realizing that my lawyering background limited my approach to family matters, I began integrating these other approaches into my practice and writing.

My evolution from a mediator who facilitated settlements to promoting family peace took many years. My three greatest sources of inspiration were *Bringing Peace into the Room* (Daniel Bowling and David Hoffman), *The Making of a Mediator* (Michael Lang), and *Calm in the Face of the Storm* (Nan Waller Burnett). Starting with a series of articles discussing how we could go beyond mediation to peacemaking, building on a 1999 Symposium on Training Mediators for the 20th Century, my article "Lawyer as Peacemaker: Building a Successful Law Practice Without Going to Court" in Family Law Quarterly (fall 2009) marked my transition to peacemaking.

With the support of my faculty colleagues at UCLA School of Law, I not only included peacemaking in my mediation course but also launched two new law school courses, Lawyer as Peacemaker and Non-Court Family Law Practice. This classroom work led to my editing Family Court Review's Special Issue on Peacemaking in 2015. Judge Elizabeth Potter Scully and I followed up this special issue with peacemaking sections in our books *The Complete Guide to Mediation* (ABA 2015), *Unbundling Legal Services* (ABA 2017), and *Effectively Representing Clients in Family Mediation* (ABA 2023, adding Lara Traum as co-author).

Throughout the last ten years, peacemaking initiatives in Collaborative Practice and Mediation have added this dimension to the settlement transaction orientation of mediation so that professionals from all fields of origin are now receiving peacemaking curriculum in their mediation training, and consumers are offered a new array of approaches by professionals to both resolve conflicts and form new family relationships through Collaborative and Mediated Premarital and Postmarital as well as surrogacy and planning family estates and business partnerships.

Some highlights regarding peacemaking in the last decade include:

- Establishment of the Webb-Mosten Lawyer as Peacemaker Award in 2024 by the Pennsylvania State Bar
- In 2013, Patrick Kelly, president of the California State Bar, personally endorsed a special issue of the California State Bar Journal on Lawyer as Peacemaker:

  > I've devoted much of my career to the peacemaker's role through alternative dispute resolution and peer mediation such as the Los Angeles County Bar Association's Dispute Resolution Services, now known as the Center for Civic Mediation.

Through that work, I became acquainted with many of the leaders in ADR. One such leader, Forrest Mosten, a mediator and UCLA School of Law professor, is an expert on the subject. He has written a companion column in this month's California Bar Journal about how his law practice thrived after he decided to be a non-court lawyer.

He also helped involve some of the best and brightest thinkers on the subject to offer their insights on this issue. I'd like to thank these columnists for their valuable contributions and urge each of our members to carefully review their thoughts and suggestions for the evolution of our practice to one that thinks of client needs and problem solving as our highest priority. To give you a brief review of these contributions:

- Luz Herrera, a professor at the Thomas Jefferson School of Law in San Diego, writes about how limited-scope services can play a role in serving the needs of clients and increase the peacemaking role of lawyers.
- Thomas D. Barton, a professor at the California Western School of Law, discusses the importance of preventive legal healthcare.
- Russell Korobkin, a professor at the UCLA School of Law, covers how to incorporate principles of peacemaking into the process of negotiating a settlement agreement.
- Richard Chernick and Barbara Reeves Neal, who are noted mediators and arbitrators at JAMS, give a primer on how to design an effective dispute-resolution process.
- Kenneth Cloke, director of the Center for Dispute Resolution in Santa Monica, instructs us on how to be agents of forgiveness and reconciliation.

I encourage my colleagues to read and carefully consider the guidance these distinguished contributors have given us. If we, as attorneys, can address this need ourselves, not only will the public be better served but, in time, the public will recognize better practices themselves.

At annual conferences of the International Academy of Collaborative Professionals, the conference committee routinely carves out a special program on Peacemaking to enhance the conference program.

These instances of progress are only samples of peacemaking at work in the recent past. It is our hope that this book will accelerate the integration of peacemaking not just for lawyers but in other professions as well.

Lara Traum

Mediation was sewn into the fabric of my being from childhood. A child of divorce, blessed with a blended, intergenerational family of immigrants, I was no stranger to conversations about the past, the navigation of an ever-shifting present, and musings about an uncertain future. A peacemaking identity was, perhaps, inevitable.

I began my career as a musician—first as a classical singer and pianist, then as a staff member and teen choral conductor with the Zamir Choral Foundation. Inhabiting the rests between the notes, luxuriating in the blending of different voices from different walks of life, I came to understand that peace and harmony weren't just musical ideals—they were possibilities for the world. I wanted those possibilities to exist in more spaces—beyond the stage, outside the concert hall, and in the many homes where I had witnessed strife, confusion, conflict, and frustrated abandonment. While coordinating choral retreats and preparing to conduct on stage at Lincoln Center, I studied for the LSATs under my desk, wondering if—just maybe—I got in, and if I received enough of a scholarship, I could expand the toolbox with which I was making peace.

Peace is brought to us through unexpected, spiritual interventions. We build our lives, make our plans, pursue the peace we want to see—and then something external and magical intervenes. For me, that intervention came as the silver lining to a health crisis.

Shortly after informing my beloved musical community that I'd be shifting gears and enrolling at the Benjamin N. Cardozo School of Law, I fell ill. Within a year, I had conducted my last concert and then lost the ability to work; sang my last performance and then lost the ability to walk; accepted a full-ride to law school and then deferred—all while navigating a life-altering Crohn's disease flare. It took six months before I could imagine a future. When I first stood on my feet again, they walked me into a mediation training. That training turned the light back on.

Unlike my esteemed co-author, I completed my first mediation training before enrolling in law school. That's the chronology the fates had in store. I went on to resume my studies at Cardozo, participate in the school's seminal Divorce Mediation Clinic, and absorb many of the skills I still use in my sessions today. I served as Editor-in-Chief of the *Cardozo Journal of Conflict Resolution*, competed with the ADR Team, and partnered with the endlessly inspiring Lela Love to deliver two International Advocate for Peace Awards—to Peter Yarrow and Benjamin Ferencz. I hosted symposia and events. And I met my treasured mentor, co-author, and now friend, Woody—who took a leap of faith when spotting peace-loving energy in a law student and showed me that peacemaking-in-action includes finding kindred spirits and lifting them up with wisdom, opportunity, and grace.

After graduating, I was fortunate to join my best friend—and mom—Alla Roytberg, at the law firm she had built. It was unlike any other practice where I had interned or been offered a job—grounded in a moral imperative to focus on "spreading good," rather than merely "doing well." At first, I did litigate. A lot. Drawing on my time in NYLAG's Domestic Violence Clinical Center, I fought fiercely in the courtroom—earning, with a twinkle, the nickname "tiger litigator" from a few. But that identity was short-lived. It didn't align with my soul—or with Alla's.

So there came a day—the one we often talk about—our "commitment to peacemaking" day.

It happened over lunch, in 2019. Debriefing over difficult cases, lamenting the way families were being torn apart, we exchanged a look of shared understanding. We could no longer be part of the damage. With an anxious gulp of green tea and spontaneous conviction, I pulled a pen from my bag and wrote on a napkin: "We will not accept any more litigated cases." We signed it. We notarized each other's signatures—for formality, for a chuckle, and as acknowledgment that this was no empty moment. And that was it. We wound down our open litigation cases, accepted no new ones, and became proud partners of Roytberg Traum Law and Mediation, P.C.—an entirely peacemaking, life-cycle law firm.

Since then, my commitment to peace has not faltered—tested as it has been. As assistant trainer to Woody in San Diego, I signed the Peacemaker's Pledge. I renew it each year, and have the text outlined in calligraphy at home. I became active with the New York State Council on Divorce Mediation—serving on committees, the Board of Directors, and eventually as President from 2023–2025. I launched PeaceChord LLC, committing to training others to do the same. I write about peace, think about peace, and try to cultivate peace in my community. And I continue to find peace at the piano and in song—because in finding peace, I found healing and the ability to sing on stage once more.

Join me in this work—in this identity. It is beautiful on this side of the rainbow.

About the Authors

Forrest (Woody) Mosten has spent his entire career as a tireless peacemaker working for increased legal access and dispute resolution for the underserved and diverse members of our society.

Woody is a professional mediator helping families, businesses, and organizations resolve disputes. He has mediated conflict involving schools, community boards, churches and synagogues, and nonprofit organizations.

He is the co-founder of Mosten Mediation Training Academy for online Mediation Training, which offers courses throughout the world (www.MostenMediationTraining.com).

Woody serves clients throughout the world exclusively through Zoom. Prior to converting to an online practice, he had offices in San Diego and Los Angeles and was named an Honorary Member of the Orange County Collaborative Practice Group. Woody and his wife, Dr. Jody Mosten, live in La Jolla.

Woody is in constant demand worldwide as a conference keynote speaker and expert witness on mediation. He served on the faculty from 2002 to 2022 at the UCLA School of Law (Mediation and Lawyer as Peacemaker) and he previously taught at Cal Western School of Law (Innovative Law Practice), the University of San Diego School of Law (Legal Ethics), the University of Southern California (Client Counseling), Pepperdine Law School (Mediation), Hamline Law School (Advanced Mediation and Unbundling), the University of Nevada at Las Vegas (Collaborative Law), the University of Idaho (Mediation), the University of Denver (Legal Access), Mercer Law School (Trial Advocacy and Client Counseling), and other educational institutions.

In 1972, with his partners Len Jacoby and Steve Meyers, Woody opened the first private legal clinic in the United States that is still in operation 49 years later following a California Supreme Court ruling permitting an expansion of consumer information by lawyers.

Woody was Director of Clinical Education at Mercer Law School in Macon, Georgia, where he traveled the Southern United States recruiting

African American law students as Faculty Sponsor for the Black Law Students Association.

Early in his career, Woody was a lawyer for the Oglala Sioux Nation following the Wounded Knee Occupation. He also served as a lawyer working with the United Farm Workers and has trained Asian American mediators to better serve their communities and as ACLU counsel in cases involving civil rights.

Woody has served as consultant and trainer for the Hopi Dispute Resolution Council and has conducted Basic and Advanced Mediation trainings on the Hopi Tribal Grounds. In addition, he was named to neutral and impartial mediator for major political and public policy tribal disputes.

Woody served as Director of Consumer Protection and as the Assistant Regional Director of the Federal Trade Commission. In this position, he led an investigation against real estate brokers who harassed consumer-oriented brokers who tried to help consumers. This experience led 13 years later to Woody inventing Limited Scope Legal Services, for which he is recognized as the "Father of Unbundled Legal Services."[1]

Woody is a founding member of the Southern California Mediation Association (SCMA) and was named by SCMA as Peacemaker of the Year and has twice served as keynote speaker at the SCMA Annual Conference and has keynoted the SCMA Family Mediation Institute with Judge Elizabeth Potter Scully, who is also Woody's co-author on three ABA books. Woody is the recipient of the 2017 SCMA President's Award. In 2020, SCMA presented Woody with its Inaugural Forrest S. Mosten Star Award for Innovation and Achievement in Mediation.

In 2024, the Pennsylvania State Bar established the Stu Webb/Forrest Mosten Peacemaker Award. Woody keynoted and was principal trainer at the Pennsylvania State Bar Peacemaker Conference in Philadelphia in 2018.

Woody has chaired many committees and projects in Peace Education. In 2008, the Association of Conflict Resolution appointed Woody to chair its Task Force to establish a National Peacemaker Museum. He has served as a conflict resolution consultant and facilitator for the Burnham Center for Community Advancement in San Diego

Woody is a Charter Member of Mediators Beyond Borders and was spotlighted in March 2024.[2]

In 2019, Woody received a Life Career Achievement Award from the Academy of Professional Family Mediators (APFM). In 2020, APFM established the

---

1. *Unbundled Legal Services*, Wikipedia, https://en.wikipedia.org/wiki/Unbundled_legal_services (last visited Sep. 25, 2025).

2. https://mediatorsbeyondborders.org/a-lifelong-pursuit-of-peace-member-spotlight-forrest-woody-mosten/

Forrest (Woody) Mosten Diversity, Equality, and Inclusion Training Scholarship Diversity, Equity & Inclusion (apfmnet.org).

Woody was awarded the Lifetime Career Award by the New York State Mediation Association and has been recipient of the ABA Lawyer as Problem Solver Award, ABA Lifetime Legal Access Award, and the Los Angeles County Bar Louis M. Brown Conflict Prevention Award.

Woody is the author of eight books and numerous articles on mediation and other dispute resolution topics. In 2022, Woody was named as honoree of Whose Who in ADR. https://www.adrtimes.com/whos-who-in-adr-forrest-woody-mosten/ He has served as editor of four special issues for the Family Court Review. In 2020, he was named chair of the Mediate.com Task Force on Online Mediation Training, and is the co-author of the Task Force's Final Report OnlineTaskForceReportAug6c.pdf (mediate.com).

Since 1989, Woody has served as chair of the International Client Consultation Competition involving 25 countries including India, Poland, Sri Lanka, Malaysia, Indonesia, Ukraine, Nigeria, and other countries from Western and Eastern Europe www.BrownMosten.com.

Woody can be reached at www.mostenmediation.com for mediation services and at www.mostenguthrie.com for mediation training. Woody's bio is also at https://en.wikipedia.org/wiki/Forrest_S._Mosten.

Lara Traum, Esq., is a collaborative attorney, mediator, parenting coordinator, and conflict resolution educator. She practices as an attorney in New York, New Jersey, and Connecticut and as a mediator nationally and internationally.

As partner at Roytberg Traum Law & Mediation, P.C., Lara co-leads a mission-driven "peacemaking life-cycle" firm that specializes in family and matrimonial law, estate planning, and cross-cultural dispute resolution. Her work extends from prenuptial and postnuptial planning through divorce mediation, parenting coordination, and trust and estate mediation, always guided by values of integrity, productive pathways to resolution, access to services, and deep human connection.

Lara earned her JD, cum laude, from the Benjamin N. Cardozo School of Law, where she concentrated in family and matrimonial law and received the prestigious Jacob Burns Medal for scholastic excellence. As Editor in Chief of the *Cardozo Journal of Conflict Resolution*, she led scholarly discourse on conflict transformation and family mediation. Lara also distinguished herself in competition, taking first place at both national and international Cyberweek eMediation contests, and securing second place in the Northeast ABA Representation in Mediation Competition.

Lara began practicing as a mediator in 2013 under the Part 146 approval of the New York State Unified Court System. She completed comprehensive mediation training with the New York Center for Interpersonal Development

(Berner/Stadler), the Cardozo Divorce Mediation Clinic, and Mosten Mediation Training. At the Mosten Mediation Training, she served as an assistant trainer under Forrest S. Mosten, mentoring new mediators herself and contributing to the field's growth. She now serves as a mediation skills trainer for the New York State Council on Divorce Mediation, and at her own training business, PeaceChord LLC.

An accomplished writer and author, Lara co-authored the 2023 ABA book *Effectively Representing Clients in Family Mediation* (with Forrest S. Mosten and Hon. Elizabeth Potter Scully). Her scholarly chapters and articles are found in books and journals published by the American Bar Association, New York State Bar Association, *Cardozo Journal of Conflict Resolution*, and *Family Court Review*, covering themes such as interdisciplinary teamwork, integration of cultural considerations in mediation, preventive conflict wellness, and modern mediation strategies.

Lara holds leadership roles in numerous professional organizations. She is the immediate past president of the New York State Council on Divorce Mediation (2023–2025); an officer on the Board of Directors of the Zamir Choral Foundation; a director on the Board of COJECO (Council of Jewish Émigré Community Organizations); and a member of Long Island Collaborative Divorce Professionals, International Academy of Collaborative Professionals, New York Association of Collaborative Professionals, Association of Family and Conciliation Courts, Academy of Professional Family Mediators, and other organizations.

Before her legal career, Lara was a classical singer and pianist, and an administrator and conductor with the Zamir Choral Foundation. She performed at venues including Carnegie Hall and Lincoln Center, and conducted a chapter of the HaZamir teen choir.

Lara is fluent in Russian and brings deep cultural nuance to her practice, serving clients across diverse communities in Queens, New York, internationally, and in interfaith contexts. She is committed to accessible conflict resolution and promotes "moderate means" sliding-scale access to services.

Lara Traum can be reached at www.goodlawfirm.com for mediation, legal, and parenting coordination services and at www.peacechord.com for training and strategic planning services.

Chapter 1
Family Lawyer as Peacemaker

Exiled in Brazil, the day before ending his life, Stefan Zweig penned the final pages of his renowned homage to the golden age of liberalism, peace, and reason in *Vienna: The World of Yesterday.* It was 1942.

Published in protest by an anti-Nazi firm in Stockholm, Zweig's writings did not prevent systemic ills from unfolding throughout the world. But the book was there, lying in wait. A memoir about peace gained, peace venerated, peace manipulated, and peace expunged. The book was written at a time when the world was aching, and the author himself was raw and exhausted. But peace would return. As it always does. As it always must.

A couple of years ago, the American Bar Association accepted a book proposal for this "peacemaker" text—a guide to our professional community on all the practical, pragmatic, and paradigm-shifting ways to build legal careers grounded in the pursuit of "peace." In 2022, Russia invaded Ukraine. In 2023, the Middle East erupted in hateful massacre. Violence continued to devastate Somalia. Antisemitism grew rampant throughout the world. And so, our book about peacemaking for family lawyers faltered at the starting gate.

But it is in such times that we must recommit ourselves to the promised missive—to invite those who work with families to think more deeply not just about working for settlements, but for preventing conflict in the first instance. We need to develop spaces and practices that lighten the load. As professionals who work with families, we have a responsibility to bring peace into the lives of those who will ultimately bring peace into the world. Because peace starts at home—even homes in which parents live separately.

***

Our journey toward peacemaking begins with the question: Why did we become family lawyers? Did we fall into working with family conflict accidentally? Was there an inspiring professor in law school offering a reprieve from narratives about codes and regulations in the form of human stories? A formative personal experience in our own childhoods or later? Did we embark on conscious journeys toward one of the most creative and intersectional fields of law, or are we realizing now, for the first time, the boundless scope of our profession?

When combing through daily to-do lists and routines, we may not have (or take) the opportunity to pause and reflect. In this first chapter, let us start with that reflection. Let us pause, set our ever-buzzing mobile phones to "do not disturb," and consider—why did we become family lawyers? Why do I do what I do every day? Do I like what I am doing? Do I like how I am doing it?

The practice of family law sits at the intersection of nearly all aspects of life and society. We are tasked with being expert creatives that understand ever-changing matrimonial and domestic constructs, the interplay between property and psychology, the impact of complex business holdings and international assets, the realities of intimate partner violence and access to justice, tax impacting, cross-cultural parenting logistics, and so much more. We address the past, support the present, and plan for the future. We family lawyers are modern-day polymaths—Renaissance women, tasked with knowing as much as possible while remaining responsible for knowing what we do not know.

Tolstoy began Anna Karenina: "Happy families are all alike; every unhappy family is unhappy in its own way." Mother Teresa famously chimed in: "Peace and war begin at home. If we truly want peace in the world, let us begin by loving one another in our own families. If we want to spread joy, we need for every family to have joy."[1] As family lawyers, we truly understand what they meant. We meet families at their most conflicted. We are at the front lines of process navigation, conflict prevention, and party empowerment—we are tasked with holding space for new frameworks in which families can shift from war and strife toward joy and peace. What a privilege it is to do this work.

Practice Areas? Peacemaking Practices Focus on Process Offerings

Family lawyers have always been at the forefront of guiding parties through the complex and emotionally charged terrain of family restructuring. However, while practitioners may have decades of experience, practicing on "autopilot" can be lethal. The role of the family lawyer requires constant vigilance. As society evolves, so too does family law—constantly adapting to reflect new realities and shifting cultural dynamics. Family law has undergone significant transformation, shaped by changes in divorce and separation practices, child custody

1. Mother Teresa, *In My Own Words*, comp. José Luis González-Balado (Liguori Publications, 1996/1997), 25, section "7. Home and Family."

arrangements, spousal support norms, asset division considerations, intimate partner violence support, collaborative adoption processes, and a growing understanding of identity and cross-cultural issues. State legislators and members of the judiciary have contributed to the normalization of peacemaking with revised statutes and administrative regulations stressing mediation and consumer-friendly approaches. Today, family lawyers are tasked with responding to an expanding range of client needs, requiring not only legal expertise but also innovative approaches and fresh perspectives to help repair and rehabilitate. Some lawyers have embraced these changes with success, while others are stymied by the learning curve of this dynamic field. To embrace change while harnessing our existing expertise, we need to shift our focus from the practice areas that define our field to the process options that help families navigate through their journeys.

Practice Areas

As we create our websites and think about advertising our businesses, we family lawyers often describe our services by providing a standard list of "practice areas." These areas reflect the core issues that families face when navigating legal transitions and conflicts, such as:

- **Separation and Divorce:** the stage of life where families seek to disentangle partnered relationships by addressing a litany of topics such as property division, spousal support, and parenting logistics.
- **Child Custody and Visitation:** the legal and logistical designations, often in dispute between parents or other family members, defining their custodial and visitation rights, aspirationally maintaining the best interests of the children involved.
- **Child Support:** a financial framework, developed by legal code, deviation from legal code, or subsequent modification, for families to ensure that their children's needs are appropriately funded.
- **Spousal Support:** a financial framework aimed at recognizing the marital and financial realities of a married couple and ensuring that cash flow is appropriately identified to support each individual's future needs.
- **Property Division:** the process of dividing shared assets and debts, including real estate, bank accounts, businesses, investments, personal properties, as well as any liabilities.
- **Adoption:** the facilitation of a legal process to adopt a child nationally or internationally, in compliance with related laws and regulations.
- **Paternity:** the navigation of parental identity and rights for unmarried parents.

- **Intimate Partner Violence and Restraining Orders:** representation and support for victims of domestic or intimate partner violence, extending to obtaining restraining orders and providing related legal support and safety planning.
- **Prenuptial and Postnuptial Agreements:** preparation of contracts outlining the financial rights of spouses before or during their marriage.
- **Guardianship and Conservatorship:** the process of establishing legal guardianship over minors or incapacitated adults to substitute judgment on their behalf.
- **Surrogacy and Reproductive Technology:** the development of legal agreements surrounding surrogacy, sperm/egg donation, and other reproductive technology–related issues.
- **Same-Sex Marriage and LGBTQ+ Family Law:** specialized representation of parties in same-sex and LGBTQ+ family relationships navigating unique legal and regulatory complications surrounding marriage, adoption, and divorce.
- **International Family Law:** representation and navigation of cross-border family issues, including matters such as international child custody disputes and international adoption.

We've all seen the standard list of family law practice areas, and we know that they only scratch the surface. In reality, countless unique issues arise in family law that no comprehensive list could ever fully capture. What about bankruptcy during a divorce? Post-judgment co-parenting disputes over vaccinations of young children? Navigating international parenting plans in a world shaped by global conflict? Or the complexities of cohabitation and cost sharing for polyamorous partners and group families? In our ever-changing world, the once "clear" boundaries between these issues blur and lose their significance. The family lawyer, in this context, becomes the ultimate "specialist generalist"—meeting each family where they are and, rather than relying solely on prescribed solutions, asking the more essential question: *What do the individuals in **this** family truly need?*

As family lawyers, when we look into the eyes of clients who are confused or overwhelmed and reflect on *what this family needs*, we are already making a critical shift. Instead of rigidly categorizing their challenges into traditional practice areas framed by adversarial posturing, we recalibrate our approach to focus on process options. We move beyond thinking of a client as simply "needing more custody," "paying less support," or "needing adjustments for asset dissipation." Instead, we look at the broader picture, considering the family as a whole and matching them with the process that best aligns with their unique situation. Some families may benefit most from collaborative, interdisciplinary teamwork that fosters holistic resolution; others may thrive in a mediated environment that emphasizes mutual understanding. For some, coaching and unbundled legal support may be the right path, empowering them to survive and even thrive through a pro se litigation process. By shifting our focus from outcomes to process, we tailor our guidance to each family's distinct needs, offering a path forward that is as unique as their journey. With this in mind, we family law peacemakers have pivoted and our "list of services" has changed to a list of process options rather than practice areas:

- **Mediation:** A neutral third party facilitates communication and negotiation between the parties to help them reach a mutually acceptable agreement, with or without attorney representation.
- **Collaborative Law:** An interdisciplinary team of lawyers, financial experts, mental health professionals, and coaches works together with parties to resolve issues outside of court.
- **Unbundled Legal Services (Limited Scope Representation):** A lawyer provides specific legal services for part of a case, while the client handles the rest on their own.
- **Coaching:** A family law coach provides advice, strategy, and guidance to pro se, self-represented individuals.
- **Arbitration:** A neutral third party hears evidence and makes binding or nonbinding decisions on the disputed issues.
- **Parenting Coordination:** A neutral professional helps parents, often high-conflict parents, resolve day-to-day disputes related to parenting time, child custody, and other co-parenting issues.
- **Negotiation/Settlement:** Attorneys help parties negotiate directly, with or without the help of a third-party facilitator, to resolve disputes and reach an agreement outside of court.
- **Post-Judgment Modifications:** Neutral professionals or attorneys help parties modify the terms of the agreement if there are substantial changes in circumstances, such as changes in income, relocation, or the child's needs, or if the parties simply jointly wish to make a change.
- **Litigation:** Litigation is the classic courtroom approach, where each party presents their case to a judge who makes decisions on contested issues (e.g., divorce, custody, support).

And so, the modern family lawyer's services are packaged differently. Gone are the days of "I will tell you what your process should be, what your strategy should be, what your position should be, and what deal you should accept." Instead, our websites now feature process options and detail our expertise as mediators and/or litigators and/or collaborative professionals. Conflict prevention and peacemaking are no longer the language spoken by family mediators alone—all family lawyers who wish to stay current and maintain flourishing practices are tasked with becoming family peacemakers and conflict prevention specialists.

What Is Peacemaking and How Does It Help Families: Lara's "Four P's of Peace"

I am a peacemaker. What does that mean?

Google offers us a quick, multi-dictionary comparison. Oxford defines a peacemaker as "one who makes peace, especially by reconciling adversaries," while Merriam-Webster takes a softer approach, describing a peacemaker as "one who makes peace, especially by reconciling parties at variance." Yet, as family lawyers, we may find ourselves questioning whether this applies. Are we truly in the reconciliation business? Not often . . .

In the Abrahamic faiths, peacemaking is often viewed as an outward-facing role—one focused on resolving conflicts between others. In these traditions, the peacemaker is seen as an intervening third party. In Jewish Rabbinic tradition, Psalm 34 directs, "Seek peace and pursue it." In Islamic teachings, the Qur'an instructs, "If two parties of the believers quarrel, make peace between them."[2] Christian theology adds a divine dimension, suggesting that a peacemaker's duty is not only to reconcile people with one another but also to "reconcile people to God." In these religious traditions, the peacemaker's mission is to restore peace for others—it is a role that looks outward, focused on resolving the disputes of others.

In contrast, Eastern traditions encourage the peacemaker to look inward. In Buddhist thought, the belief is that when we cultivate peace within ourselves, it naturally radiates outward, influencing the world around us and fostering a collective sense of harmony.[3] Similarly, in Hinduism, peace is seen as a "reflection of spiritual consciousness," with violence viewed as a sign of a soul that has yet to engage in meaningful self-reflection or spiritual growth.[4] Both Hinduism and Buddhism recognize peace as an inner journey, one that every soul yearns for and is capable of achieving. This path to peace is paved with humility, compassion, and a sincere commitment to helping others. Through this inward journey, the peacemaker not only transforms himself but also contributes to the broader healing of the world.

Spiritual communities are not the only ones that reflect deeply on peace. One need not possess religious faith to appreciate the value of peace or to actively promote it. Leo Tolstoy, whose writings have inspired millions, including renowned peacemakers like Mahatma Gandhi, Martin Luther King Jr., and James Bevel, comes to mind. Tolstoy's works (particularly *War and Peace*) echo his own personal moral struggles with organized religion—a struggle that

---

2. Translation from Maulana Muhammad Ali, The Holy Qur'an 1006 (Lahore and US: Ahmadiyya Anjuman Ishaat Islam, 1991).

3. Juichiro Tanabe, *Buddhism and Peace Theory: Exploring a Buddhist Inner Peace*, 21(2) Int'l J. Peace Studies (Fall 2016).

4. https://www.himalayanacademy.com/the-hindu-ethic-of-non-violence/.

transcends time, space, and culture—while still carrying a universal call for a world inhabited by peacemakers. His literary philosophy underscores what we know to be true: that the work of peace is twofold—it is both an internal challenge and an outward responsibility. As Tolstoy once said, "Without knowing what I am and why I am here, life is impossible." True peace begins with self-awareness and a commitment to living purposefully in the service of others.[5]

So, what is peacemaking? It is a way of life. It extends to the way we carry ourselves inside and outside of our offices—from our innermost thoughts to our general outlook. It extends to the way we interact with family and friends and colleagues. And for us, as family lawyers, it infuses the work that we do as we prevent conflict, promote communication, and improve the worlds of the families who invite us into their lives.

Peacemaking helps families. Even in the most amiable of families, there is still conflict that could benefit from peacemaking support. Idyllic depictions of family life in Norman Rockwell paintings tirelessly capture the essence of family energy, marked by cacophony and chaos at crowded tables with heads turned in different directions. Families are a collection of individual persons, with individual perspectives, needs, and natures. Families need peace and peaceful interventions. Imagine if only a trained mediator were seated at that Norman Rockwell dinner table . . .

When we as family lawyers take the time to carry peace within us, processing our secondhand (or firsthand) traumas, meditating, and exuding calm, we model peace and hold space for those currently struggling. We see the light at the end of the tunnel when they cannot. We embody calm when they are in crisis. Families facing conflict need this desperately.

How do we help, and what exactly do we harness when providing peace-informed intervention? Peacemaking professionals commit to amplifying four essential steps, which Lara likes to refer to as the Four P's of Peace: Pause, Process, Plan, and Prevent.

1. Pause

One of the hardest things to do in crisis is . . . to pause. We have all received that client call. "I need to get a divorce yesterday." "How quickly can you prepare an agreement—we agree on everything—I just need this one small change!" "I need my own space." "I need vindication." "I need vengeance." "I don't know what I need but I need something . . . and I need it immediately."

When prospective clients call to inquire about our services, the caller is often aching with urgency. This distressed state is lethal to sound decision-making.

5. Leo Tolstoy, Anna Karenina. This is our second citation in this opening chapter of Tolstoy and his monumental literary contribution. Perhaps as lawyers, we might add such literature to our required professional reading.

Whether the caller is navigating a fight, flight, or freeze response to stress, a thoughtful pause to consider the status quo and select the right path forward may be beyond the caller's cognitive bandwidth.

As family lawyers, we are uniquely positioned to help inject that pause. We can serve as the conduit for that pause, the one who helps them step out of the maelstrom of emotion and into a more deliberate, measured space. A pause is not a delay—it's a crucial, restorative breath. It's a moment of acknowledgment. "That sounds like an incredibly challenging experience." "It seems like you've been in limbo and are ready for a change." "Thank you for sharing how overwhelming this must be."

Rather than rushing into legal strategy or immediately offering a solution, we can offer something far more valuable: a moment of emotional understanding and validation. A mere minute spent together in this space of shared pause often works wonders. "I hear you, and I will let you take a moment to realize that you've been heard and understood and accepted exactly as you are, right here, in this moment." In just 60 seconds, we can provide them the relief of exhaling. The physical effects are powerful: lowered heart rate, reduced blood pressure, and a calmer, more open state of mind. This small gesture often helps them to begin digesting the complexities of their situation in a way they couldn't before.

A pause, whether brief validation during an initial consultation or a quiet moment in the heat of negotiation, is a profound peacemaking tool. By offering space to reflect, we promote de-escalation, rational thinking, and productive dialogue. We create the conditions for peace to emerge. As family lawyers, if we remember to gift our clients with a moment of pause, we don't just help resolve disputes—we help to lay the foundation for possible long-term healing and stability.

2. Process

The power of process is twofold. When we speak of "process," we are referring both to the journey the parties in conflict must travel (as a verb) and the framework through which they will resolve their disputes (as a noun).

As a verb, "process" refers to the personal work that parties need to do to digest what is happening to them. It's an opportunity to step back and truly understand the legal information they're receiving, the options available to them, and the potential consequences of each choice. In the midst of emotional turmoil, this cognitive processing is vital. Without it, decisions are often impulsive, emotionally driven, and later regretted.[6]

---

6. Bowen's theory of differentiation describes an individual's ability to maintain a clear sense of self while remaining emotionally connected to others, particularly within the family system.

As a noun, "process" refers to the structured approach or method by which parties will resolve their dispute. Whether through litigation, mediation, collaborative law, or other methods, the chosen process is the pathway that will guide the family to a resolution. The process is not just a procedural necessity; it's the vehicle that can transform conflict into resolution.

Supporting families in choosing the right dispute resolution process, modifying those processes to suit each family's unique needs, and continuously evaluating whether the selected process remains the best fit for the situation—that is at the heart of a family lawyer's role as a peacemaker. Matching the right process to the family's needs, and delivering that process effectively, can be the difference between a harmful, prolonged conflict and an imminent peaceful, productive resolution.

In building a peacemaking practice as a family lawyer, thorough process knowledge and the ability to clearly explain process options is key. How can unbundled services and legal coaching support pro se litigants? How do collaborative teams further productive and thorough contracting? How does mediation ensure informed consent and structured self-determination? What process options are most helpful if I am valuing complex businesses? Navigating a reluctant or recalcitrant spouse? Struggling to secure a safety plan for my self-harming preteen transitioning into two homes? What is the time spent in a given process? The cost? The amount of work done by the party and the amount of work done by the professional?

The intricacies of process are where the professional can shine. It's already difficult for families in conflict to figure out what they want and need; our job is to help them understand *how* they can achieve those goals through the right processes.

3. Plan

Antoine de Saint-Exupéry said, "A goal without a plan is just a wish." I want to get divorced. I want to be the primary residential custodian. I want the house, and I am willing to liquidate all retirement assets to buy it out. I want to stop living in limbo as soon as possible. I don't care about the details. I want what I want, and I want it today. I will figure out tomorrow . . . tomorrow.

Planning is difficult. Planning is especially difficult when navigating the uncertainty of unresolved family conflict. Perhaps the process has already

Those with high differentiation can manage their thoughts and emotions under stress, while those with low differentiation tend to be more reactive and emotionally fused with others. This concept is foundational in Bowen Family Systems Theory and is linked to patterns of emotional functioning passed through generations. *See* Murray Bowen, Family Therapy in Clinical Practice (1978).

been selected—the parties will be mediating, or the collaborative team has been established, or the pro se petition has been drafted and filed in court. We already selected the process. And, once the process has been selected, the goal is to ultimately be done with the process as efficiently as possible. But what is the plan?

Planning is difficult. Planning is particularly challenging when navigating the uncertainty that unresolved family conflict often brings. The emotional stakes are high, and the landscape is constantly shifting. While the process may already be selected—mediation, collaborative law, or court-based proceedings—the journey toward efficient and sustainable resolution can still unravel and drag. Efficiency requires planning.

There are two major kinds of "plans" that we, as practitioners, are tasked with creating: professional plans and subject-matter plans.

Professional plans help streamline a structured process—how do we manage meeting schedules and calendar meetings efficiently? How do we establish and maintain an appropriate agenda? How do we ensure that all necessary persons are participating in the process in all necessary ways?

Subject-matter plans, on the other hand, ensure that we address the heart of the dispute with precision and thoroughness, ensuring that minimal loopholes remain. When a goal of "joint decision-making" is set for co-parents, for example, subject-matter planning helps families dig deeper: What kinds of topics might you find yourselves co-parenting in the future? What are your values around private school education? Religious observance? Use of screens and devices? How will you navigate unforeseen topics? What will you do when you disagree? When your new significant others disagree? Planning is often where the greatest value of a family lawyer is realized. It's not just about putting out fires in the present; it's about preparing the family for a healthier, more stable future.

4. Prevent

Perhaps one of the most critical, yet often overlooked, aspects of our role as family lawyers is conflict prevention. While our clients are understandably consumed with their immediate challenges—move-out dates, custody exchanges, and the details of day-to-day survival—our responsibility goes beyond just putting out fires in the present. We must look ahead.[7]

As family lawyers, we are called to think about the future with clarity and foresight. We need to consider the issues that may arise down the road—college decisions, new relationships, changes in living arrangements, and many

7. *See* Forrest S. Mosten & Lara Traum, *The Family Lawyer's Role in Preventive Legal and Conflict Wellness*, 55 Fam. Ct. Rev. 26 (2017).

other scenarios that may seem distant but are guaranteed to come into play. We must introduce these future topics calmly, with curiosity and an open invitation to prepare for the road ahead.

While these conversations can be difficult, our role is not just to protect the family members in the present but to equip them with the tools to handle challenges as they arise. Conflict prevention is a delicate dance—one that requires empathy, foresight, and the ability to calmly guide families into a future they can feel prepared for. By preventing conflicts before they flare up, we help to ensure that families don't just survive their current crisis but are also positioned to thrive in the future.

Borrowing Strategies from Therapeutic Practice, Peace Studies, and Nonviolent Communication to Help Families in Transition

The Four P's of Peace help us frame the task at hand. However, we don't just strive to understand the work—we strive to do it *well*. While many family law professionals come from traditional legal backgrounds, shaped by law schools and courtroom experience, the most effective strategies and tools we use have evolved from distinct fields—therapy, peace studies, and nonviolent communication. These disciplines offer profound insights and practical methods that allow us to approach family conflict with greater empathy, understanding, and a focus on resolution. By integrating these diverse influences, we can do more than simply navigate disputes; we can facilitate meaningful, lasting peace for the families we serve.

When families are in flux, journeying through a divorce, separation, or other life-altering change, emotional tides overwhelm. It is easy for words to become weapons, and for well-meaning intentions to be clouded by pain and fear. It is here, in these delicate moments, that the wisdom from therapy, peace studies, and nonviolent communication can offer transformative relief. These strategies aren't just about solving problems—they are about creating spaces where healing can unfold.

By weaving in therapeutic approaches, professionals can help families navigate the chaos of change with compassion, offering not just legal guidance but emotional support that helps parties reconnect with themselves and one another. Taking tips from therapists, family law professionals can learn how to develop safe and neutral environments for negotiation and dialogue, allocate time to identifying underlying emotions and needs through validation and respect, model active listening and guide parties toward calmly using "I" statements during charged moments, and reinforcing positive progress despite challenges and potential impasse.

Peace studies teach us that conflict does not have to be destructive. In fact, if approached with a mindset of understanding and cooperation rather than aggression, conflict can be an opportunity for growth. When families are in the midst of transition and emotions are running high, parties can easily slip into patterns of blame, anger, and defensiveness. Peace studies show us that resolution does not come from fighting to be right but from learning to listen, to step into the other person's shoes, and to find common ground. For families in crisis, these peace-building tools offer the promise of not just surviving the transition but of moving through it with grace and respect.[8]

Nonviolent communication adds another layer of depth to this process. It shifts the way we speak to each other from a place of judgment and accusation to one of empathy and understanding. Imagine a parent in the throes of a custody battle, feeling unheard and overwhelmed. Instead of saying, "You don't care about the kids," nonviolent communication invites them to express their emotions in a way that opens up a dialogue, not a confrontation: "I feel anxious when I don't know how the kids will be cared for, and I need reassurance." This small shift in language can transform the tone of the entire conversation, turning it from a power struggle into an opportunity for connection. Nonviolent communication helps family members articulate their deepest needs without placing blame, allowing them to speak from a place of vulnerability and to build trust.[9]

For professionals working with families in transition, incorporating tools taken from therapy, peace studies, and nonviolent communication means offering more than just legal advice. We provide families with a road map

---

8. *See* Johan Galtung, Peace by Peaceful Means: Peace and Conflict, Development and Civilization 9–20 (1996) (Galtung distinguishes between "negative peace" (the absence of violence) and "positive peace" (the presence of justice and equity), arguing that sustainable peace requires addressing structural violence and systemic inequality); Adam Curle, Making Peace 12–25 (1971) (Curle emphasizes the importance of transforming unpeaceful relationships through awareness, education, and dialogue, framing peace as a dynamic and developmental process.); Elise Boulding, Cultures of Peace: The Hidden Side of History 45–60 (2000) (Boulding advocates for fostering peace through everyday practices, particularly in families and communities, and stresses the role of imagination and inclusive participation in peace-building); Séverine Autesserre, The Frontlines of Peace: An Insider's Guide to Changing the World 45–67 (2021) (Autesserre examines grassroots peace-building efforts, highlighting how local actors and communities can play pivotal roles in ending violence and fostering sustainable peace.); and Rebecca L. Oxford, Ed., Understanding Peace Cultures 12–29 (2014) (Oxford explores the concept of peace cultures, emphasizing the importance of cultural contexts in shaping peace-building practices and the need for culturally sensitive approaches to conflict resolution.).

9. *See* Marshall B. Rosenberg, Nonviolent Communication: A Language of Life 1–25 (3d ed., 2015). Rosenberg introduces a communication model based on empathy, honesty, and compassion, emphasizing that conflict can be reduced when people learn to express their needs without blame and listen with deep understanding.

for emotional clarity and a path to healing. When family members feel heard, when they understand their own emotions and those of others, they can begin to make decisions not out of fear but out of wisdom. These tools empower families to reclaim agency over their situations. Rather than seeing each other as adversaries, family members begin to see each other as partners in the shared goal of creating a healthier, more stable future for everyone involved.

The beauty of these strategies lies in their ability to transform conflict into a catalyst for growth and understanding. Therapy, peace studies, and nonviolent communication don't just teach families how to avoid fighting—they teach them how to embrace conflict as an opportunity for healing. They show us that conflict does not have to tear us apart; it can help us come back together. And in the case of families in transition, this is perhaps the greatest gift: the chance to emerge from difficult times not only intact but stronger, more compassionate, and more united than before. When we offer families the tools to manage their emotions, express their needs, and resolve differences peacefully, we are not just guiding them through a transition—we are empowering them to build a foundation for a more harmonious and resilient future.

Values of Peacemaking: Empathy, Nonviolence, Collaboration, and Justice

Peacemaking goes beyond resolving conflict. Peacemaking fosters understanding, facilitates healing, and empowers collaboration. Peacemaking honors the dignity of each individual, recognizing that every person's voice, experience, and perspective matters. Peacemaking creates environments where compassion and respect can thrive, even in the most challenging of circumstances. These values shape how we approach conflict, encouraging us to seek solutions that preserve relationships and promote lasting peace. Empathy, nonviolence, collaboration, and justice form the foundation of peacemaking.

In every conflict, especially those within families, it is easy for individuals to become entrenched in their own feelings and views. Peacemaking, however, invites us to step outside of our own perspectives and truly understand the emotions, needs, and fears of others. This doesn't mean agreeing with every viewpoint, but rather acknowledging the validity of another's experience. By practicing empathy, peacemakers create a space where people feel seen, heard, and understood, which is often the first step toward resolution.

Peacemaking harnesses nonviolent communication and engagement techniques to transform aggression and hostility into constructive dialogue, helping individuals shift from a mindset of "winning" the conflict to one of finding mutual understanding. Nonviolent communication teaches us to speak with kindness and clarity, addressing the issue at hand without resorting to blame or attack. In doing so, we preserve the humanity of everyone involved, ensuring that the process of conflict resolution itself does not cause further harm.[10]

Rather than approaching conflict resolution as a zero-sum game where one party's gain is another's loss, collaboration in peacemaking emphasizes cooperative solutions. It encourages individuals to see each other not as opponents but as partners in creating a shared, sustainable outcome. Collaboration means seeking win–win solutions, where all parties can walk away feeling that their needs have been acknowledged and addressed. It involves working together to find creative, flexible solutions that respect each person's needs, interests, and values.

Finally, as peacemakers supporting productive outcomes, we must realize that justice is not in conflict with peacemaking. In fact, justice is paramount in peacemaking. Justice in the peacemaking context is not about retribution or punishment but about fairness, accountability, and the restoration of balance. It recognizes that, in any conflict, true peace comes not from ignoring differences, but from addressing them with integrity. Peacemaking encourages parties to take responsibility for their actions while creating opportunities for healing. It is about ensuring that no one is left unheard or marginalized, and that every individual's rights and dignity are appropriately upheld throughout the process.

Empathy, collaboration, and justice guide us toward creating environments where conflict leads to growth, understanding, and lasting peace. In a world where tensions are high and divisions often run deep, the values of peacemaking offer a hopeful and transformative path forward. We are excited that you are joining us, in optimism and in peace.

---

10. Examples of Nonviolent Communication (NVC) in practice include co-parents resolving scheduling conflicts through empathetic dialogue that avoids blame; workplace colleagues using NVC to address missed deadlines collaboratively; neighbors employing NVC in mediating property disputes; and couples improving understanding by expressing needs without criticism. These applications demonstrate how NVC fosters clarity, compassion, and mutual respect across varied conflict settings. *Id.*

Cleaning Our Own Mirrors by Archana Medhekar[11]

On behalf of the Ontario Association for Family Mediation (OAFM) Board, our Executive Director Mary-Anne Popescu, and the staff, it is my privilege as a president, to welcome you all to the 2025 Family Peacemakers Conference.

We have gathered in Ottawa, our nation's capital, a fitting place to celebrate our strength: *social cohesion* and our *shared sense of community*.

Recently, I was visiting an indigenous friendship center in Thunder Bay, where I was introduced to the Indigenous teaching of "Two-Eyed Seeing." It means learning to see the world through two eyes: one eye with the strengths of Indigenous ways of knowing, and other eye through Western approaches. In the world of family mediation, this Indigenous teaching calls on us—to hold space for multiple truths, our diverse identities, and the power of human connection.

Truly speaking, mediation is not about fixing people. It is about seeing them and helping them see each other again. That begins with us. As mediators and collaborative professionals, our role is deeply human. To bring insight for our participants, we must clean our own mirror first. It means self-awareness, sitting with discomfort, and realizing that conflict is never static. It evolves, just as people transform. Our humility in navigating the space between "letting go" and the "new beginning" is what makes this work rewarding.

This conference is about humanizing our work by lifting people up and being creative. A heartfelt thank you to our dedicated organizing committee. Your hard work and vision to bring vibrant topics together makes this conference memorable. Also, thank you to all our presenters for sharing their innovative ideas, helpful tools, and valuable experience with us.

There is one thing that connects us all, we have seen it time and again: Behind every dispute is a human story, and every resolution

---

11. President, Ontario Association for Family Mediation, Opening Remarks (Family Peacemakers Conference 2025).

offers a chance to heal. I have learned from my international peace-building work that conflict is the delta (the gap) between *where we are now* and *where we want to be*. Let's work together to close that gap with compassion, connection, and collaboration. Specially now when the world around us desperately needs it.

On behalf of OAFM, I am deeply grateful for all your in-person presence. I hope that you will enjoy this insightful conference. Let us continue to build peace—together.

Thank you, Merci, Magwitch
Ottawa, Ontario, Canada
May 2, 2025

Chapter 2

Building a "Successful" Peacemaking Practice from the Inside Out

Patrick Kalscheur

Peacemaking. Let it begin with me.
—Kevin Scudder (1960–2023)

In this chapter we explore the concept of practice building, specifically building a peacemaking practice. In doing so, it is helpful to take a look at models of successful practices. But what is a successful peacemaking practice? We can imagine that success equals many things: a steady flow of clients, positive (profitable) revenues, a completely out of court non-litigious practice, working with a dynamic team of professionals, meeting different goals and metrics we set for ourselves, having a large following online and on social media, publishing articles and books, leading trainings filled with participants, and on and on. Every single one of these things is positive and worth striving for.

As I sit here to write the names of the practices that emulate this success, they do not come to mind. But I have no trouble identifying the *peacemakers* that embody peace. There are, of course, the amazing peacemakers in our world such as Mahatma Ghandi, Rev. Desmond Tutu, Dr. Martin Luther King, and Mother Teresa. Closer to home, we can also see successful peacemaking family lawyers such as Stu Webb, Woody Mosten, Jacinta Gallant, David Hoffman, and the late Kevin Scudder. While it is safe to assume each of these family lawyers as peacemakers built a successful peacemaking practice, what stands out is the fact that each of them became successful peacemakers. But what does "successful peacemaker" mean?

If you have had the good fortune to meet one of these peacemakers, attend one of their trainings or workshops, or read one of their books or articles, you will know they possess certain characteristics, including clear communication, excitement (passion even) for the work they do, curiosity in what you have to say, a calm demeanor, patience, confidence, and a general sense of joy to be with you. While I have not had the good fortune of working on a case with any of these peacemakers, I imagine they bring the same characteristics into their client work as they provide in their trainings and writings. What better way to create peace for families in conflict than to:

- Communicate clearly with everyone in the room;
- Show curiosity in what each person has to say;
- Remain calm amidst the storm of conflict;
- Model patience when clients feel distress;
- Project confidence where clients feel uncertain about outcomes;
- Show clients that joy still exists at a time when they may feel their most unlovable.

What these models of successful peacemakers have done is to create peace inside themselves. They demonstrate the characteristics of, they embody, what peace looks like. David Hoffman and Daniel Bowling have written about the importance of *Bringing Peace into the Room*[1] and how the personal characteristics of a mediator impact the outcomes in mediation. In this chapter, we explore how the personal characteristics of the peacemaker impact the development and, ultimately, the success of the peacemaker's practice. In short, the more peace that you create inside yourself, the more peace you can create in your practice: To have a successful peacemaking practice, try to become more peaceful.

Don't fear, we are not setting you up for an impossible task. Internal peace exists on a continuum. There is no expectation that you must always be peaceful; rather, the goal is to develop the ability to identify when you are not experiencing peace and to apply tools to bring yourself back into a peaceful state. In fact, you are learning to make peace. As we begin to make more peace internally, we begin to see more clearly how to make more peace externally. We will have developed the foundation upon which to build out our peacemaking practices. The peacemaker's purpose comes into focus and can be communicated clearly to potential clients and professional referral sources. As peacemakers experience excitement and passion for their work, they become more confident, calm, and patient. The peacemaking family lawyer feels genuine joy in his work, connects to the families he is helping, and becomes someone families seeking peace want to hire.

1. Daniel Bowling & David Hoffman, Bringing Peace into the Room: How the Personal Qualities of the Mediator Impact the Process of Conflict Resolution (2003).

Self-Awareness Practices as a Foundation for Peacemaking

When one hears the term "practice building," the mind quickly turns to concepts such as marketing, networking, training, and other business concepts to support a practice. These are all important; however, they all focus on what the practice looks like externally. Successful peacemakers realize that they must first learn to make peace inside before they build out their practice. This is an internal process; peacemaking happens inside the peacemaker first.

A house with big, beautiful rooms cannot stand without resting on a strong foundation. A peacemaking practice with a beautiful website, active social media pages, and lots of followers will not be sustained unless the clients experience some peace when they are with you. That is why this chapter does not provide a list of external to-do's but, instead, offers different tools—tools that, if consistently implemented, develop peace from within first. From there, peace can radiate out into the world of potential clients.

Next we will explore a subset of tools that you may want to utilize in your practice. You may want to try one or all of these tools. The key is to develop a daily personal routine, outside of the presence of your clients, and to practice, practice, practice. Just as a lawyer wouldn't espouse knowledge of the law without having done the necessary legal research, peacemakers who want to cultivate peace in their clients must learn how to make peace first.

Leaders in the field such as Nan Waller Burnett have written about the benefits and importance of developing a daily practice of peace for conflict resolution professionals.[2] Here are some tools with brief descriptions to consider as you develop your peacemaking practice.

Tool #1: Meditation

There are many forms of meditation. The most common form that most people envision when they hear the word meditation is sitting in silence with your eyes closed, following the pattern of your breathing. As thoughts arise, the meditator notices the thoughts and how one thought leads to another, eventually releasing the thoughts and coming back to their breathing. You may also practice a walking meditation, where you focus on the rhythm of your movements in connection with your breathing, noticing your thoughts as they arise, and coming back to the rhythm of movement and breathing. When you are meditating, you are seeking to become more aware of the natural peaceful

---

2. Nan Waller Burnett, Calm in the Face of the Storm: Spiritual Daily Practice for the Peacemaker (2007).

state of your being (breathing, moving) and of how thoughts impact those natural states (create more or less peace).

As you develop your meditation practice, you may become more aware of the interplay of how your thoughts create emotional reactions that create more thoughts that begin to create stories. With practice, you may learn to notice the story is not real but being created by you, and to come back to your breath, back to your body, and realize that you are simply sitting in a chair with your eyes closed. A state of peace returns.

Peacemaking lawyers who meditate learn to slow down. They observe their thoughts about and emotional reactions to their clients experiencing conflict. They reflect on the efforts of other professionals involved. They find their breath, return to a peaceful state, and model that to their clients who may have been overcome by their own emotional reactions to the maelstrom of conflict in which they find themselves. With practice, peacemaking lawyers who meditate do not take on the burdens of their clients and can hear more clearly what each party is saying and how to spot options for creative peaceful resolutions.

Tool #2: Body Scans/Physical Cues

Another tool for you to develop is a greater awareness and understanding of how physical sensations in your own body indicate whether you are in a state of peace or have been trapped in the conflict of the people you are trying to help. To perform a body scan, sit quietly with your eyes closed and internally go through your body from the tips of your toes to the top of your head, seeking any painful or pleasurable sensations. When you notice a sensation in one part of the body, pause and bring greater attention to the sensation and ask a series of curious questions. Is the sensation pleasurable or painful? Is there an emotion present? Can I label that emotion (fear, joy, anger, pain)? Is this a familiar sensation for you? Is there a story behind it? Then gently release your attention from this sensation and resume your scan through your body to see if there are other sensations present. If so, pause and bring the same awareness and curiosity to that sensation. Repeat this process until you feel complete and ready to continue. This can be done privately or shared with your client(s).

When this practice is done regularly, you begin to notice patterns. Certain physical sensations in specific parts of the body indicate similar emotional states are present. For example, you may notice a tightness in your chest that indicates fear is present; you can inquire about what stimulus is creating the fearful reaction, tend to any needs, and with gentleness bring peace back into your body and emotional state.

If you develop an awareness of such physical cues and patterns, you can utilize this information when working with clients. If a specific physical cue arises when with clients, you can pause, inquire internally about whether the emotion is present, discern if this emotion is your own or perhaps absorbed from the clients, and choose more intentionally how to engage or not engage. If the emotion is a trigger arising from your personal life, gently self-soothe internally through mindful and meditative techniques, bringing yourself back to a peaceful state without adding your own emotions to the already emotionally crowded room. If the emotion is arising from the clients, you can lead with curiosity. Is the topic at hand informing the emotion? Is it something else? Gentle questions create safety for the person experiencing the emotion to communicate more authentically, and authentic emotional release opens more doors for peaceful resolutions.

Tool #3: Internal Family Systems/Parts Work

Internal Family Systems (IFS) is a therapeutic model developed by Dr. Richard Schwartz and a wonderful overview can be found in his book *Introduction to Internal Family Systems*.[3] Briefly described, the IFS models states that we all have different parts within ourselves operating simultaneously, with each of these parts playing different roles. Core wounds may arise from childhood trauma. Painful experiences create and inform internal parts of ourselves known as "exiles," while other parts of ourselves provide balance and protect our exiles from re-injury and the challenging emotions and painful feelings associated with them; these parts are aptly named "protectors." Meanwhile, our true Self, according to the IFS model, remains in a peaceful state. When we journey inward and access the true Self, we can unburden the exiles and protectors, creating a state of freedom, wholeness, and harmony from which we gain the ability to see all of our different inner qualities with curiosity, compassion, creativity, confidence, courage, or calmness.

If you want to work with the IFS model to create more peace, you can add this to your meditation or body scanning exercises. For example, when performing a body scan, you may inquire whether a certain sensation is associated with an exile or a protector. You might then access Self energy, which is indicated if you feel one of the "c" words just mentioned (curiosity, compassion, etc.) toward the exile or protector. You can then engage with nonjudgmental inward curiosity. What is the protector's job? How long has the protector been doing that job? What would it need to be at ease and to relinquish that job? After spending some time exploring this, see if you can access some gratitude for the hard work all the parts of you do to help you function, and allow yourself to return to a peaceful state.

3. Richard C. Schwartz, Introduction to Internal Family Systems (2d ed., 2023).

A peacemaker that develops an IFS-based practice can utilize these tools for themselves as well as for their clients. When you feel triggered or sense a strong emotional reaction to something happening with clients brewing inside you—check in. See if one of your "parts" is activated and what is needed to come back to Self. When working with families in conflict, the language of parts (exiles and protectors) is very accessible. Spouses going through a divorce have many competing impulses, emotions, and reactions. A part of them may feel angry, hurt, shameful, and so on, *and* another part of them chose mediation or the collaborative process because they want a peaceful resolution, a positive co-parenting relationship, or to feel less pain. When a peacemaker can confidently acknowledge the protector part that is activated, that part can be soothed, and the peacemaker can encourage the part of the client that wants a peaceful outcome to state its needs and desires. By helping clients access Self, you can help them find internal mediators and, from that place, generate the peaceful outcomes that the family is seeking.[4]

Tool #4: Journaling

For many lawyers becoming peacemakers, the tools just described may feel unfamiliar and uncomfortable. Journaling, however, may feel more comfortable for you.

In developing a daily journaling practice, begin by noting those experiences that create peace for you. Write about some of the memories in your life when you felt the most at peace. What were you doing? Were you alone or with others? What role does nature play in these experiences? What did these experiences feel like in your body? Can you access those feelings now? Spend some time remembering and writing about as many of these experiences as you can recall and look for any patterns or common threads.

A journaling practice can move forward each day with an exploration of what you are experiencing that day, whether you feel at peace or not, and what may be causing these feelings. Finding a similar time of the day each day (morning, evening, or both) is a good practice to keep consistency as well. Journaling can also be an excellent supplement to any of the other tools discussed here. Writing about the experiences we have in meditation or as we explore our parts helps solidify those practices and may allow you to feel a greater sense of confidence in using what you are learning as you develop your own peacemaking practice.

4. For a more detailed discussion of how to apply IFS principles to mediation, see David A. Hoffman, *Mediation, Multiple Minds, and the Negotiation Within*, 16 Harv. Negot. L. Rev. 297 (Spring 2011).

Tool #5: Visualization Exercises

Visualization is a tool that many highly successful people and high performers such as athletes use. Visualization can be either proactive and creative or reflective. Proactive visualization, at its core, is an opportunity for you to see what a successful outcome looks and feels like, thereby accessing new ways to create those desired outcomes. To try this, before an upcoming mediation, meeting with a client, or even a court appearance, set aside some time to imagine what outcome you want to create. See yourself acting in the manner you wish to act; see yourself communicating clearly; see yourself moving through the experience in a state of peace. As you do this, take note of what the experience looks and feels like. Do you take a certain posture? Do you see yourself speaking often or little? Do you notice any sensations in your body?

Visualization is also a tool that can be used to reflect on either a positive or challenging experience. If you have completed a successful meeting, take some time to see yourself and the others in that meeting. What worked well? How did you engage with others in the room? Do you notice any physical sensations as you remember this experience. When reflecting on a meeting that didn't go well or felt more challenging for you, see yourself in the room and remember the moments when things became difficult. What was the first moment that happened? Were you speaking or listening to another speak? How did you experience that challenge physically or emotionally? How did you respond to this? How did that feel? Now see yourself making a different choice. What do you do differently? How does making that different choice feel, emotionally or physically? Do you feel more peace?

As you develop a visualization practice, you will begin to learn from past moments where you did not create peace either in yourself or in your clients and develop new strategies for creating more peace in the future. Old patterns become clear as new pathways emerge. This is particularly effective when coupled with a journaling practice.

Tool #6: Talk Therapy

While some of the other tools mentioned are inherently solo in nature, some find that they process and pursue peace best with another person, another soul. Therapy creates a safe space for the peacemaker to explore, with another person, how to identify emotional dysregulation and develop tools to regulate themselves. In other words, we can examine what takes us out of a peaceful state and how to return to peace. There are many different types of therapy, and I encourage you to explore the type that speaks to you.

As you develop a therapeutic relationship with your therapist, you might develop trust and the ability to explore deeper levels of reactivity in relational dynamics. For example, if you feel a particularly strong emotional reaction to a client or another professional, therapy can be a safe and confidential place to examine this with a well-qualified and caring professional. You can obtain strategies to engage differently and find more peace in those relationships, with therapeutic role plays and other techniques. As you explore peacemaking tropes in dialogue, old narratives that historically prevented success may emerge. These can include internal mistaken beliefs such as "I am not good enough," "I don't deserve success," "Nobody wants to hear what I have to say," or "I am at my core, a lawyer, not a peacemaker." Having a therapist to assist in reframing these limiting beliefs can be one important step toward developing a successful peacemaking practice.

All of the tools identified here are just a sampling of the many options available to the family lawyer seeking to develop a peacemaking practice. You may already have other practices that create peace in your life. The key is to build consistent daily practice where you can reflect on when you are and are not in a peaceful state, and, over time, you will begin to bring more peace into your peacemaking practice.

Finding Your Why

Once you have begun to develop a practice for making peace internally, the next step is to identify why you want to be a peacemaker for others—why you want to work with families in conflict, and what purpose is driving you to this work. Developing clear answers to these questions will allow you to build a peacemaking practice to serve others that is aligned with your purpose. When your work and your purpose are aligned, work may become more pleasurable, and you may become more attractive to potential clients and other professionals. You may begin to emulate the characteristics of successful peacemakers mentioned earlier in this chapter—passionate, joyful, curious, calm, and confident.

There is no one way to approach accessing your peacemaking purpose; however, this is a critical step in building a sustainable peacemaking practice. Woody Mosten and Kevin Scudder have written on the topic extensively in what they describe as the importance of developing your practice signature.[5] Mosten and Scudder ask the peacemaker to take stock of their personal life

5. Woody Mosten originally developed the peacemaking signature in his books *Mediation Career Guide* (2001) and *Collaborative Divorce Handbook* (2009); it was further developed by Kevin Scudder in his chapter *Redefining Your Practice Signature and Creating a Profitable Peacemaking Practice*, *in* Building a Successful Collaborative Practice (Mosten & Cordover eds., 2018). See our Appendix for your own copy of this Peacemaker Self-Survey.

and their professional life by examining their core values, the events that have shaped those core values, and how the peacemaker's personal attributes can be incorporated into their peacemaking practice. I strongly encourage you to examine your values and identify your peacemaking signature. This may lead to the creation of your mission statement, business plan, and other actions that help you build your practice.

Another way that you can identify your purpose is by understanding what it *feels* like for you when you embody and truly live as your true peacemaking self. While there may be common sensations (slow rhythmic breathing, tingling, or other pleasurable sensations), your peacemaking experience—what you feel—will be unique to you. When you step into your peacemaking self, you can ask yourself deeper questions and begin to see why you want to do this work more clearly. The answers to these deeper questions will also be unique to you.

Try It Out: Meditation, Visualization, and Journaling

The following is an exercise to assist you in identifying what it feels like for you to be a peacemaker and why you want to do this work. The exercise uses a combination of the meditation and visualization tools noted earlier, followed by some questions you can use as journaling prompts. If one of the other tools resonates more for you, then I encourage you to modify the exercise to fit into your peacemaking toolbox. This guided meditation is more effective when you don't have to stop in the middle of it to read the prompts that follow. Therefore, I recommend that you read through it first to become familiar with the prompts. Alternatively, you can record yourself reading the meditation and replay the recording or video while you meditate.

Meditation: Finding Your Why

Settle into a comfortable seated position.

Take a few deep breaths in through your nose and out through your mouth. Notice your body sitting in your chair, your arms resting comfortably. Begin to notice the rise and fall of your breath. Notice your feet resting on the ground. Breathing in and out.

Now I invite you to bring your attention to the center of your chest, into your heart space; breathing into that space, allowing your heart to feel open; allowing yourself to feel love; love for yourself; love for others; just breathing in openness and love.

Now I invite you, with your mind's eye, to remember a time where you felt totally aligned as a peacemaker; when you felt fully in flow; when you did really good work; when you just knew that you were doing what you are called to do. Take some time to notice the details of this experience. Where are you? What are you doing? Who is present? Are you taking a more active or passive role? What does this experience feel like? Do you notice any sensations in your body? Let yourself really feel this experience.

Now I invite you to ask yourself, "Why do I do this work? Why do I want to be a peacemaker? How do I want to impact families?" Allow some time, just breathing, noticing, and feeling, for any answers to come to you. Take a few moments to appreciate this experience, to feel true gratitude for having it.

When you are ready, begin to come back to your breath, back to your heart, back to your body sitting in your chair. Allow small movements to return to your hands or feet, and when you are ready you can open your eyes.

Journaling Prompts: Finding Your Why

Once you have completed the meditation, I recommend that you spend some time writing about your meditation experience. You can use the questions listed in the meditation as your journaling prompts, repeated here. If needed, repeat the meditation more than once. The more times you do the meditation, the clearer your purpose may become, the more memories you will access, and the more likely patterns will emerge. Writing about the meditation by using the following prompts will also reinforce your confidence in your "why" for being a peacemaker.

1. Start by writing about your meditation experience. What was that like for you? Were you able to access a memory?
2. What role were you playing in your memory? Were you in an advocacy, advisory, or neutral position?
3. Do you prefer to work with a team of professionals or on your own?
4. What sensations did you feel in your body when you did the meditation? Can you pause, close your eyes while writing and access those sensations now?
5. Did answers to the questions come when you asked yourself about your purpose? Sometimes these answers come in the form of words, sometimes in images, and still other times in new sensations. What happened for you during the meditation?

Taking Inventory of Your Practice

Once you have clearly identified your "why," the next step is to begin a thorough investigation into your practice to see how you can start to feel your purpose more frequently. It is also important to identify how often your clients and the professionals you work with are experiencing you in your purpose and the outcomes you intend and hope for them.

Following is another series of journaling prompts to consider as you begin the examination of your practice. If you find one of these prompts particularly intriguing or challenging, I encourage you to explore the question with whichever peacemaking tool resonates most with you. For example, you could create your own meditation or visualization exercise around the question or talk about it in therapy. Be as creative and have as much fun as you can with this exploration.

1. How often, in your current practice, do you feel like you are aligned with your purpose?
2. What activities could you add to your practice to feel your purpose more often?
3. Which tasks could you remove from your practice to free up more of your time to do the tasks that create your purpose?
4. Who are your ideal clients?
5. If you were fully aligned with your purpose during a new client consultation, how would you look, feel, and act? How is this similar to or different from how you currently approach consultations?
6. Examine your practice from the perspective of a client. How often do they experience you aligned with your purpose? What can you change to allow them to experience that more often?
7. Examine the professionals that you typically work with. Is it easy or difficult to feel your purpose when you work with them? What makes it easy or difficult? What can you change to make this easier?

Once you have completed this examination of your practices, consider what changes you might want to make for yourself, for your clients, and for the professionals you work with. Then keep coming back to these exercises. Do an annual, quarterly, or even monthly assessment of the health of your peacemaking practice where the fundamental question you are asking is how aligned is your practice with your purpose? (You will not lose your peacemaking card if you also examine the financial trends of your practice alone, or with a financial professional.)

The more time you spend refining your understanding of why you want to be a peacemaker and aligning your practice with your purpose, the more clearly you can articulate your "why" to potential clients and referral sources. With this clear understanding, you can develop a website, write a blog, work with marketing professionals, and so on. Your message as to why you are a peacemaker is clear, and you begin to embody the professional you always wanted to be; you begin to build the practice you always wanted to have.

Making Your Practice Financially Sustainable

One of the biggest challenges for family lawyers making the transition from litigation to peacemaking are fears that this new practice may not provide ample financial rewards to support you and your family. That unease is what makes us slip back into old patterns. Those family lawyers still in transition take on clients and cases that keep them away from the practice they ultimately want to have. Old fears emerge and inaccurate limiting beliefs come back. Finding compassion for yourself and relying on your daily peacemaking practice(s) in these moments is essential. Check in with yourself to see how aligned your practice is with your purpose at these times of doubt. Perhaps there was a recent client or situation that moved you away from your purpose; see if you can honor this experience without making it bigger than it really is. See if you can recall other clients or situations in your practice where you were aligned with your purpose.

Working with families in conflict is hard work. Acknowledge that. Even when we are aligned with our purpose, there will be moments when the situations we are addressing sadden us. We are emotional human beings assisting other human beings during times of heightened emotions, trauma even; it is natural for that to impact us. That is why taking care of ourselves and balancing how much we are engaged with families in conflict with other activities is so important to sustainability.

Before I began my peacemaking practice I worked at a large litigation-based law firm. Making a lasting transition from the courtroom meant that I needed to make more changes to my life than simply the forum in which I worked with my clients. To fully step into my new practice, I had to envision how I could make my personal life and my work life flow together in a congruent way where the one didn't feel so separate from the other. I wanted to bring joy and happiness into my work and my personal life. The key, I found was identifying the activities in my life that brought me that joy and happiness and ensuring that I made time for them every day. For me that meant making time for my family, time in nature, time for my peacemaking practices, and time developing the type of practice that was aligned with my purpose, which is to create healing spaces for families to navigate difficult conversations.

I encourage you to examine the activities that bring you joy and happiness in your life. What fills up your cup? What nourishes your soul? From there identify how you can experience moments of that each day. For example, if time in nature is important to you, schedule time each day for a walk. If time with your family is important, create space each day to connect with them. If travel is something you love, you can set aside time to plan trips, read about places you might want to go, or talk about past trips with those you have traveled with. Small windows of time can be sprinkled throughout your day.

It is also important to spend some time realistically looking at how much time you really need to work. Get clear about the amount of revenue you need to generate to support your financial goals. If you find that you need to work more hours than are realistic, perhaps you are undervaluing your services and need to consider charging more. Or perhaps you need to reevaluate your financial goals so they become aligned with a life filled with time for joy and happiness. These are personal decisions. Choose what is most important to you, what will bring you the most peace. Once you have identified the pieces most important to you and how much time you need to spend on billable work, set aside some time to visualize what an ideal day in your life would look like.

When I began my practice, I did a visualization exercise where I envisioned what my ideal day would look like. Here is the chart that I created.

Patrick Kalscheur, Visualizing an Ideal Day in the Preferred Lifestyle

(a) Early Morning Practices (5:30–7:00 am): meditation, yoga, reading, journaling
(b) Morning Family Prep (7:00–8:30 am): be with boys, help prepare them for school, make family breakfast, etc.
(c) Time in Nature (8:30–10:00 am): hike, bike, walk the dog, etc. Take time to feel fresh air and prepare for the day.
(d) Billable Work (10:00 am–12:00 pm): mediation, collaborative cases, etc.
(e) Lunch/Nature/Shop (12:00–2:00 pm): eat lunch, take a walk, hike, bike ride, etc. or go grocery shopping as necessary.
(f) Work (2:00–5:00 pm): some of this billable, some time spent exploring new avenues for practice growth, idea generation.
(g) Family/Cook/Nature (5:00–8:30 pm): cook dinner, eat with family, take a family walk or bike ride, read, enjoy a fire or other family activity.
(h) Easy work/wind down (8:30–10:00 pm): read articles or other inspiring materials, spend time with Anviksha (my wife).
(i) Evening meditation (10:00–10:30 pm): relaxation and release of the day in preparation for sleep.
(j) Sleep (10:30 pm–5:30 am): sleep and dream.

Initially, it was very important for me to adhere to this schedule as it kept me committed to making a full transition out of litigation and into a full-time peacemaking practice. Over time, I have been able to let go of rigidly keeping such a schedule as I now can simply feel when any elements of my life get out of balance. When this happens, I look for what is out of balance, and I come back to my purpose and identifying those things that create more happiness and joy in my life. This does not mean that doubts and challenges never arise—they do. But by integrating work and life together in a way where one flows more naturally from the other and ensuring that I am creating space for happiness each day, I am able to come back to a peaceful state more quickly and naturally.

Concluding Note

While some of the activities recommended in this chapter may seem new to you, I am hopeful that you will consider them and try them—both for yourself as a peacemaking individual and for how you work with families going through conflicts. At the core of this chapter, I am asking you to tune in to what is most important to you, to make sure you are taking good care of yourself, and to visualize the outcomes that will create as much joy and happiness as possible for you and for your clients as they navigate big changes in their lives. Moving from a court-based practice to a peacemaking practice is a big change for a lawyer, so please bring the same care and attention to your practice that you would encourage your clients to bring to their lives. If you do, you will be modeling how to make peace for your clients.

Patrick Kalscheur worked for many years in large and midsized law firms before leaving to open Kalscheur Conscious Family Law in 2017. Patrick saw the need for families undergoing divorce to feel more supported, to help them restore peace, and to guide them to amicable outcomes they could feel good about many years later. In addition to his role at Kalscheur Conscious Family Law, Patrick is the Director of the Family Restructuring Center at Introspective Family Wellness, where mediation and mental health professionals support the whole family system as families navigate separation and divorce. Patrick also trains other peacemakers on their paths to peace through his innovative Integrated Professional Training workshops, classes, and mastermind groups. Contact: patrick@chicagoconsciouslaw.com or patrick@introspectivefamily-therapy.com.

Chapter 3

Lawyers as Peacemakers: A Personal Journey

David Hoffman[1]

I'm a lawyer. I started my law career as a litigator. That's the only area of law that interested me. I thought litigation was a good way to fight for social justice and make the world a better place.

I was inspired by the courtroom victories for civil rights and civil liberties in the years when I was growing up in the 1950s and 1960s—most notably in *Brown v. Board of Education*, in which the Supreme Court said that forcing students to attend separate schools, segregated by race, was unconstitutional.

For the past 31 years, I have been a courtroom lawyer. I have had my share of exciting cases where I tried to make the world a better place, which brings me to a question: Should you just say "no" to litigation and stop going to court? (See Chapter 4 for a discussion on whether to both litigate and have a collaborative practice.)

It's not that we don't need courts. On the contrary, we need them very much—to tell us what the law is and how to apply it. Pursue those important cases. However, many more cases are in the courts than should be. Furthermore, the cost of this unnecessary litigation is not just in time and money but also in unnecessary acrimony and the destruction of families.

You probably know what mediation is—but in case you don't, it's quite simple. Mediation is "facilitated negotiation." The mediator is not the "decider" (such as a judge or arbitrator). Instead, the mediator helps the parties communicate and problem-solve more effectively.

I have seen mediations where an apology settled the case. For example, I mediated a dispute between a doctor and nurse who had worked together for several years in the sorely underfunded medical clinic of a homeless shelter.

---

1. This chapter is an edited transcript from a TEDx Talk delivered by peacemaker David Hoffman on April 24, 2016.

The dispute arose when the nurse walked off the job in the middle of a shift as a protest: She had been trying to get the management of the shelter to do a better job in equipping the clinic, and management had turned a deaf ear. During the mediation, I was surprised when each party expressed genuine appreciation for the other as a professional and as a principled person. The nurse took responsibility for leaving the doctor in the lurch. "I am truly sorry," she said, "that I put you in an awful spot, but I hope you realize that I did it for a good reason." She expressed her admiration for the doctor, who, she pointed out, could have been earning far more in private practice. The doctor, too, was sorry. "I felt horrible about firing you for leaving during your shift," he said. "You're an amazingly talented nurse and totally dedicated to the patients." At that point, the doctor and the nurse looked at each other and got a little tearful. The case settled because there is an inherent logic—some call it magic—to mediation when people truly listen to each other with open hearts.

After I got my mediation training in 1992, I started doing more mediation and less litigation each year. Then in the year 2000, I got trained in a new process called collaborative law. In collaborative law, each party has a lawyer, but the lawyers and clients agree that the lawyers are in the case solely for negotiation. If the negotiations reach an impasse, the clients can go to court, but they are required to hire new lawyers. The collaborative process gives both the lawyers and clients an incentive to resolve the case by agreement. In addition, the lawyers and the clients in collaborative law agree to share all relevant information, negotiate in a cooperative manner, and, if experts are needed, hire them jointly.

In the last 25 years, thousands of lawyers in the United States and other countries have been trained in collaborative law. In my own practice, I have seen many dozens of cases settled using that process. With each passing year, more divorce professionals realize that our legal system needs fewer litigators and more peacemakers.

Here's a useful analogy: Think of the medical arena, where surgeons play a role similar to the role that litigators play in our legal system. Surgeons are often desperately needed when routine medical procedures are insufficient. But would we want a medical system that had mostly surgeons and only a few internists? Probably not. Neither should we have a legal system with great multitudes of litigators and only a few peacemakers.

Gandhi once said, "Be the change that you wish to see in the world"—which brings me to the decision that I made. Beginning today, I will no longer be accepting litigation cases. I am happy to refer such cases to colleagues of mine, inside my firm and outside my firm. My new job description is now mediator, arbitrator, collaborative law attorney, and "full-time peacemaker." (See Chapter 2 for a discussion of financial and other reasons to give up litigation.)

In taking this step, I want to acknowledge the hundreds—perhaps thousands—of other lawyers around the United States and other countries who have made the same decision. My colleague and mentor, Woody Mosten, who practices law in San Diego, took this step long ago and is leading the movement for lawyers as peacemakers. Stu Webb from Minnesota founded the collaborative law movement, and Pauline Tesler from California wrote the first textbook on collaborative law. Both stopped going to court to pursue peacemaking full time. In my own backyard in Boston, I was preceded in taking this step by many friends and colleagues—all of them excellent lawyers who do not go to court anymore. All of them are full-time peacemakers.

One of the reasons that I have decided to just say "no" to litigation is summed up in the following conversation that I had with my colleague Dan Finn just after he made this same decision. I asked Dan, "Why did you decide not to go to court anymore?" He said that it struck him one day, as he was standing in front of the judge in a divorce case, that his job was to portray the opposing party as a worse person than she really was, and to portray his own client as a better person than he really was. Dan said, "This feels morally wrong."

I agree. Our litigation system incentivizes the harshest of attacks on the opposing party. This is not unique to our legal system. Our political system has sadly sunk to the same sorry level. We see it in the presidential campaigns and in Congress. Sociologist Deborah Tannen accurately described our society as an "Argument Culture," in which highly polarized debate is viewed as the best way of getting at the truth. This may work well enough in a courtroom battle between two multinational corporations. However, it is far from ideal when the litigants are parents getting a divorce, siblings trying to sort out the estate of their parents, or business owners whose partnership is coming apart at the seams.

Peacemaking is underutilized in our legal system, but it has a good lineage there. Abe Lincoln, before he became President, was a country lawyer with a knack for settling cases. He wrote: "Discourage litigation. Persuade neighbors to compromise whenever you can. . . . As a peacemaker, the lawyer has a superior opportunity of becoming a good [person]."[2]

The late Supreme Court Chief Justice Warren Burger made the same point: "The entire legal profession . . . has become so mesmerized with the stimulation of the courtroom contest that we tend to forget that we ought to be healers of conflict."[3]

---

2. Abraham Lincoln, *Notes for a Law Lecture, July 1, 1850*, *in* THE COLLECTED WORKS OF ABRAHAM LINCOLN, VOL. 2 at 82–83 (Roy P. Basler ed., 1953).

3. Warren E. Burger, *Burger Urges Lawyers to Polish Ethics, Help Unclog Courts*, CHRISTIAN SCI. MONITOR (Feb. 13, 1984).

Practice Tips

1. Although collaborative practice may be your process of choice, respect and support for the courts remains essential, especially in their protection of expanding the reach of justice for minorities, women, and same-sex couples.
2. Moving away from litigation can reduce acrimony and destruction of relationships both for clients and for you.
3. An essential benefit of collaborative practice is the speed of resolution.
4. Collaborative professionals understand that an apology can be one of the most effective conflict resolution tools.
5. Collaborative practice understands that feelings are as real as facts. Accordingly, collaborative professionals work with clients to increase understanding of the emotional aspects of disputes and work out solutions that deal with complex and nuanced emotional situations.
6. Collaborative professionals stress listening to the clients for direct communication and self-determination of their lives.
7. Clients do the heavy lifting with the support of collaborative professionals.
8. Collaborative practice is not a rose garden or a "Kumbaya" experience. It is difficult work and requires you to manage your own emotions. Collaborative practice opens up the universe of resolution options well beyond the parameters imposed by the law.
9. Get ready for a bumpy ride. Collaborative practice is not magic, and you will sometimes be blamed for not solving an insoluble and intractable problem. A thick skin helps.
10. Sometimes calmness and lack of defensiveness when attacked can be a collaborative professional's greatest tool.
11. You need training, training, and more training to be a successful collaborative practitioner.
12. To fully focus on staying out of court, you may wish to follow the lead of David Hoffman and many other collaborative professionals in becoming a full-time peacemaker.
13. As a collaborative practitioner, you will not be required to portray the other client as worse than he or she really is, or to portray your own client as better than he or she really is.
14. Remember the wisdom of Abraham Lincoln who urged people to "Discourage litigation. Persuade neighbors to compromise whenever you can. . . . As a peacemaker, the lawyer has a superior opportunity of becoming a good person."
15. Follow the advice of the late Supreme Court Chief Justice Warren Burger to become a "healer of conflict."

By the way, there's an important role that you can play in fostering peacemaking. There comes a time in your life when you ask yourself: Is this job, where I spend so much of my time, fully aligned with my values and beliefs? Am I doing the work that God put me on this planet to do?

So, I encourage those of you who are still looking for the work that you were meant to do—keep your minds and hearts open. You will find your way, and hopefully it won't take you as long as it took me.

I want to conclude with an invitation to become a peacemaker. You can do this at work and in your community. Take a mediation training, which should be a universal part of the curriculum in our schools and universities. Read the book *Getting to Yes* by Roger Fisher, Bill Ury, and Bruce Patton and learn about principled negotiation. Build a support group of fellow mediators and collaborative practitioners.

These skills are immensely useful even if you do not make collaborative practice or mediation your day job. Volunteer peacemakers are needed in community and court programs. Becoming a peacemaker is a journey, not a destination, and our world desperately needs more peacemakers.

David A. Hoffman is the founding member of Boston Law Collaborative, LLC, where he serves as a mediator, arbitrator, and collaborative law attorney. He also teaches three courses at Harvard Law School, where he is the John H. Watson, Jr. Lecturer on Law: Mediation; Diversity and Dispute Resolution; and Legal Profession: Collaborative Law. David has published three books on the subject of dispute resolution: *Mediation: A Practice Guide for Mediators, Lawyers, and Other Professionals* (Massachusetts Continuing Legal Education, 2013); *Bringing Peace into the Room: How the Personal Qualities of the Mediator Impact the Process of Conflict Resolution* (with Daniel Bowling) (Jossey-Bass 2003); and *Massachusetts Alternative Dispute Resolution* (with Prof. David Matz) (Butterworth Legal Publishers 1994, 2d ed. 1996). Furthermore, David is the past chair of the American Bar Association Section of Dispute Resolution and a founding member of the Massachusetts Collaborative Law Council. David is also a member of the Peacemaking Practice Trainers. Website: http://blc.law/

Chapter 4
Resolving Conflict by Building Peaceful Solutions

Peace is not merely a distant goal that we seek, but
a means by which we arrive at that goal.
—Martin Luther King Jr.

In the past several decades, family lawyers have been educated beyond the adversarial paradigm to achieve settlements in new and different ways both inside and outside the courtroom. And yet, despite excellent law school courses, court programs featuring mediation, and continual education by bar associations and private providers, family lawyers still cling to adversarial negotiation and litigation as their methodology of choice.

The goal of this chapter is to review the key areas of lawyering with a dispute resolution commitment and how these areas can be further adapted to meet the values and attributes of peacemaking for clients.

Legal Representation in Mediation

In recent years, Family Mediation has become much more widely used both in the courthouse and in the private sector. While considered the foundation of *Alternative*[1] Dispute Resolution, mediation was first viewed as an alternative to how cases were settled in the courts. Due to the desire and need by family law judges to better administer a constantly rising caseload, mediation was inserted into court procedure as both a required and recommended alternative to judges managing the cases and making decisions following adversarial hearings and trials.

1. Some might suggest using the term "appropriate" dispute resolution; or even more clearly "consensual" dispute resolution (CDR). *See* Nancy Cameron, *Collaborative Practice in the Canadian Landscape*, 49 Fam. Ct. Rev. 221 (2011), https://doi.org/10.1111/j.1744-1617.2011.01365.x.

Mediation was (and still is) seen as an alternative to negotiation—which is far more commonplace. Although the majority of families in many jurisdictions navigate the family court system without legal representation, unrepresented parties often fail to engage in meaningful negotiation after a case is filed, due to various contributing factors. Even when self-represented parties attempt to negotiate on their own or are encouraged to do so by a family law judge, emotional stress, the difficulty of the law, or a lack of experience often prevents them from getting the job done.[2]

Progressive courts make attempts to help floundering self-represented litigants with ombudspersons, family court officers, and other staff to help the unrepresented primarily fill out court forms and in some instances provide guidance on issues to negotiate. In rarer court systems, such court officers assume mediator functions. In some communities, nonprofit or low-cost clinics outside the court system will coach one party in drafting or negotiation (see the section on limited scope representation later in this chapter).

Ultimately, most families navigate the legal system without representation—both parties are self-represented. In response, some judges take on a neutral, quasi-mediator role by facilitating voluntary settlement conferences, while others conduct mandatory settlement conferences. In these settings, the judge's role becomes a hybrid of mediator and evaluative decision-maker, aimed at encouraging resolution. Best practice dictates that a judge overseeing a settlement conference should not be the same judge who decides the case, in order to maintain impartiality and prevent exposure to settlement positions or judicial persuasion. However, in smaller jurisdictions, practical limitations often require the same judge to perform both roles.

Lawyer–Lawyer Negotiation

Even though fewer than 40 percent of family litigants hire two lawyers, the court system is designed for this model. While courts encourage lawyers to negotiate before a hearing or trial date, all too often, lawyers have not set aside time for just the lawyers to discuss and negotiate terms. Even less frequently do lawyers and their clients sit down together outside of the court setting, aka hold a "four-way meeting."

---

2. *See* JULIE MCFARLANE, NATIONAL SELF REPRESENTED LITIGANTS PROJECT. Although researching Canadian families, we believe that Professor McFarlane's findings are applicable to the experience in the U.S. and other jurisdictions.

On the day of a court hearing, judges offer (or require) different forms of negotiation to take place right in the courthouse:

A. Judge will ask lawyers to negotiate out in the hall or in the attorney conference room. Clients sit at a distance from each other but close enough either to hear the lawyers or confer with their lawyer at an appropriate time.

B. Lawyers and clients will sit down together in a four-way setting.

As the lawyers have already prepared for a hearing/trial, these negotiations are often limited in time, or feature lawyers with divided attention juggling thoughts about settling the case or having the first crack at a courtroom to conduct litigation. Lawyers and clients all feel the pressure to settle quickly, which is generally encouraged by the judge who would rather make space for a lengthy and productive negotiation rather than consume court time.

No matter the negotiation model used in court, a judge's primary motivation is often to conserve court time and resources by reaching a quick settlement instead of holding a full hearing.

Court Connected Mediation

Courthouse mediation programs have similar motivations: save court resources. These programs are generally "late stage," that is, taking place either on the day of litigation or set very close to trial. In addition to client and lawyer reluctance to mediate early, judges often mirror those attitudes due to prior experience as family litigators themselves or due to the paucity of court mediators.

Court-connected mediators are either on court staff or have private practices but serve on panels administered by court personnel. States differ as to whether a judge can order parties to participate in mediation, particularly if the parties must pay for the mediation service. In some jurisdictions, legislation or court rules require parties to participate in mediation. In other jurisdictions, where no such legal authority exists, judges are reluctant (or not permitted) to *order* parties into mediation, but some judges still note the value of working with a mediator to expedite or eventually achieve settlement.[3]

3. Due to advances in curriculum and training about mediation developed in judicial education programs, more judges now have a sound knowledge of the benefits of mediation, particularly to help court administration.

Private Mediation

You can readily see why court mediation and negotiation may be inadequate to maximize peacemaking benefits discussed in an earlier chapter. Many lawyers and parties would prefer to litigate, not mediate. Selection of a mediator by parties is nonexistent in many jurisdictions: Mediators are assigned by the court and have different levels of mediation training, or none at all. Lawyers and mediators are time pressured and under the duress of an impending court hearing. The goal of the process is to resolve cases to reduce court caseload rather than optimize party self determination and durable settlement.

Private mediation is not a guaranteed panacea for peacemaking. If parties are represented by counsel, the overwhelming choice of mediator by lawyers is a retired judicial officer or veteran litigator. Why? Lawyers have a belief (with little or no empirical evidentiary backup) that parties have more trust and confidence in judges and litigators serving as mediators who are skilled in case evaluation and power-based negotiation depending on the strength of facts and law.

Very few of such lawyer-selected mediators have had any mediation training or experience. They run a mediation as a judge would control a Mandatory Settlement Conference. This means that the parties rarely, if ever, meet together in joint session—the parties and their lawyers stay in separate rooms and rarely meet as a group, with or without the mediator. As indicated in the Riskin-Welsh article, "Is That All There Is," the conversations in such mediation tend to be rather narrow—focusing on "lawyer" issues such as the relative weaknesses in each case, how a judge might rule, and other issues with which lawyers are most familiar and comfortable.[4]

Tips for Peacemaking in Mediation

Timing of Mediation

Uncertainty about their future, continued conflict, and the drain of resources to resolve conflict all augur for the earliest resolution possible. This supports starting mediation as soon as possible rather than riding the waves of negotiation and/or court proceedings while the calendar pages continue to be turned.

Concerns about unfinished information exchange, the negative raw impact of recent separation, and permitting adjustment after separation to set in before attempting settlement are valid. Yet, they are outweighed by the pain of unresolved conflict. We recommend folding these concerns into the mediation process while still starting mediation as soon as possible.

4. Leonard L. Riskin & Nancy A. Welsh, *Is That All There Is?: "The Problem" in Court Oriented Mediation*, 15 Geo. Mason L. Rev. 863 (2008).

Significant conflict often erupts after the decision to divorce, as spouses continue to share the same cage. Wars of the Roses do happen—not infrequently. Rather than expediting court filings or permitting cold wars to continue, initiating mediation to handle cohabitation and move out issues may be the best move possible. Yes, the emotions will be raw; and blame for the demise of the relationship may be at its highest. And still, it is never too early to mediate.

Selection of Mediator

When lawyers select a mediator jointly, the parties themselves are often not consulted or included in the selection process. It is customary for the parties never to have even met the mediator prior to selection, and often not until the parties are involved in negotiation.

Having mutual agreement in selecting a mediator that both lawyers trust and respect is a benefit to clients. However, the lawyers may mutually select a mediator that *they* like, which may in many cases be a different choice than what the clients would have preferred. A main criterion for lawyer selection is often whether the mediator knows the law and can evaluate the legal strengths and weaknesses of each party's position. This legal-based skill may be an important factor in lawyer-led mediator selection, and retired judges and veteran family law litigators fit the bill on that basis.

Clients may align with the emphasis on legal experience by default, as they often are not informed of other considerations and the peacemaking choices that they might make. Some of these other considerations include:

1. **Mediators with Subject Area Experience**—such as therapists trained in spousal communication and parenting—can bring valuable subject-matter expertise to the process. When financial issues are involved, mediation can sometimes be bifurcated so that matters like accounting, corporate law, real estate, or pensions are handled by mediators with relevant expertise. To address the full range of substantive needs, many mediators work as co-mediators, combining their diverse skills into a single team. However, we have found that few retired judges or mediators who also practice litigation favor this interdisciplinary approach, even though it may be the preferred model for clients if given the option.

   Many excellent mediators may lack extensive litigation experience but possess the empathy and long-term training necessary to guide parties through dialogue rather than offering evaluative recommendations. Some facilitative mediators have legal backgrounds, including family law expertise, yet focus on uncovering the parties' underlying needs and interests to foster a broader conversation instead of providing evaluative or directive guidance. Others come from fields such as education, business, or social work, bringing strong skills in framing issues and leaving legal analysis to the attorneys. For example, the well-known "Father of Modern Mediation" Dr. John Haynes used his background as a professor of education to establish rapport and build trust with mediation parties. He used his teaching background to turn the mediation table into a classroom of client education and was a master at teasing out options and helping parties make considered decisions. Mediation scholars Professor Stephen Goldberg and Margaret Shaw published a study in the Harvard Negotiation Journal that found that the most successful mediators were not necessarily well versed in the law but did in fact establish rapport and build confidence and trust.[5]

2. **Use of Joint Sessions.** In the UCLA Law School course that Woody taught—Lawyers as Peacemakers—he once brought in a client from a family mediation to speak with his students. In the mediation she "survived" (her words, not ours), the guest lamented that during a ten-hour mediation session, she and her lawyer were locked up in one room, and her husband and his lawyer were locked up separately. They never once spoke with each other, on any issue! The mediator shuttled back and forth messengering different proposals: She complained that she was not sure that the proposal was actually what her husband intended. Her only contact was with the mediator. She conceded that the case was settled, but it left a bitter taste in her mouth. The guest surmised that if she had known other options for settlement than presented by the mediator, her settlement might have better met her long-term needs.

   Many law-dominated mediators and the family lawyers who select them are not comfortable with client emotion or interaction. There is a fear that such direct client contact could get out of control and the mediation itself would be in peril.

   Mediators and lawyers who are trained as consultant lawyers play very important roles in guiding but not controlling their clients through difficult mediation sessions.[6]

3. **Use Sequential Sessions.** In their article "Late Nights and Cancellation Rights: Bolstering Enforceability of Mediated Settlements with a Cooling Off Period," Judge Thomas Lewis, Judge Elizabeth Potter Scully, and Woody Mosten argue that traditional mediations that last into the wee hours are Petrie dishes of duress and coercion impacting clients

---

5. Ellen Waldman Goldberg & Judith Shaw, *The Secrets of Successful (and Unsuccessful) Mediators*, 23 Harv. Negot. L. Rev. 393 (2007).

6. *See* Mosten, Scully & Traum, Effectively Representing Clients in Family Mediations (ABA 2023).

to sign when their capacity to agree and understand informed consent are frayed beyond good client (or attorney) judgment.[7]

These situations stem from the single-session model of mediation—the customary format for lawyer-led mediations. Parties and counsel gather at an appointed time with the goal (stated or unstated): try to hammer out a deal today or it's on to trial for resolution. This results in long days and unnecessary extra stress due to the sense that it is "now or never," leading to late day/night concessions that can then lead to next morning remorse. The traditional lawyer mantra is: "If parties don't sign at this session, they will change their positions in the light of day, back out, and all of work will be for naught."

Peacemaking lawyers often work with family mediators who favor sequential sessions. Parties work with their mediator (and often with consulting attorneys) for shorter sessions, from 90 minutes to four hours in length, without the expectation that an agreement will be reached by the end of the session. A shorter session may focus on a single issue or attempt comprehensive agreements that parties are encouraged and expected to reflect upon and make modifications at the next session, if appropriate.

When peacemaking lawyers work in a sequential session format, support for client reflection and possible modification after the mediation session is encouraged. Clients are educated with a different mindset: "Never sign if you are not ready to do so. Take the necessary time to consider options and only sign after you have had all of your questions answered." If parties never sign after leaving the mediation session, peacemaking lawyers encourage their clients to try again, perhaps in a different format or with a different mediator, or with additional experts at the mediation table. As signing a final settlement containing 250 to 350 linked issues may be the biggest and most important negotiation of a client's life, pressuring a client rarely helps; and often hurts the resolution process and the family's future restructured relationship.[8]

4. **Encourage Clients to Make Their Own Opening Statements.** While many lawyers (and mediators) espouse client decision-making, very few mediations start with the parties talking to each other. Customarily,

7. Thomas Lewis, Elizabeth Potter Scully & Woody Mosten, *Late Nights and Cancellation Rights: Bolstering Enforceability of Mediated Settlements with a Cooling Off Period*, CAL. ST. BAR J. 36–38 (2019).

8. To view what pressure can bring about, see the seminal case of *Cassell v. Superior Court* 51 Cal. 4th 113, 244 P.3d 1080, 119 Cal. Rptr. 3d 437 (2019), in which the client, in his malpractice action, accused his lawyer of pressuring him to sign to the point that the lawyer followed Cassell into the restroom and harangued him while the client took a bio break!

the mediator (and perhaps lawyers) provides the opening introductions, goals of the mediation, protocol, and ground rules. The parties may ask or answer a question and are otherwise mute.

As a peacemaking lawyer you can encourage your client (and the other lawyer and/or mediator) to have the parties offer remarks—often based on a template that might look something like this:

1. Choose who goes first.
2. No time limit—you each can speaks without fear of interruption.
3. Speak directly to your spouse/partner.
4. Acknowledge the positive personal attributes and contributions of your spouse to your family.
5. Point out the common values that the two of you have. Describe areas of conflict that have occurred and how you would like to avoid them in the future.
6. Describe your goals for the mediation and your vision for the key components of your settlement.
7. Share your concerns about what you (and the children) need and any concerns about the actions of the other party.
8. Questions and discussion.

As a peacemaker, you can provide gentle guidance as to various ways that your client can prepare for this important conversation with this important person in their life, someone they may not have had many positive conversations with lately, or perhaps no conversations at all.

Some options you might lay out include:

- Feel free to write out your statement—you can even read it at your own pace. Many mediation participants also print out a copy for their partner to read later.
- Jot down key notes and refer to them when you want, or need, to do so.
- Speak from the heart—as little or as much as you are moved.

Many of our clients say that this chance to reset the conflict made a great difference in helping their mediation have success.

5. **Have Parties Work Together (If Possible).** Experienced mediators share opportunities for restructuring parents and partners to work for instead of against each other. Some of these options, which not only help reduce the tension but also can save them both significant mediation fees, include:

- Finding best and least costly health insurance
- Divide up furniture and personal items themselves with directions from the mediator and support from their lawyers
- Fix up the home for sale together and divide tasks of working with real estate broker, plumbers, and other service providers
- Look for their child's next school together or individually and share data
- Find a mutual way of helping or setting boundaries for children who are struggling with the separation
- Select therapists, financial advisors, and other professionals together

If you are drafting the settlement terms, summaries, or other documents, be faithful to the parties' agreement and do not try to take adversarial advantage.

6. Encourage your client to prevent future conflict by holding regular parenting meetings to check in and address potential issues early.

Collaborative Practice as Your Gateway to Peacemaking

As we have discussed, peacemaking is both a mindset and a set of values that can be integrated into the practice of lawyering. One of our great peacemakers, Ken Cloke, has the following insights toward your new path:

> Conflicts, like dreams, are made of desires and fears, honesty and doubt, passion and surrender, all of which lie beneath the surface and are revealed through a collaborative professional's questions. Our willingness to answer these same questions ourselves gives us permission to search for the piercing, dangerous moments that change people's lives, and the courage to seek them out, even in our own lives. . . . Collaborative practice is the search for the invisible bridge that connects every living being with every other. . . .[9]

As described more deeply in the next chapter, collaborative law started approximately 40 years ago by Stu Webb, a family lawyer in Minnesota who utilized all of his lawyering skills but refused to transport them to the

9. Kenneth Cloke, Mediating Dangerously 50–51 (inserting "collaborative practice" for "mediation."

courthouse. In the interim, collaborative practice has grown internationally into an approach that will welcome you to accelerate your peacemaking journey along with an interdisciplinary network that will still allow you to have an aligned relationship with your clients while still resulting in a high settlement rate with satisfied clients.

Collaborative Practice Values

A quick overview of the values embedded in the collaborative process should feel quite familiar and comfortable to a peacemaking lawyer.

1. Respect and dignity for the other party and other professionals
2. Direct and open communication with the other party and professionals
3. Voluntary and full disclosure of relevant information and documents necessary to make agreements
4. Commitment to the healing of the family
5. Use of interest-based negotiation to try to meet the needs of both parties

These values are not just aspirational: They are required by the professionals who practice and are incorporated into a client contract called a Participation Agreement, which is signed by both parties, both lawyers, and any other professionals on the collaborative team.

Other Professionals? A Collaborative Team?

These features are essential aspects of peacemaking and two of the major developments since collaborative law was founded by Stu Webb. Just as in the medical field where triage of the surgeon, diagnostician, nurse, anesthesiologist, social workers, and others provides the best patient care, collaborative practice now regularly features mental health and financial professionals in a number of roles. Unlike collaborative lawyers who are *always* aligned with their clients (yet open to helping the entire family), these other professionals are generally neutral. While the lawyers are selected by each party individually, the neutral members of the collaborative team are either jointly selected by the lawyers or the parties mutually select them (traditionally guided by their lawyers—though a new protocol of having parties select their own professionals is now gaining traction throughout the CDR community).[10]

10. Forrest S. Mosten, Bringing Informed Consent & Consumerism into Mediation: Parties Jointly Select Their Lawyers (Nov. 13, 2023), https://mediate.com/bringing-informed-consent-consumerism-into-mediation-parties-jointly-select-their-lawyers/.

Lawyer Disqualification Contract

The single most important innovation in collaborative practice (and the only required protocol among an array of collaborative models) is the four-way agreement involving both lawyers and parties stating that if either party terminates the collaborative process or initiates an adversarial court action, both collaborative lawyers are *permanently* disqualified from representing their clients any further—both in the private collaborative process and in any court proceeding involving these parties. This requirement is not waivable by the parties. As a double dose of informed consent, the engagement agreement with each client and collaborative lawyer should contain a client acknowledgment about the use and impact of the Disqualification contract.

Some critics of collaborative law see the Lawyer Disqualification as an abandonment of clients who have invested money and trust in their lawyers only to be forced to pay another retainer and establish a new relationship with a lawyer for the balance of the legal journey. Commissioners of the Uniform Collaborative Law Act (UCLA) see the disqualification clause in a much more positive (aka peacemaking) light: This clause permits parties to form trust in both the other party's lawyer and the collaborative process with the assurance that *nothing* the party says or does in the "safe container" will ever be used against her in a court of law. This permits generosity in settlement proposals and protection in letting parties share their fears and concerns not just with their own lawyer but also with the other party's lawyer as well.

The cloak of confidentiality of collaborative communications is another feature of the process as mandated by the UCLA. Such communications, including settlement offers, are not later admissible in court should the collaborative process not ultimately end in a full agreement. While nearly 30 states have adopted the UCLA to date, nearly half the states in the U.S. still do not have this confidentiality protection. While some states have extended mediation confidentiality to collaborative matters, confidentiality protections should be explicitly included in all Participation Agreements.

Interdisciplinary Teams

A key peacemaking feature of collaborative practice is its adoption of the team triage approach to helping the family. By including mental health practitioners to assist with party communication and parenting, lawyers let their clients know that these needs will be met by trained experts rather than by legal practitioners schooled in the law. This modesty and acknowledgment of our limits as well as willingness to trust other professionals to help our clients is a different and satisfying message to our clients. Few (if any) lawyers have undergone the 3,000 hours of supervised client work that all of our licensed mental health colleagues have. As in unbundling, clients get the help that they need at a lower price point. (Actually, collaborative law *is* an unbundled service because court work is not part of the full scope lawyering package.) In the same way, the current and financial needs of clients are met by the inclusion of a collaborative financial professional on the team.

As there is no "I" in "team," the collaborative team approach differs greatly from your role as a family lawyer. While a collaborative lawyer has all the same ethical lawyer obligations for client care ("Yes, we are real lawyers!"), the collaborative lawyer is not a sole operator: He is a member of a team. Not the team leader but a co-manager and decision-maker in the process. Instead of going it alone, the collaborative lawyer joins his teammates (not just the other lawyer, often referred to as a "collaborative partner") for pre-brief and post-brief sessions that are explicitly confidential from the clients in order to promote a freedom of team communication for the clients' welfare free of client oversight or anxiety. This is a truly different atmosphere, veering away from a need to have clients briefed or second guess team decisions. Just like a surgical team would make technical decisions of how to operate, the collaborative team is dedicated to client welfare but not obligated to share all ideas and views of other team members. While some clients may be reluctant to cede control when they are paying the bill, given the 86 percent success rate and lawyer duty to provide client informed consent as to the collaborative process (including confidential team meetings), client satisfaction with collaborative practice is quite high—particularly due to the commitment of collaborative professionals to provide deep-rooted agreements that will help prevent conflict in the future.

Peacemaking Going Full Circle: Protocols Combining Mediation, Collaborative Professionals, and a Committed Interdisciplinary Team

In this chapter, we have discretely discussed peacemaking possibilities utilizing lawyer–lawyer negotiation, unbundled legal services, mediation with and without consulting attorneys, and collaborative practice. In addition to saving money and gaining control over their own lives, clients can benefit by choosing any of these options.

But what happens if we use them together? For example, mediation may be the process of first choice with parties opting to use collaborative professionals as co-mediators, consulting counsel, and consultants. On the other hand, parties my choose the aligned guidance of collaborative lawyers in a team approach with the use of a mediator to hold the neutral space and utilize either a facilitative or directive style to help get a settlement agreement.

Mediators are used in a variety of stages of the collaborative process. Mediators are now more frequently being admitted as active members of collaborative practice groups—and many practice groups require mediation training in addition to collaborative training for membership in these groups.[11]

The first stage of mediator involvement (and the least frequently utilized) is for the collaborative lawyers and/or full team to work with clients in bringing on a mediator at early in the process. Rather than to act as a referee or deal maker when there are disputes between parties, the mediator helps the team and parties set an agreed agenda and set up a process that works for both parties. A distinct advantage of early use of a mediator is that it frees the collaborative lawyers from joint management and settlement duties in order to concentrate on advising and supporting clients through the process. Clients often appreciate their lawyers aligned care rather than having the lawyers attempt to be neutral in bargaining both process choices and deciding on settlement terms.

A second stage of mediator involvement in an otherwise collaborative process is to name a mediator in negotiating the Participation Agreement. This mediator could be brought off the bench whenever one or both parties feel conflict overcoming progress or otherwise becoming stuck in an effort to reach settlement and avoid termination of the collaborative process.

A third stage is requiring mediation after notice termination of the collaborative process by one or both parties. Collaborative lawyers would be authorized to serve as mediation counsel with client consent and not otherwise be disqualified given the termination.

A new synergistic development of combining mediation and collaborative practice is a protocol requiring disqualification of the consulting lawyers if the mediation terminates for any reason.[12] Mirroring the purpose of the collaborative attorney disqualification clause, parties must make this choice for attorney disqualification. Since many parties choose mediation because they want to limit the involvement of lawyers; this protocol fits nicely with their overriding motivation and goals. This termination clause generally is adopted when parties enter mediation without lawyers rather than having the lawyers steer the matter into mediation.

This protocol to limit involvement of lawyers in mediation can have an additional add-on if adopted by the parties: Rather than have consulting

11. See the International Academy of Collaborative Professionals website www.collaborativepractice.com for a full list of collaborative practice groups worldwide.

12. See a sample attorney disqualification agreement in the Appendix.

counsel initiate interaction between them that might drive up costs or increase conflict, lawyers and parties can agree that all communication and negotiation will involve the neutral mediator, selected by the parties to keep the impartial tone and space of the mediation. Consulting lawyers focus on consulting with their clients to educate, advise, and implement strategy. Lawyers and their clients are encouraged to meet with the mediator separately, and lawyers are encouraged to meet with the mediator jointly. This method ensures that the mediator will remain in control of the design and management of the mediation, while lawyers work with the mediator on those tasks. It also limits the lawyers' hijacking of the mediation in those situations in which lawyers who are brought on by the mediator and parties no longer believe that the mediator's neutrality is worth the extra fees.

Conclusion

Choosing the appropriate peacemaking option is a nuanced and often challenging decision. However, since each option can lead to different—and frequently more successful—outcomes than the traditional lawyering approach, understanding and applying these various models can provide clients with more informed and often longer-lasting benefits.

Chapter 5
Helping Clients as a Peacemaker

The opposite of war is not peace, it's creation.
—Jonathan Larson

Most family lawyers in the United States practice in a paradigm that blends the roles of "solicitor" and "barrister" in the English model. Family lawyers are "solicitors" in that they directly work with clients to understand their needs and goals and attempt to negotiate favorable settlements as advocates in the shadow of the courthouse.[1] Using litigation as both negotiation leverage and as the next step following incomplete settlement talks, the family lawyer works also as a "barrister": an expert in court tactics and skills utilizing a positional-based method of negotiation.

While this combined solicitor–barrister model results in low consumer satisfaction (one loser, two losers, and rarely a winner), it is by far the most well-known and utilized model for resolving family disputes.

The model is familiar, but true peacemakers always struggled to conform. The binary was insufficient to foster peace and healing. Families needed something different.

A few unique thinkers, ahead of their time in many ways, acknowledged that peacemaking could only be furthered through process adjustment. There needed to be a paradigm shift within each practitioner as well as a new procedural format to catch the newly inspired peacemaker with a functional a road map for serving families differently. Mediation, collaborative law, and unbundled representation were born of necessity—envisioned by creatives yearning for better pathways to peace.

1. *See* Mnookin & Kornhauser, *Bargaining in the Shadow of the Law*, Yale L. Rev. (1977), following up on the historic Pound Conference convened by Supreme Court Chief Justice, Warren Burger, Professor Frank Sander, Reporter.

The Birth of Collaborative Practice: Peace Shifts in Baby Steps

In 1990, a Minnesota family lawyer, Stu Webb, conceived of a new model. In their seminal ABA treatise, Building a Successful Collaborative Practice, authors Adam Cordover and Forrest Mosten provided the following historical backdrop to Stu Webb's work:

> In 1990, a Minnesota family law attorney named Stu Webb began promoting what he deemed "Collaborative Law," or the practice of law separating out trial work and creating negotiation specialists. Collaborative Law is now used in Tampa Bay, throughout Florida, and around the world, as families have realized that they don't want to be placed in the adversarial proceedings of trial practice for divorce and other personal matters.
>
> On February 14, 1990, Webb wrote a letter to The Honorable A.M. "Sandy" Keith, a Justice of the Minnesota Supreme Court, describing Collaborative Law. Below is the text of the letter:
>
> *Dear Sandy:*
>
> *I met you at a party at Steve & Marilyn Erickson's several years ago. I was interested in your involvement with mediation. I also heard you talk last November at the Conference for Dispute Resolution Practitioners Seminar.*
>
> *I, too, took Steve and Marilyn's mediation training and have done mediation, mediation wrap-ups and, generally, have been vitally interested in exploring alternative dispute resolution in all its manifestations.*
>
> *I think I've come up with a new wrinkle that I'd like to share with you. One of the aspects of mediation that I feel is a weakness is that it basically leaves out input by the lawyer at the early stages (sometimes that's an advantage!). By that I don't mean adversarial, contentious lawyering, but the analytical, reasoned ability to solve problems and generate creative alternatives and create a positive context for settlement. Of course, these attributes of good lawyering are not utilized greatly in the usual adversarial family law proceeding either.*
>
> *But you and I have both experienced, I'm sure, those occasional times, occurring usually by accident, when in the course of attempting to negotiate a family law settlement, we find ourselves in a conference with the opposing counsel, and perhaps the respective clients, where the dynamics were such that in a climate of positive*

energy, creative alternatives were presented. In that context, everyone contributed to a final settlement that satisfied all concerned—and everyone left the conference feeling high energy, good feelings and satisfaction. More than likely, the possibility for a change in the way the parties related to each other in the future may have greatly increased. As a result, the lawyers may also develop a degree of trust between them that might make future dealings more productive.

So, my premise has been: why not create this settlement climate deliberately? I propose doing this by creating a context for settling family law matters by, where possible, removing the trial aspects from consideration initially. I would do this by creating a coterie of lawyers who would agree to take cases, on a case-by-case basis, for settlement only. The understanding would be that if it were determined at any time that the parties could not agree and settlement didn't appear possible, or if for other reasons adversarial court proceedings were likely to be required, the attorneys for both sides would withdraw from the case and the parties would retain new attorneys from there on out to final resolution.

I call the attorney in this settlement model a collaborative attorney, practicing in that case collaborative law.

The advantages of this collaborative-law model:

1. *Each party is represented by an attorney of his/her choice. (This is usually not the case in mediation until after the mediation has been completed.)*
2. *This allows the lawyers to be focused in the settlement mode without the threat of "going to Court" lurking just around the corner. In the normal situation, settlement is often by-passed initially while the parties posture and the lawyers work on discovery.*
3. *There is continuity between settlement and processing the final dissolution. (This is usually not the case in mediation with the resulting problem of the lawyers not liking the mediated settlement.)*
4. *With the focus on settlement and avoiding court, the lawyers and clients are motivated to learn what works to achieve settlement; how to problem-solve without getting "plugged in" to the emotional content (a la "War of the Roses"). Lawyers who participate in this program will be motivated to develop win-win settlement skills such as those practiced in mediation (just like they now focus on sharpening trial skills).*

5. *Lawyers are freed up to use their real lawyering skills, i.e., analysis, problem solving, creating alternatives, tax and estate planning and looking at the overall picture as to what's fair.*
6. *Four-way conferences become the norm with positive energies being generated (because that's where the creative solutions lie) as all work collaboratively for a fair settlement. As in mediation, the potential is high for the clients to have a lot of input.*
7. *Clients and potential clients get an orientation in which they are advised of the advantages, including cost savings, of this approach and the kind of attitude and frame of mind that is most likely to achieve fair, prompt, efficient and positive settlements that work for both parties.*
8. *When cases don't settle and new attorneys are retained for trial, the clients have had the best shot both ways, i.e., a settlement specialist and a trial specialist (in my experience they usually don't come in the same package).*
9. *Settling matters on a collaborative basis is just more fun!*

Practically, I am in the process of having lunch with some of my family law attorney-friends and inviting them to be open to participate in a collaborative model, should the occasion arise. The only requirement, as I've said, is an understanding by all concerned that the two attorneys would withdraw at such time as further settlement efforts appeared fruitless. The reception I have received has been encouraging.

Eventually there might be a referral listing for use by prospective clients enumerating lawyers willing to handle a matter on a collaborative basis.

Personally, about four months ago, I made the final moves to abandon my trial practice (which was already slanted toward settlement) to devote myself exclusively to a family law settlement practice. This means that I have unilaterally declared that I will not go to court in an adversarial matter. My practice is fun again!

Among other things, I spend a lot of time educating clients and prospective clients on the merits of settlement—however that can be achieved—and of avoiding unnecessary or premature use of the courts. I also stress the mindset that is optimal for settlement. Enclosed is an article I published which I hand out and find useful in helping clients center themselves for productive settlement work.

Because of your interest in this field and the fact that we both know there's "got to be a better way" of resolving most of these matters, I wanted to give you the above outline of what I'm up to. I would be most happy to discuss this—or other settlement alternatives—with you further at your convenience if you should wish to do so.

I apologize for the length of this letter. If nothing else, however, it has helped me to get my thinking on this subject somewhat organized.

Very truly yours

Stuart G. Webb[2]

Cordover then provided a personal coda of this historical moment:

> I have now decided to take Stu's lead and practice exclusively in out-of-court dispute resolution with a focus on Collaborative Family Law. In this way, I want to help families stay out of the adversarial court system and resolve their disputes privately, in a respectful setting.[3]

Webb's vision of a two-lawyer process focusing on non-court settlement created quite a stir among family lawyers worldwide. Currently, the International Academy of Collaborative Professionals[4] has membership in 24 countries and a cadre of cases, statutes, and even a Uniform Law that has been adopted by 26 states as of the date of publication of this book.

As will be further discussed in this chapter, the two-lawyer model has evolved into an interdisciplinary team that approximates triage care rather than a uni-disciplinary legal approach.

Paradigm Shift

Webb's original vision of collaborative law was to provide clients with a "safe container" away from litigation based on an agreement between lawyers not to go to court if settlement did not jell. This was the beginning of the extinction of the blended solicitor-barrister model by removing the "barrister" component.

2. https://familydiplomacy.com/the-origins-of-collaborative-divorce-stu-webbs-letter/. You can also learn more from a book written by Stu and fellow collaborative attorney, Ron Ousky, called *The Collaborative Way to Divorce: The Revolutionary Method That Results in Less Stress, Lower Costs, and Happier Kids–Without Going to Court*. The book is easy to read and geared toward spouses who are considering divorce.

3. www.collaborativepractice.com.

4. Rule 9 of Uniform Collaborative Law Act: Rule 9. Disqualification of Collaborative Lawyer and Lawyers in Associated Law Firm. (a) Except as otherwise provided in subsection (c), a collaborative lawyer is disqualified from appearing before a tribunal to represent a party in a proceeding related to the collaborative matter.

Over the next 20 years, the lawyer agreement to avoid court was supplanted by a more sophisticated contractual tool called the Attorney Disqualification Agreement[5] included in a Collaborative Participation Agreement[6] signed by all parties and all lawyers.

Original Paradigm Shift

Webb's innovation brought with it a view that collaborative law practitioners required a shift in their thinking and role. Essentially, avoid court and concentrate on settlement. Court was (and is) always seen as an option for anyone at any time. However, four-way meetings between clients and lawyers were used as the primary method to seek and achieve settlement.

Very little else was different. The basic tenant was to avoid court hearings and the procedural world that preceded them: motions, compulsory discovery, and meeting court rules and deadlines. Lawyers still dominated these four-way meetings. Positional negotiation still was the key method of discussion. Clients selected collaborative law because of what they did not want. This was seen as good enough.

Evolution of the Paradigm Shift

As collaborative training developed and interdisciplinary teamwork grew, the paradigm shifted some more. Not just stressing what collaborative law was not, the process morphed to what other benefits awaited clients and collaborative professionals, lawyers and nonlawyers alike. Even the name changed to collaborative practice—connoting a more inclusive process.

We credit past International Academy of Collaborative Professionals (IACP) president Nancy Cameron, a Canadian barrister, for pioneering a modified new paradigm in her brilliant book *Collaborative Practice: Deepening the Dialogue*. Here are a just a few samples of Cameron's wisdom:

- One of the most difficult aspects of change is not learning new skills, but unlearning old ways of being.
- What is new is this: we now have a framework—collaborative process—designed specifically for families to resolve disputes outside of the adversarial framework.

---

5. "Collaborative law participation agreement" means an agreement by persons to participate in a collaborative law process, Collaborative Law Act.

6. Nancy Cameron, Collaborative Practice: Deepening the Dialogue 91–92 (Society of British Columbia, 2004).

- Lawyers in collaborative practice have to be intimately aware of their own individual adversarial behavior and of our professional adversarial norms.
- We have constructed professional schemas that group certain behaviors as good practice. Professionally, we share lacunas that are often well aligned with our personal defenses. We have lived in a professional climate that has an extremely heightened sense of "attack or defend."
- Into this complicated milieu, we must bring our deeply ingrained professional sense of risk aversion, which also summons defensive behavior.
- Lawyers also have to redefine our relationships with professional colleagues—with the other lawyer and any other team members involved with the family.
- Helping our clients meet their respective needs, often takes us to edge of our comfort zones, which makes us anxious. Once I become anxious, I fall into my known, comfortable, adversarial behaviors. . . . As I collapse into the comfort of my old role, it takes great courage to explain this to my colleagues.[7]

New Paradigm: Working for Present and Future Peace

Building on the shoulders of Webb and Cameron, this book urges yet another redefinition of the new paradigm. Going beyond Webb's aversion to court and accepting Cameron's groundbreaking description of the professional and personal challenges of practicing law in different way, we challenge our lawyer readers to adopt a positive and needed new paradigm: to work for present and future peace in the families that we serve.

A powerful tool for exploring the complexities of collaborative divorce practice lies in the work of the late Gay Cox and Linda Wray. Drawing on self-reported data from IACP members, Cox and Wray identified the variables most commonly present in the 14 percent of collaborative law cases that did not result in settlement. Their findings, compiled under the title "Top Difficulty Factors Identified in Collaborative Cases," offer valuable insights.

The most frequently cited factor (59 percent) was: "Clients rarely or never trust the other client or one or more professionals." At the other end of the spectrum, the least-cited factor (16 percent) was: "One or both clients invaded the privacy of the other."

---

7. *See* Forrest Mosten, *Bringing Informed Consent & Consumerism into Mediation: Parties Jointly Select Their Lawyers*, MEDIATE.COM (Nov. 13, 2023).

Rather than focusing solely on these findings as predictors of failure, we as peacemaking lawyers can use them as guideposts for intervention. Each difficulty identified in Cox and Wray's study is an invitation: an opportunity to apply a proactive, compassionate approach to collaborative work. We've reframed these "difficulty factors" into a three-part model:

- **Learning theory:** The identified difficulty
- **Strategy:** The lawyer's goal in working with the client(s)
- **Intervention:** Practical steps to achieve that goal, often involving specific tasks or reframing techniques

Here are our suggestions:

Difficulty: "Clients rarely or never trust the other client."

Peacemaking approach: Work to build trust between the parties
Strategy: Explore ways to have parties work together to meet each other's needs
Intervention: Find a task requiring involvement of both parties that will be necessary to meet the unmet nets of each party

Illustration: Neither party wants wife to remain as dependent on spouse's health insurance, and both parties want spouse to have her own health insurance.

Task: Both parties research possible coverage opportunities, fill out application either together or sequentially, and arrange for payment of first premium.

Illustration: Both parties want the higher earner to buy out spousal support of lower earning party with a one-time lump-sum payment.

Task: A neutral CPA experienced in family law and finances will need to be engaged.[8] Parties could interview possible candidates together and work with professionals in customizing the protocol, scope, and terms.

Difficulty: "Clients rarely or never trust one or more professionals."

Peacemaking approach: Work to build trust between the parties and the other collaborative lawyer
Strategy: Find an opportunity for lawyers representing the other party to treat that party with respect and dignity
Intervention: Both lawyers could reframe concerns of other party with accuracy and compassion to demonstrate empathy

8. The following section is based on Mosten, *supra* note 7.

Difficulty: Both parties show an extreme lack of empathy toward the other party (50 percent of cases).

Peacemaking approach: Work to develop more empathy between the parties

Strategy: Explore ways for parties to realize that they are dependent upon each other to reach a settlement—cannot have a deal unless they both sign on

Intervention: Find a task in which each party is dependent upon the other

Illustration: Parties have agreed to split the net proceeds of the sale of their family residence. Lawyers work with parties to gain cooperation to fix repairs, put house in showable condition, and cooperate during the negotiation to obtain the best sale price.

Difficulty: One or both parties have unrealistic outcome expectations of process (45 percent of cases).

Peacemaking approach: Provide information so that informed consent of process is obtained

Strategy: Provide best information possible about time needed to resolve matter and fee variables of professionals

Intervention: Provide a written fee estimate for all professionals involved along with stages of settlement involved

Difficulty: One or both parties have unrealistic outcome expectations of ultimate terms of settlement (45 percent of cases).

Peacemaking approach: Provide alternatives for various terms so that informed consent of settlement terms is obtained

Strategy: Discuss options of in-kind division or buy out of non-employee interest and the need to engage appropriate professionals (pension lawyer for in-kind division or actuary to determine after tax present value for buy-out option)

Intervention: Both lawyers prepare presentation of options, costs, professionals, and methods of selecting and working with professionals

Illustration: The parties have joint interest in a defined benefit plan of one of the spouses.

Difficulty: Clients attribute little or no value to the contribution of the other (41 percent of cases).

Peacemaking approach: Educate John on how Linda's behavior has helped him

Strategy: Educate John on how Linda has helped him in his career and the children with her actions

Intervention: Have the parties discuss the time and benefits of Linda's contributions keeping the children healthy: learning about nutrition, finding and shopping for the right foods at the best price, locating and make appointments with the most helpful doctors

Illustration: John complains that Linda refused to work, spent too much, and does not understand that two homes can afford even less than before.

Cox and Wray point out other difficulties that you can rethink in similar ways: mental health issues of the parties (41 percent of cases), cooperation of the parties always or almost always impossible (40 percent of cases), one or both parties acted unilaterally (39 percent of cases), verbal abuse (20 percent of cases), and one or both clients invaded the privacy of the other (16 percent of cases). Difficulties that were once markers of failure are the peacemaker's guideposts for opportunity.

Representation in Mediation: Peace Means Never Being Stranded

Most mediation participants "go it alone" because they believe that the use of lawyers is not just unaffordable but that the participation of lawyers will hurt the mediation and the long-term relationship of the parties.

The truth is that while some (many lawyers) act contrary to the peacemaking goals of mediation, the key is for mediators to educate clients about the helpful roles of lawyers, selecting those lawyers trained to help mediation parties, and how the selection process can work within mediation.

First, let us briefly look at the options for joint party selection.[9] The typical method is for parties to separately decide that a lawyer would be helpful and each of them conduct their search, make their selection, and either the party or lawyer introduces the lawyer into the mediation process. There are generally no agreed criteria for background, approach, or cost of the lawyers. The clients (and mediator) play the cards that are dealt. Some lawyers selected by the

9. Adam M. Kahane, Collaborating with the Enemy, How to Work with People You Don't Agree with or Like or Trust (Berrett-Koehler, 2017).

parties truly help the process; others, less so. The lack of thoughtful reflection about attorney selection is in part responsible for the negative attitude toward lawyers held by many mediators.

Another approach is to discuss the use of lawyers within the mediation process with possible agreements made to guide the selection. Often, mediators will provide information about the difference between "mediation-friendly" lawyers and those lawyers who are essentially litigators who participate in mediation in an adversarial-based model. Other litigators play a passive role or absent themselves from their clients' mediation experience, essentially leaving clients to fend for themselves. Neither domination nor absence by lawyers sufficiently helps their clients participate successfully in mediation.

Another approach is for the mediator to facilitate a discussion as to what criteria for consulting lawyers the parties can mutually agree to use in their selection. For example, lawyers who have themselves taken family mediation training (or better yet, a full 40-hour course) may better understand how to work the mediation process on behalf of their clients and the entire process. Another source of effective and supporting consulting lawyers are local collaborative practice groups. Almost every community hosts groups of trained collaborative lawyers who are committed to and support mediation and are trained to be excellent collaborative lawyers.

Building on a party agreement to use "mediation-friendly" lawyers, many parties are very open to working with lawyers with whom the mediator has worked successfully in the past. If parties want to interview and select their lawyers outside of mediation, they could request the mediator to provide a list of consulting lawyers and supporting background information on each lawyer. This mediator intervention can facilitate the search for clients, as trying to navigate a long list can be frustrating.

There are several ways mediators can provide recommended lawyers:

1. Separate lists for each party
2. One list and have parties divide it up
3. Parties can agree to have one of them use the mediator's list and the other party can then interview and engage all those lawyers not selected by the first party

The protocol unveiled in this chapter is to have the parties partner with the mediator in lawyer selection. The essence is that parties together interview lawyers recommended by the mediator in a mediation session and then select the two lawyers and which lawyer will represent each spouse. Not only do parties approve of this protocol (often selecting a mediator who will offer it), but most lawyers report a favorable response to be requested to meet directly with both parties as a new method of being engaged to work in mediations.

There are several reasons that clients and lawyers like this protocol:

A. While written resumes and bios provide useful information about the training and experience of potential lawyers, none of these resources replace face to face discussion. Clients appreciate the opportunity to assess eye contact, interest and passion for the work, listening ability, and the way that potential lawyer candidates answer client questions and concerns during the interview. The online experience can be personal and by comparing the way three or four lawyer candidates respond to similar questions, clients seem to have a much better sense of comparison to help their selection.
B. Lawyers find that online interviews give them the opportunity to meet both clients with a minimum of time investment. Little or no preparation is required, and the time commitment rarely totals over 30 minutes for emails with the mediator and the interview itself. I have never had a lawyer unwilling to donate this time without a fee given the lawyer's opportunity to be hired for a paying assignment.
C. By having a joint interview, the clients increase their opportunity for having two lawyers that they feel will contribute positively to the mediation experience. Also, it helps minimize common antipathy toward the other party's lawyer. If Linda's lawyer makes a request or demand of John, while John may not be thrilled with the request or demand, since John selected Mary's lawyer with her, John will be less likely to blame Mary's lawyer personally or assume that the lawyer has a personal bias against him.

Steps in Protocol of Joint Party Selection of Lawyer in Mediation

1. Parties agree that they want mediator to recommend consulting lawyer candidates.
2. Parties agree that they want mediator to convene the lawyer selection process.
2. Mediator contacts four to six lawyers by email whom she believes would be appropriate for the parties to ascertain interest and availability and to set date and time for the interview. The mediator sends lawyers the suggested protocol for their review.
3. If the parties have agreed the potential lawyers must sign litigation disqualification clauses if the mediation terminates, the mediator sends a copy of the Consulting Lawyer Litigation Disqualification Agreement for review and approval.

4. Three to four lawyers are booked in 10 to 15 online interview sessions to conclude interviewing process in an hour of mediation time.
5. Once lawyers confirm, mediator provides parties with an interview schedule, lawyer bios, and sample questions that they may use as examples.
6. Interviews are conducted online with mediator introducing each lawyer to parties, the lawyer providing a short overview of her practice, and the parties and mediator asking questions of lawyer. Parties alternate in asking questions. Fees are always part of the discussion.
7. After all interviews, parties and mediators discuss the strengths and weaknesses of each lawyer. Parties will select two lawyers and determine which lawyer will represent each party. If both parties want the same lawyer, mediator will attempt to resolve issue or another lawyer is selected.
8. Mediator contacts lawyers selected requesting their engagement letters be sent to parties.
9. Mediator contacts lawyers not selected thanking them for their time and contribution to the parties.

Limited-Scope Coaching (Unbundling)

Coaching is different from representation. Instead of suiting up yourself and playing in the game, you are on the sidelines with a whistle, clipboard, and encouragement, helping your player (client) make the best decisions and use the best strategies possible.

What Is Limited-Scope Coaching

The "full bundle" of legal services includes (1) gathering facts, (2) advising the client, (3) discovering the facts of the opposing party, (4) researching the law, (5) drafting correspondence and documents, (6) negotiating, and (7) representing the client in court.

A peacemaking lawyer who is engaged in a limited-scope role is contracted to conduct one or more of these but not all. Examples of limited scope services include the following:

- *Advice*: Advice can be purchased at an initial consultation or throughout their case as determined by the client with input from the lawyer. The lawyer and client collaborate to help the client decide if and when further consultations may be needed.

- *Research*: The lawyer will provide research in person or electronically. Research may take as little as 15 minutes or many hours. The client is in charge of determining the scope of the job and who will do the work—the lawyer, the client, or a negotiated collaborative effort between the two. The lawyer should communicate with the client before undertaking a major project and come to an agreement on the number of hours to spend on a particular project.
- *Drafting*: Lawyers may be engaged to send a letter on behalf of the client on their law-firm letterhead or to ghostwrite letters or court pleadings for the client to transmit, or they may review and comment on documents the client has prepared.
- *Negotiation*: The lawyer can teach the client how to negotiate with their spouse or the spouse's lawyer directly in preparation for a settlement meeting, mediation, or other dispute resolution process. Or the lawyer may be engaged to conduct some or all of the negotiations either with or on behalf of their client.
- *Court appearances*: A lawyer providing limited scope representation (LSR) may appear at one or more court appearances, hearings, and other court-related processes on limited issues or on all issues.

Coaching Requires Informed Consent and Excellent Communication

Attorneys may limit their legal services when there is client informed consent and a written agreement in every state, and in many Western countries informed consent must cover an understanding of litigation, options to litigation, and a comparison of the benefits and risks of each process option. This must be done in writing at the start of the representation and updated if the scope of services is modified. You must discuss in detail the services they intend to provide and the services that are not included. This discussion is essential and must explain to a client the division of tasks to help them understand the division of labor in LSR. The lawyer must thoroughly explain when their work will be complete and when they will no longer represent the client. Attorneys should confirm this status through a letter or court notice confirming modification of scope of services or disengagement.

The lawyer–coach and client together are in charge of determining the scope of representation; courts, other parties, and their lawyers are required to honor their decision. When a lawyer is engaged for a single issue only, clients will either represent themselves or engage another representative to handle other issues. Every time a lawyer writes a single letter instead of three possible letters, drafts one agreement instead of five possible agreements, or makes one phone call instead of several possible phone calls, the lawyer is providing limited scope services. "Second opinions" are also classic unbundled services. You must create strong boundaries with your clients. If the client decides they would prefer more services or full representation, the attorney–client relationship can transition to handling other responsibilities or their complete case, including negotiation and court appearances, only after the paperwork has been amended to include the new limited scope or full representation.

Each of these coaching models may include conversion from one scope of service delivery to the other throughout the divorce process:

- The client starts self-representing and then engages a limited scope lawyer.
- The lawyer–client limited scope engagement converts to full-service representation.
- The full-service relationship scales down to limited coaching.
- Coaching might terminate, and the client starts or returns to self-representation.

Limited Scope Lawyer Serves as an Advisor and Coach: By providing advice on how to tamp down the conflict and take positive steps to improve the overall family situation, a limited-scope lawyer–coach can make an important contribution to the peacemaking capacity of clients in a number of ways.

Lawyers Can Teach Clients About Divorce Dynamics: By hiring a lawyer on a limited basis, clients can learn about the communication patterns that lead to conflict between divorcing spouses. When lawyers teach clients about the four distinct divorce relationships (emotional, physical, financial, and legal), it helps them better understand and implement a successful negotiation process. This knowledge can benefit spouses, the children, and the entire family system. For example, if the emotional divorce is in early stages, it might be too hard to negotiate parenting issues without help. If it is well underway, the couple will probably be less raw and reactive toward each other, and they can focus on resolving their parenting and financial issues. Similarly, teaching the client about the long-term effects of anger may make it easier for the client to avoid blow-ups with the other spouse, lowering conflict levels as they go through their divorce.

Assessing the Legal Strengths and Weaknesses of Each Party's Position: A lawyer–coach can help the client learn the importance of making this assessment and coach them how to do it. The lawyer may be able to help the client see beyond their legal and negotiation positions to the underlying interests that they and their former partner mutually want to realize. The client can then use this knowledge to increase success in divorce negotiations.

Analyzing the Personalities of the Parties, Communication Dynamics, Emotional and Financial Leverage: The lawyer–coach can also help the client understand negotiation dynamics. By sharing impressions and teaching the client how to appreciate and empathize with the underlying needs and goals of their spouse, lawyers can help their clients to maximize their effectiveness in formulating and presenting their proposals. Experienced negotiators utilize these skills at the negotiation table to insightfully read their clients, opposing parties, counsel, and others involved in and affected by a negotiation. In addition to their own professional experience, family lawyers know and have access to negotiation resources that can help a client prepare for an upcoming negotiation. Helping clients to recognize the behaviors that set them off and understand what behaviors they may set off in their spouses can reduce conflict overall.

Teaching Negotiation Theory and Techniques: Regardless of their formal negotiation training, lawyers can provide their clients with a customized crash course in relevant negotiation skills to help reach settlement. A lawyer can recommend appropriate or client-friendly negotiation books and videos available for client study. An otherwise unrepresented client can greatly benefit from reading negotiation and divorce books for the lay public.

Develop a Negotiation Plan: Regardless of the skills that a client might have or develop, developing a negotiation plan and pre-meeting preparation are the keys to a successful outcome. Coming up with an initial settlement position is often the most difficult task a client faces when trying to get through their own negotiation. A lawyer can help develop a plan with several backup options and prepare responses for anticipated concerns raised by the other spouse or their lawyer. The client can benefit by rehearsing a negotiation and then receiving constructive feedback from the lawyer–coach to prepare for the meeting with the other spouse. This type of rehearsal can be conducted in front of the client's friends or even the lawyer's office staff to get comments that might help clients in perhaps one of the most important conversations of their life. Recording the simulation with the client's cell phone can provide the client with a good resource to rehearse before an important negotiation. Although remaining on the sidelines, the lawyer–coach can remain available by telephone or text during (or shortly after) a spousal meeting to serve as a resource and emotional support for the client as needed.

Whether in collaborative law or mediation, as core professional or as a sideline coach, the role of the peacemaking lawyer is ever evolving. We are no longer limited to adversarial roles; instead, we can serve as builders of understanding, designers of processes, and coaches of positive change. By translating obstacles into opportunities—through empathy, strategy, and thoughtful intervention—we help clients not only reach settlements but reshape their family relationships with dignity and respect. We are peacemakers.

Utilizing Dialogue to Enhance Peace by Nancy Cameron

"Lawyers as Peacemakers" has called to hundreds of lawyers tired of working in an adversarial model, convinced that there is a better way to practice, a process more aligned with their personal values. The concepts and underlying values of lawyers as peacemakers continues to call to a younger generation of professionals, many of whom have, from the beginning of their careers, intentionally decided against the notion of adversarial dispute resolution, particularly in the family law context.

We are trained in a profession that gives lawyers an agency so powerful that we are collectively "called to the bar," a euphemism for that railing in every courtroom that divides lawyers and judges from the rest of the public. We wear these robes of agency (and in Canada, the robes are more than figurative) with pride. Making certain that justice is done is part of our calling. As we consider our shift to peacemaking, I urge us to consider how that role calls for something that explicitly recognizes the individual agency of those we work with. This includes moving away from our own notion of what peace is to a definition of peace that is inclusive of the clients' needs. We are building together—not only with our colleagues, but most importantly, with our clients. A courtroom takes most of the agency away from clients. I believe that, at the heart of this work, it is imperative that we embrace and support the agency of everyone involved.

As peacemakers, we can help create the conditions for building peace. A key tool is to become skilled in different types of communication, with a deeper understanding of the purpose served by each type.

Adam Kahane, in *Collaborating with the Enemy*,[10] explores four different ways of talking and listening. None of these are new, although the fourth is probably less familiar to us. The four methods he describes are downloading, debating, dialoguing, and presencing. Each of these has a vital role in certain circumstances. Individually, we have a tendency to be drawn to one or another of these communication styles. Each of these can produce different results.

10. Peter Senge et al. Presence: Human Purpose and the Field of the Future (Crown Currency, 2008).

Communication Vignettes

Downloading

A few days ago, my husband came back to our cabin after a trip to town, carrying a bag with the silky ends of fresh corn sprouting from the top.

"Did you buy corn?" I admit this was more of a snipe than a question. We had just hosted a number of people for the last eight days, and I was tired of preparing food. The last thing I wanted to do was start shucking corn.

"Yes!"

"How many ears did you buy?" This time, it was more like an interrogation than a snipe. I wasn't really curious; I was fueling my indignation.

"A dozen. They were a good deal."

"We'll never be able to eat a dozen ears of corn!"

"I thought you'd be happy," he replied. "We don't have to eat them all; we can give some away."

In this short exchange, I was clearly downloading. All of us have done it. We've all been the subject of others' downloads.

When we download, we don't listen. Although I asked, I didn't really care how many ears of corn he brought home; I did not want to deal with any more food.

We have one intention when we download, which is to get our story across. My story was simple (though not quite transparent). I did not want to think about food, let alone prepare it or find room in the fridge. I did not want to plan the week's meals based on a surplus of corn.

This is not my proudest example of downloading. I am a trainer, and sometimes downloading is necessary in order to describe certain concepts. I am a writer, and every time I tell a story I am downloading. This chapter is an example of downloading.

Clients usually want a legal opinion. Whenever we tell them about the law, we are downloading.

When I first meet clients, and ask them what brought them to my office, I am encouraging them to download. I make notes. I find there is often a treasure of information, and if I am curious, these small gems will yield much important context and help me discover my client's deeper fears and longings.

Downloading has a place in peacemaking and peace-building. It is likely a small place, and should only be used intentionally.

Debate

I never belonged to a debate club. As a lawyer who spent years in a courtroom, this was a skill I had to learn. Debating is central to what we have been taught in law school—that the truth is best uncovered by two equal advocates presenting evidence and debating before an impartial third party.

What we have learned from brain science completely contradicts this core legal assumption. We know that there is no such thing as an "impartial third party." We are all subject to a litany of biases based upon our past experiences, our values, our beliefs, and our cultural upbringing. We know that "two equal advocates" is not the norm in today's courts, especially with so many litigants without professional representation, so we must question what influence this inequality has to do with the court's mission to discover the truth and to rule on the side of justice.

Yet debate continues to be a central tool in the lawyer's repertoire. The fundamentals of debate—expressing one point of view—allows for more nuance than downloading. Debate includes listening closely to what the other person has to say, although this listening is often confined to parsing out how one will respond in order to bolster one's opinion.

When lawyers are involved in making and building peace, debate may sometimes occur. Two lawyers may have very different views of the law. Parents may have different views about the best schools for their children. We know that debating can push us toward polarization, so it is important, if debate arises in our work, that we find some ways to nudge the debate into dialogue. Curiosity is often the gateway through which debate can move to dialogue.

Dialogue

The day after he arrived home with the corn, my husband said, "I was thinking about taking some corn to the neighbors."

"How many ears were you going to take to them? I was thinking of making a corn soufflé tonight."

"I thought I'd take eight. Do you think that's enough? I'm not sure how many people they have over there."

"Eight should be enough. There are a lot of little kids, and they probably won't eat more than half a cob each. And that leaves four ears, which is perfect for the soufflé. Do you mind shucking four cobs for us?"

As short as this dialogue was, it represented many of the important features of dialogue. Each of us was interested in what the other one wanted to do, and were invested in listening to the other.

Dialogue requires empathy and self-reflection. It also involves more nuanced listening than either downloading (which centers listening within the person who is downloading) and debating (where listening is simultaneously paired with thinking about one's response).

Dialogue encourages us to be curious, and encourages us to ask questions we do not know the answers to. As mentioned earlier, when my client downloads in my office, there are often gems that I can later mine for more personal information. If I listen carefully to someone who is downloading, I can later encourage a dialogue with a simple question, such as "tell me more about . . ." or "I am curious to know what you mean when you say . . . ."

As peacemakers and builders, dialogue is one of our most valuable communication skills. It encourages our creativity, helps us dip into brainstorming, and is key to be able to work with colleagues and clients to problem solve.

Presencing

I had neglected too much at the office, frantically rearranging my to-do list to tackle those items that felt most urgent to me, and dropping other matters lower down the list. My oldest sister's son, Jason, was dying in Montreal, hours by plane away from my home in Vancouver. My sister had passed away a few years before, and I valued the strength of my relationship with my nephew and his family.

I tried not to cover Jason in snot and tears as I choked out my good-bye. I hugged his thin body on the sofa where he blanketed his own pain so he could comfort me. I am not certain I had ever been knifed so ferociously by grief as I kissed him, knowing I would never see him alive again. I tried not to bury him in my sobs. I wandered back to my hotel, doing what my great-niece called the "Montreal Shuffle," a slow, deliberate, planting of each booted foot in the dirty, ice-encrusted snow. The crunch of each footstep revealed the softer snow below.

I had been back in the office two days, and had hurriedly worked to complete a separation agreement so that I could get it out to the other lawyer, and then to our clients, prior to our collaborative four-way meeting the following day. Tangled with my grief was a not-so-healthy dose of shame and guilt for having let this agreement linger on my to-do list, but at least I got it out before our meeting. I rationalized my delay with the assumption that, since these clients had waited years after they separated before consulting lawyers, a few extra months would not be a big issue for them.

It was one of those January days when the mountains outside my office window were regal in a new blanket of snow. I was grateful that the other lawyer was one of my favorite collaborative lawyers. Her client (I will call him Ned) was seated on the sofa that looked out the window. He usually was very amicable during the meetings, but I knew he tended to download his frustrations on his lawyer after they left. My client (I will call her Elaine) was seated next to me, and the other lawyer was in a chair across the small table from Ned.

We had exchanged pleasantries, and were getting ready to review the draft agreement together when the dam that had been holding back the husband's frustration broke. He laid into me with a classic download. He complained about how long I took to complete the agreement, and the fact that I only got it out to everyone the day before.

I could feel tears beginning to pool in my eyes. My own grief was so raw and deep it wanted to throw up a defensive shield and lash out, word for word. I willed myself to stay in the chair and listened for not only what Ned was saying, but also for what was lurking behind his words. His lawyer was leaning forward in an attempt to calm him. Elaine had withdrawn into her protective "Can we just get this over with" mode.

I could feel the desire to cross my arms over my chest to protect my skittering heart. Instead of crossing my arms I sat up a little straighter and pulled my shoulders back to help me concentrate on opening my heart. I turned my attention to keeping my bum in the chair instead of fleeing the room. I looked at Ned, noticed the color of his eyes, inhaled and exhaled, and then responded. "It sounds like you're really frustrated because you have been paying support all this time. Instead of getting credit for voluntarily paying support, the fact that I delayed finishing the agreement feels like it's punishing you, and you're not getting any recognition for the fact you have continued to pay."

Instead of a broken dam, the room suddenly felt like a still, deep pool. Ned nodded as he acknowledged his frustration. I said something about how we could take what he had been paying into account so that it wasn't penalizing him, and together the four of us worked out an adjustment that worked for both Ned and Elaine, and helped us complete the agreement. Perhaps one of the gifts of grief is its ability to meld us to the present moment.

I share this incident not because I did anything special (other than resist the immediate urge to defend myself or run out of the room), but because it is one of the few times in my work as a lawyer that I felt what Otto Sharmer and Peter Senghe refer to as "presencing."[11]

In my experience, presencing is rare. It requires aligning attention, intention, and agency in order to allow the potential future to manifest. It involves an intentional holding of the space, listening with our mind and our heart, to explore the future. Presencing is the magic we get to glimpse when we commit to working as peace-builders. It requires us to practice being centered so that

11. Otto Scharmer & Katrin Kaufer, Presencing: 7 Practices for Transforming Self, Society and Business (Berrett-Koehler, 2025).

in even the most difficult circumstances, we can come back to our center. It requires us to honor everyone's agency. It requires us to work not only with focused attention but also with a clear intention.

I believe that our justice system must evolve in order to meet the changing needs of the population. When I refer to the justice system, I am not only referring to courts, I am also referring to the statutes that support the courts, to the many services that support families going through separation and divorce, services that are often hidden because of the siloes we have created, and to the processes that we, as lawyers, routinely bring to clients. We know that any system that is incapable of necessary evolution and change will collapse. We are in the midst of profound planetary change. Hundreds of thousands of people, involved in different systems, are working for systemic change within the particular systems they are familiar with. I am confident that peacemaking lawyers who are drawn to developing the necessary skills to work as peacebuilders are also those who can help bring both intention and attention to the systems change necessary for the justice system to be more responsive to the needs of common people. These facilitators of peace are creating what Otto Scharmer refers to as the social soil necessary for systems change. Presencing is an important skill for deep systems change, and is explored in detail in Otto Scharmer's book: Presencing: 7 Practices for Transforming Self, Society and Business.

I encourage you to think about which of the communication skills tend to be your default. Where do you automatically go if you feel threatened or uncertain? If you can't decide this, pair up with a colleague that you trust and that you work with regularly and share with each other what you see as the other's default communication style. If your default tends to be downloading (yes, I am looking at you, the lawyer who loves to regale the group with personal stories) or debate (yes, you, the lawyer who was president of the debate club and further honed those skills in court), practice the art of dialogue. If you are well versed in the art of dialogue, perhaps lean into another style for a challenge. Communication is essential to our work. Stay curious, and practice listening with your ears and with your heart.

Nancy Cameron is a lawyer, writer, and educator. She has been deeply involved with systems change in the family justice system, and is a member of the Collaborative Strategy Committee of British Columbia's Transform the Family Justice System Collaborative. She teaches and trains in the interdisciplinary model of collaborative practice, as well as other subjects in dispute resolution. She has been an adjunct professor at both the University of British Columbia Law School and a continuing adjunct professor in the LLM for Dispute Resolution program at Hong Kong University Faculty of Law. Ms. Cameron has written numerous articles on collaborative practice, as well as a book: *Collaborative Practice: Deepening the Dialogue.* She received her Queens Counsel Designation in 2005 and in 2019 received the BC Law Society Excellence in Family Law Award.

Chapter 6

A New Way Forward: Using Mediation to Create Marriage-Friendly Prenups[1]

Laurie Israel

The Disconnect Between a Loving Relationship and a Prenuptial Agreement

Attorneys commonly experience many challenges in representing clients during prenuptial-agreement negotiations. However, lawyers' challenges are dwarfed by the challenges experienced by the future spouses themselves.

A couple is engaged to be married. Like most engaged couples, they are excited about the prospect of marriage and spending their lives together. At that moment, they are experiencing a "high" of deep fondness and affection for each other. Then one partner informs the other that a prenuptial agreement must be in place before they marry. The request is typically unilateral, made by only one of the future spouses. It's not actually a request but a demand, without which the already-planned marriage cannot proceed.

While the prenup requirement may not be a surprise to their fiancé, it is usually an unwelcome prospect. Most people getting married would prefer to proceed without one. Having a prenup wasn't their idea of how a good marriage should start out.

1. Excerpted with author's permission from "Mediating Prenups: A Better Path Forward for Marriage-Positive Prenuptial Agreements" (Integrity Registry Press 2025) Ó Laurie Israel 2025. All rights reserved. In sharing insights about her prenuptial and postnuptial mediation experiences, Laurie captures the essence of a peacemaking approach—harnessing empathy, productivity, and the power of attuned conflict prevention at every turn.

The fundamental problem with prenups is that they are generally inconsistent with marriage's core principles of mutual faithfulness and complete commitment. Marriage entails caring about the other person both personally and financially. The obligation for mutual financial care between married spouses is termed a "fiduciary duty." The basic premise underlying this legal concept is that the married couple should protect each other financially. Isn't that part of what marriage is? Prenups often remove this obligation of financial loyalty without replacing it with anything else. As a result, the upcoming marriage is damaged and becomes weakened as it proceeds.

Wedding vows often embody this ideal of personal faithfulness and fiduciary duty. Words such as "All I am I give to you" and "All that I have I share with you" are frequently spoken in a marriage ceremony. With these words, a couple promises total personal and financial sharing, the spirit of unconditional generosity and mutual loyalty. This is what sustains long-term marriages.

Standard prenuptial agreements undermine these fundamental marital principles by tearing at the very fabric of financial security implicit in marriage itself. By design, such agreements prioritize individual financial protection over mutual economic well-being. The inherent emotional pain of being part of such negotiations, and the ensuing marriage based on these terms, reveal the deep relational harm these documents can inflict.

When the subject of a prenup arises, early attorney involvement often transforms prenup negotiations into adversarial proceedings. Lawyers representing the wealthier spouse typically adopt an uncompromising stance, advising their client against concessions. Their reassurance that the document will "remain in a drawer" rings hollow, as it will be activated in the future at divorce or death. This undermines any sense of security. Memories of what's in the document can serve to poison the marriage.

The wealthy spouse's attorney's negotiating stance often becomes "take it or leave it," creating an inherently imbalanced dynamic. Despite the challenging terms, most couples remain committed and reluctant to dissolve their engagement. Consequently, the marriage often proceeds with compromised terms, leaving underlying emotional wounds.

Alternative solutions can and do exist. Prenuptial agreements can address genuine concerns equitably, protecting both parties' needs and interests in regard to security and fairness. While prenup lawyers typically fail to address the potentially harmful personal consequences of their legal advice, a more collaborative process can transform these agreements into constructive, healing experiences. This alternative process generates a more balanced prenup and leads to a better marriage, in which having a prenup makes sense and may serve a particular couple well. In a good prenup, the deeply held concerns of both spouses should be adequately addressed. In the traditional lawyer-driven process, this is frequently not the result.

The traditional legal approach reveals a critical irony. While ostensibly pursuing "risk protection" for the wealthy spouse, the process fundamentally undermines the interests of the other party. Risk to the marriage itself is not taken into consideration at all. The attorney-led approach thus paradoxically *creates* marital risk instead of mitigating it. It's the opposite of risk protection in one important aspect—the supporting of the health of the upcoming marriage.

Risk protection in a prenup is a valid goal, but it should be applied to the interests of *both* parties. When it only applies to one party, it is damaging. The fundamental question becomes what's more important—the money or the marriage? An effective prenup must balance equity and security for both parties through an open, collaborative process—ideally through beginning with mediation at the outset.

The Mediation Alternative

About 15 years ago, after having witnessed numerous distressing legal negotiations close up as an attorney representing clients, I began mediating prenuptial agreements. At that time, very few attorney/mediators were mediating prenups. While divorce mediation was well-established in Massachusetts, my jurisdiction, prenuptial-agreement mediation remained rare.

I saw this scenario as presenting an opportunity for a more constructive approach to creating a balanced agreement when people sought a prenuptial agreement. I think part of the resistance to prenup mediation on the part of attorneys was the idea (widespread at that time) that a lawyer representing prenup clients should vigorously promote their own client's separate interests as an advocate, similar to functioning as an attorney in a contested divorce.

In the typical attorney-led negotiation, an attorney's ideas of what a prenup should contain and what type of process was to be followed predominated. The prenups that came out of this process were generally quite similar in their approaches. They conferred control, benefits, and protections to the more moneyed spouse while taking away rights conferred by state laws, from the other partner, leaving that future spouse in a less secure position.

But couples preparing for marriage often want to discuss their financial arrangements with each other without having any lawyer involvement at the outset. The very idea of engaging two (opposing) lawyers in the process during the tender time at which they have committed to each other and having begun readying themselves for marriage is jarring and unwelcome for most couples.

Every couple begins their union with the hope and belief that it will last forever. Yet young couples often lack insight into the factors that sustain marital success and commitment. If they are working toward having a prenuptial agreement, without nuanced guidance, they might inadvertently include prenuptial terms that could ultimately undermine their relationship.

The truth is, the approach of direct client–client discussions without mediation as the first step when discussing terms of a prenuptial agreement has two significant flaws.

First, the couple needs to discuss and negotiate their terms with a clear understanding of what legal rules pertaining to marriage are before they start changing them via a prenup. Because, in essence, that's what prenups do—change applicable state laws. This makes direct client–client negotiations problematic because the couple likely doesn't know what the laws relating to their upcoming marital status are. It's important for them to obtain this information early in the process. If they fail to understand the existing legal framework, couples risk making uninformed decisions about their rights.

Second, the direct client–client negotiation process is impaired by the fact that there is typically a substantial power imbalance between the engaged parties. This is particularly true when there are significant disparities in the couple's individual levels of wealth, and financial experience and acumen. As a result, some couples unknowingly waive important legal and practical protections. Others might propose overreaching terms that, although potentially enforceable, could ultimately undermine the marriage's stability and longevity.

For these reasons, it is optimal to start the process by engaging a neutral mediator. A mediator can provide legal information, help create decisional possibilities for the couple, and assist with power imbalances.

When I start working with a couple, they invariably have already had some difficult and painful discussions about the possibility of having a prenup when they marry. At the first session, I encourage them (at least, for a while, during our work together) to pause their face-to-face discussions about the prenup terms. This helps so that all discussions, at least initially, will be moderated with the assistance of the mediator. This goes a long way to decrease conflict and anxiety, and lets the couple focus on the positive things—their love for each other and the upcoming marriage.

The topic of spousal support frequently emerges as a hot topic during prenuptial negotiations. The discussion is often colored by cautionary tales of perpetual alimony payments that one of the parties may have heard about from friends or colleagues. In fact, often a party's primary motivation for a prenuptial agreement is to have the other party waive their marital support rights in the event of divorce—even in first marriages. Without proper guidance, parties might hastily waive alimony rights entirely, failing to fully comprehend the long-term implications of such a decision.

When a less financially secure future spouse feels pressured to waive alimony rights, it may signal to them an underlying lack of commitment to the relationship. Just the prospect of that relinquishment could potentially harm the relationship and ensuing marriage. When discussing spousal support within mediation, mediators can present many possible options that are available, drawing from prior experience in handling other prenup cases.

Providing critical legal information and facilitating productive dialogue is better than beginning with an all-or-nothing proposal (and/or acceptance) of an alimony waiver. This black and white paradigm often occurs when the clients engage attorneys instead of a mediator as their first step. Mediation serves to help the couple develop a more nuanced and informed consideration in evaluating the alimony issue as well as all terms of the prenup, before they engage lawyers—by discussing issues in real time, face-to-face, with a knowledgeable facilitator: the mediator.

Most core terms of prenuptial agreements address potential ramifications if the marriage ends in divorce. This is very disturbing to most couples, but this work must be done to formulate a fair prenup. I feel for them, but as I tell couples during the mediation, "In order for me to do this mediation fully, I have to kill you and divorce you."

It is true, discussing divorce terms is essential. But prenuptial mediation can extend beyond divorce-related matters. Mediation gives the couple an opportunity to discuss how they will manage their finances during their marriage. This can prove invaluable. Such discussion helps a couple develop a mutual understanding and can foster shared financial strategies—even if the details of these conversations don't directly make their way into the final agreement.

Modern prenuptial agreements increasingly incorporate inheritance provisions—a departure from prior practice, when attorneys typically recommended addressing such matters in post-marriage estate planning documents. While estate planning can (and should, in my opinion) be put into place later, critical decisions about inheritance are most effectively discussed during the process of formulating the prenup.

In order to make such provisions secure, estate planning requirements should be integrated directly into the prenup. This helps ensure that the couple's intentions are legally binding when the marriage ends in the death of one of them. Typical attorney advice that says, "You can do the estate plan later, it doesn't have to be addressed in the prenup," fails to provide post-death security for either spouse.

The Mediator's Role

Given the legal intricacies of prenuptial agreements, an attorney practicing within the clients' jurisdiction is generally the most suitable mediator. Such a professional can provide insight into existing laws and their purposes. The mediator should also provide comprehensive context regarding how various arrangements would be treated under state law in the absence of a prenuptial agreement.

A mediator's role in providing legal background is fundamentally informative. The goal is to expand the universe of potential options and to provide comprehensive insights into the legal and practical implications of the terms under consideration.

Mediators, however, must carefully distinguish between sharing legal information and providing legal advice. Direct legal advice to either individual or to the couple as a unit may not be offered; doing so would violate established ethical guidelines for attorneys (if the mediator is an attorney) as well as disregarding standard mediation practices. The ultimate decision-making authority should rest entirely with the clients. The mediator serves as a knowledgeable guide, facilitating understanding without prescribing specific courses of action.

Mediation clients deserve accurate legal information, making it crucial for mediators to possess comprehensive knowledge of state laws governing marriage, divorce, and inheritance, in addition to the laws of prenuptial agreements. When mediators encounter legal complexities beyond their expertise, they can engage a neutral consulting attorney to provide more specific information. Clients may also independently consult their own attorneys during the mediation process to evaluate potential agreement terms.

Most non-collaborative prenup attorneys focus narrowly on their individual client's interests, overlooking the marriage's long-term health. This lack of vision is particularly damaging for younger couples entering their first marriage.

As a prenup mediator, I identify four interconnected interests in every prenup mediation that I need to be aware of: each party individually, the couple as a unit, and—critically—the marriage itself. It's this last interest that gets left out in the usual attorney-led process. The mediator's challenge is to correlate these concerns into a constructive prenup plan. During the process, in my view, one of the roles of the mediator is to provide marriage guidance for the couple.

This approach might appear to impose the mediator's perspectives on marriage. However, mediators can ethically share insights drawn not only from legal expertise but also from practical experience. Like traditional "counselors," mediators can offer guidance that transcends pure legal information and dispute resolution. This can provide a holistic perspective that helps clients navigate complex personal and legal decisions related to their upcoming marriage.

Although a lawyer/mediator is not functioning as lawyer per se during the mediation, it is helpful to look at the ethical rules pertaining to lawyers to understand why lawyers have traditionally been called "counselors."

The American Bar Association addresses this counselor role in Model Rule 2.1: Advisor. This rule allows lawyers to consider not only legal matters when rendering advice, but also other considerations, such as "moral, economic, social and political factors that may be relevant to a client's situation." The Rule's commentary ("Counselor: Scope of Advice") explains that advice limited to "narrow legal terms" may prove inadequate. There may be other relevant considerations when providing legal advice, including practical considerations such as the "cost or effects on other people." This would seem to include family members, such as a spouse.

This language in the Model Rule can be highly useful to mediators. While mediators do not provide legal *advice*, they can offer guidance about the relational implications of the decisions the future spouses are making affecting an upcoming marriage. This is both appropriate and a valuable feature of mediation.

The mediator's unique position in the optimal first step in creating a prenuptial agreement allows mediators to provide nuanced, practical insights into the ramifications of the choices the couple will be making. These choices will be fundamental to the couple's marital foundation. In my experience as a mediator, this guidance is highly sought after and greatly valued by mediation clients.

A Framework for Mediating Prenuptial Agreements

The foremost benefit of mediating prenuptial agreements is the facilitation of face-to-face three-way discussions between the mediating clients and the mediator within the safe setting of the mediation process. There, the mediator can help clients express their thoughts, fears, and goals about the upcoming marriage's financial terms. The couple becomes part of a team with the mediator. Collectively, the team will (hopefully) explore all perspectives to find solutions to address any concerns regarding all aspects of the prenuptial agreement.

The first session with the clients is primarily focused on fact-finding. While some discussion of prenuptial terms may naturally arise, I intentionally avoid having the clients choose specific terms in this fact-finding session. Instead, I gather comprehensive information about both parties' families of origin, personal histories, and financial situations. This includes understanding the existence of any business interests, family wealth, or existing irrevocable trusts that may benefit either or both clients (the particulars of which will come later in the process).

This background is strategically important in understanding the clients and in beginning to address the question of what will be included in their agreement. This approach not only yields richer information but also establishes trust and rapport between the clients and the mediator, which is vital for effective mediation.

I believe that diving directly into prenup terms during the initial meeting is counterproductive. It bypasses crucial background information and hinders a deeper understanding of the couple's personalities, concerns, and interpersonal dynamics. I find that the insights gained from these preliminary discussions invariably prove essential to our mutually crafting appropriate prenuptial terms.

Many attorneys and mediators provide clients with questionnaires to complete prior to the first meeting. While questionnaires may seem efficient, I think they have some flaws, and therefore, I don't use them. I believe face-to-face discussion is essential for meaningful unearthing of relevant issues. In-person dialogue reveals nuanced details and unexpected information that questionnaires often miss. Through natural conversation, clients tend to share important facts and personal insights about their finances, concerns, and objectives that might otherwise remain undisclosed when questionnaires are employed as the first step.

Clients typically arrive with preconceived notions about what the terms of their prenuptial agreement should be. These are formed without legal counsel or professional guidance. While they may have specific provisions in mind, this short-circuits the process of developing a sound and thoughtfully constructed prenup. At this early stage, the parties lack any comprehensive understanding of how common prenup issues are typically resolved. They have not yet had wide-ranging discussions with a mediator regarding all available options and discussions (and helpful guidance) about the ones that might be best for them.

I encourage clients to approach this process with an open mind—a "Zen" mind, if you will. Starting with a clean slate allows the couple to explore all available options before evaluating and selecting their ultimate terms. Through this approach, clients might retain some of the original ideas they came up with in the first place, but with more thoughtful and nuanced consideration. During such discussions, clients benefit from a deeper understanding of the consequences and the significance of their choices.

The negotiation phase of a prenuptial agreement often generates considerable anxiety and fear for the future spouses. Clients tend to fixate on worst-case scenarios. As a neutral mediator, one of my most critical roles is to help clients manage their anxiety throughout the process, particularly during the initial stages.

I accomplish this through a series of reality checks. For example, if a client expresses concerns about financial security in case of divorce after a long-term marriage (e.g., if they are middle-aged at that time of divorce), I validate their concerns and work together with them to find solutions. While resolutions may not be immediate, the mediation context allows all three of us to collaborate on addressing these worrisome issues by carefully evaluating all aspects of the problem to be solved. This mediated process goes far in alleviating anxiety and leads toward finding solutions.

If one party is making significant life changes to enter the marriage, such as relocating across the country, leaving a job, or giving up an affordable living situation, special consideration is needed. Such potential losses can create substantial anxiety that has a legitimate basis in reality.

These issues must be addressed in the prenup terms. Prenuptial agreements can include reasonable and workable provisions to help restore the spouse who changed their financial position to marry and enable them to return to their pre-marriage financial situation, if necessary and appropriate, as an essential part of the prenuptial planning process.

In our second meeting, I share a blank document with clients titled "Financial Plan for Marriage." This framing, rather than calling it "Prenup Terms" or a "Term Sheet," often provides immediate relief—although in actuality it *will* be the term sheet for the prenup. By the time couples begin mediation, they've typically accumulated significant stress from discussions with friends and family about prenups. The term "prenuptial agreement" (or "prenup") itself carries heavy, negative connotations and causes great anxiety—which it invariably does. However, at its core, a prenuptial agreement is simply a financial plan for marriage.

I structure the Financial Plan for Marriage document to contain four main sections:

1. During marriage
2. Marriage ends in divorce
3. Marriage ends in death
4. General provisions, including alternative dispute resolution (ADR) provisions

We begin with the "during marriage" section in our second working session. This approach follows my philosophy of starting with manageable steps (one might call them baby steps) at first. These first steps are easier to discuss during this initial prenup planning stage. This method builds confidence in the process and allows the parties to achieve a feeling of success early on.

The "during marriage" discussion covers several key areas regarding the management of finances during the marriage:

- Treatment of earned income and retirement contributions
- Handling of premarital property—its growth over time and any earnings generated from it
- Joint and separate bank account arrangements
- Guidelines for shared expenses

- Housing arrangements and ownership options
- Personal spending and gift-giving
- Financial support for children from previous marriages

For more complex situations, we also address the following:

- Employment benefits, such as stock options and restricted stock
- Business interests and business earnings, when one spouse has an ownership stake in a company in which they are playing an active role
- Family wealth structures, including irrevocable trusts and family business entities
- Existing wealth distributions through inheritances, expected inheritances, and family gifts

This initial discussion of managing money during marriage naturally tends to flow into thinking about divorce or death provisions. However, at this point, it's best to not yet settle on terms dealing with these two topics. I guide the clients to back away from specific discussion of these issues, as the process will ultimately lead to these issues at a more appropriate time.

Starting with the topic of money management during marriage offers a relaxed approach to formulating the terms of the agreement. While these "during marriage" arrangements might not appear in the final prenup, they provide crucial context for the overall discussion and help clients plan for their upcoming financial life, once married.

This part of the mediation typically takes one session, although fact-finding in complex situations involving businesses, family trusts or family businesses requires additional time and attention, plus document-gathering and review between sessions. It is important to take the time for all three of us (clients and mediator) to fully understand these financial complexities; the ensuing discussion may take considerably more time over several sessions. Throughout these meetings, I educate clients about the relevant legal and financial concepts that these assets are subject to, as well as family wealth structures that might be present in one, or both, of the future spouses' situations.

For example, when reviewing family irrevocable trusts, we examine the actual trust documents together. Often, the mediation client who is the beneficiary of such a trust hadn't fully grasped the details of the structure of the trusts or understood its potential distributions during their lifetime. In mediation, there can be a full discussion about how the trust will impact their lives and upcoming marriage plus that of future generations.

Third-party irrevocable trusts aren't typically considered marital property. This is a principle universally reinforced in the prenup—in fact, it is the driving reason for the prenup in many cases. However, the trust's impact on the marriage cannot just simply be ignored.

Often a family wealth advisor takes the position that the couple should overlook the family wealth. The theory they present is that the wealth does not belong to the beneficiary (or the couple) but is intended for future generations. However, the income and assets flowing from these trusts to one spouse during the marriage are real and can't just be ignored. Addressing this requires thoughtful planning by both parties. The benefit of mediation is that this planning will be collaborative.

The neutral mediator guides the couple through the process of determining how the parties will manage trust-derived wealth throughout their marriage. These conversations help the couple develop an understanding of the trust's provisions pertaining to distributions and how they might plan for these distributions during their shared financial future.

When a family business is involved, or if a future spouse is engaged in and owns an ongoing business, it's important to address how business earnings and profits will be handled within the marriage. This requires thorough fact-finding about the nature of the business, future prospects for it, and how benefits flow to the spouse family member or spouse business owner. These conversations naturally evolve into a development of financial guidelines for the marriage, which can eventually be included in their prenuptial agreement.

At an appropriate point, I transition clients to the next major topic. I typically address "marriage ends at death" before discussing divorce provisions. Ironically, clients generally find death-related planning less emotionally challenging than divorce terms, particularly in first marriages. Deciding on death provisions in second marriages, however, can be complex—but solvable—although potentially quite fraught in the mediated discussions.

This gradual approach—taking small, manageable steps—proves more effective than tackling difficult topics immediately. When couples encounter challenging decisions early in the process, I often suggest postponing addressing them. By building momentum via the discussion of less difficult topics first, couples become better equipped to handle more complex decisions later.

Why Add the Extra Cost of Mediation to the Costs of Generating a Prenup

It should be recognized that a prenuptial agreement is often the most significant financial contract a person will ever sign in their life. Not only that, but it goes to the very heart of the marriage, which is one of the most primary relationships a person has in life. It's important to get it right. Embarking on mediation as the first step makes this crucial outcome of a beneficial contract much more likely to happen.

Some people view mediation as an unnecessary and expensive first step in creating a prenuptial agreement. However, mediation tends to provide a more effective beginning for the process. In addition, it provides a great deal of work product that replaces the time and cost of the attorney-led paradigm as the process unfolds.

Much of an attorney-led process (which usually starts with a draft of a prenuptial agreement) consists of back-and-forth negotiations about the terms of the agreement. Aside from creating corrosiveness between the marrying couple, due to the adversarial nature of the positions taken, this negotiation takes significant attorney time at much potential emotional cost. The attorney costs for this segment of the process are often quite significant.

In the mediation-first process, decisions about the terms of the agreement are accomplished in mediation, saving the cost of dual attorney representation. The attorneys will, of course, provide input to their clients in their review of the terms. But mediation has the benefit of peacefully accomplishing this crucial first step in the prenup construction. When done by opposing attorneys, this step usually results in an unpleasant (and memorable) negotiation.

And, of course (at least in my view), prenuptial agreements are only appropriate when there's significant wealth involved—either accumulation of prenuptial assets, family money, or inheritances—and also if it is a second marriage or a situation where a spouse is actively involved in a business. It doesn't make sense to me to try to save money by foregoing the best process option, when by doing so could likely create a negative effect on the resilience of the upcoming marriage.

Taking the Next Step: Selecting and Working with Reviewing/Drafting Attorneys for the Mediation Process

After the creation of a term sheet in mediation, each party will have the proposed terms reviewed by separate attorneys. The attorneys are generally the professionals who will draft the agreement. They might suggest modifications, add additional terms, or suggest that certain terms be omitted during this process. The parties can mutually adjust terms based on their lawyers' input. It is expected and usual that lawyers make constructive refinements to the agreement, which should be welcomed by the parties and the mediator.

As every attorney and mediator working in this field knows, attorneys make or break prenuptial agreements. In fact, a significant part of my practice involves helping couples repair damage caused by traditional attorney-to-attorney negotiations. That's why the choice of attorney is so crucial in the prenup process. When negotiations become adversarial, clients suffer. As a result, I view that an essential part of my role as a prenup mediator is to help my mediation clients find suitable attorneys to represent them.

Selecting appropriate counsel requires judgment and skill. Attorneys approach prenups differently based on their values, experiences, and practice philosophies. Some view their role as adversarial, focusing on maximizing financial benefits for their client without considering the impact on the other spouse or on the marriage itself. Others rely on standard boilerplate language without examining its implications or other options. Neither approach is beneficial to the future spouses. Starting with a mediated term sheet (subject to the attorneys' independent review with their clients) helps avoid these pitfalls.

Attorney referrals from friends or family often prove problematic or useless. Recommended attorneys may lack prenup expertise or experience with non-adversarial approaches. When family wealth is involved, often the family or the family office will recommend a specific attorney to a future spouse. However, attorneys representing the wealthy families may have a fundamental conflict of interest between the family-of-origin's interests and the future spouse's interests and desires, which might not coincide.

The selection of reviewing attorneys requires extraordinary care. Attorneys who prioritize aggressive rights bargaining can potentially derail the mediation's constructive progress and the parties' previously existing good will toward each other. Almost always, the attorneys I choose from are collaborative divorce attorneys who are active in the collaborative law bar in their jurisdiction. I believe collaborative attorneys (i.e., attorneys trained and experienced in collaborative law techniques) can better understand the delicate balance of protecting individual interests while preserving the health and viability of the marriage itself.

I find that this type of attorney has a greater understanding of marriage, what makes a long-term marriage tick, and they work within a non-adversarial framework. Often when I am compiling a list, I will ask one of the recommended attorneys (who may have successfully served as a client attorney during one of my past mediations) to suggest other attorneys they feel comfortable working with. This can be a very good source of attorney referrals.

Attorneys from various practice fields (e.g., divorce, business, and estate planning) can and do handle prenups. However, I invariably recommend divorce attorneys who practice mediation and collaborative law to fill this role. These professionals typically demonstrate greater sensitivity to the values of marriage and are more capable of creating terms that support successful marriages. Within the mediation and collaborative law bar, I choose carefully. If I have worked with someone successfully in a prenup representation situation or a mediation, I ask that person to recommend others who they trust and feel comfortable working with.

I then present my recommendations during a meeting with the clients. Together we review the websites of each of the potential attorneys and discuss them. I ask my mediation clients to pick a first and second choice from the list. Generally, they have a good sense of who they wish to approach for the next stage of the process. However, often their choices surprise me, which is why, as a mediator, I have learned (and relearned) to let the clients decide and not to let my personal views affect their decisions.

After clients select and engage their attorneys, I arrange a joint meeting directly with the attorneys. This is a three-way meeting without clients present. Before this meeting, I share all relevant documentation with the attorneys and include the mediated term sheet.

During the meeting, I brief the attorneys on the background of the case, client perspectives, and the reasoning behind the chosen terms. For complex cases involving trusts or businesses, I present detailed information about these assets and interests. We review the relevant trusts, tax returns, financial reports, operating agreements, and trust documents together. This comprehensive briefing will save the attorneys significant (and duplicative) fact-finding time. It brings the attorneys quickly up to speed and ensures that they understand the context of decisions made by the clients during the mediation.

After the attorneys consult with their clients, I ask them to collaborate on a single "almost final" draft incorporating the term sheet provisions, any agreed upon changes, and suggested improvements. This approach prevents "draft fatigue" due to the dissemination and review of multiple revisions. While I typically step back after passing the work on to the respective attorneys, I do remain available to clarify points or mediate new issues if needed.

In this way, it is a client-centered mediation process that addresses both parties' needs while protecting their relationship, followed by a structured, productive (and peaceful) attorney review/drafting phase to complete the process of creating a prenuptial agreement.

The Importance of the Marital Home

In a first marriage, typically the focus is on the development of marital property creating marital wealth. Couples in first marriages value sharing and supporting each other in all aspects of life, including economic. Generosity and mutual support are key factors that make marriages thrive. That's why couples should make thoughtful decisions about how separate property is treated in a marriage during the prenuptial agreement construction phase.

If a separate property contribution to marital property remains distinct (as found in standard prenups), that separate component of the asset continues to generate gains, losses, and income proportionate to its percentage of ownership. This approach essentially turns the spouse contributing separate property into a business partner pertaining to that asset during the marriage.

Does this dynamic feel right in a first marriage between relatively young people? Usually not. This arrangement may be acceptable in second or later marriages, but it's not typically what partners feel is right in a first marriage. Marital partners are much more than business partners.

The negative implications of tracking and accounting for separate property that has been added into marital property are particularly pronounced when it comes to the ownership and financing of the marital home. This is true especially in first marriages of relatively young people. Joint ownership of the marital residence plays a crucial role in bonding for most younger married couples and helps strengthen their connection during the inevitable ups and downs of married life. A home is not just an investment; it's the center of the married life.

If one spouse can walk away from the marriage without economic consequences, this can easily undermine the resilience of the relationship to be able to overcome the inevitable obstacles that will be faced by the couple during the course of a long marriage. This is especially pronounced with respect to the marital home. If neither party can financially walk away from the marriage without gravely impairing their economic prospects, it strengthens the possibility of a long-term marital commitment. Unfortunately, prenups, particularly for the wealthier spouse, can allow exactly that: the ability for one partner to leave without facing negative economic consequences.

Having a truly shared marital home is so important to the strengthening of a first marriage. My view is that it's a mistake in a first marriage to structure a prenup in a way that one spouse owns the marital home, or for one spouse's separate property to form the basis of its purchase. Similarly, if the marital home is funded by parents who retain ownership, or if it's held in a third-party family trust, this can also be problematic. The home should be a symbol of shared investment and commitment, not a source of potential division. Rather, it should create a lifetime of connection, support, pleasure, achievement, and shared responsibility.

Having the marital home in joint names as part of the couple's shared venture is beneficial titling. If the house at the time of the marriage is owned by one of the parties, it may make sense to purchase a new marital residence. Alternatively, the couple could gradually vest the separate property component of the marital home into marital property over a number of years as the marriage proves its durability.

If premarital property or family wealth is available for a home purchase, it might be preferable for the couple to adjust their expectations and fund the home themselves, with a joint mortgage and joint ownership. They might not be able to afford what they may with family help (or premarital property), but they will be establishing a mutual personal and financial investment in the foundation of their domestic life—the home itself.

Assuming the marital home remains sacrosanct as owned by both parties with no separate property contributions, there may still be other assets into which separate property contributions might be made. In such cases, there are various options for handling these contributions, ensuring fairness and balance while respecting the source of the separate assets. The key is to find a solution that maintains the integrity of the marriage while acknowledging the individual contributions made by each spouse.

Instead of implementing the strict boilerplate rule regarding tracking separate property contributions to the marital home, there are less extreme options to consider. One option would include a term in the prenup that ensures the separate property contribution is returned dollar-for-dollar upon sale or the dissolution of the marriage. If there is a loss, it can be assessed against the marital portion first, with any remaining losses absorbed by the separate property component.

This dollar-for-dollar approach does gradually reduce the real value of the original separate property component over time due to inflation. However, if a spouse (or their family-of-origin) has the means to make a separate property contribution to the home, it's reasonable to assume that they can absorb a loss in value due to inflation. Moreover, any marital gain would presumably be equally shared between the parties.

Another option for clients to consider is to treat the separate property contribution as a loan, with an interest rate tied to a benchmark such as the overnight banking funding rate (OBFR) or the 30-year fixed mortgage rate. This provides an alternative from handling the separate property component as a business-like partnership between the marital interest and the separate interest, where the separate property component would be entitled to a proportional loss or gain upon disposition, death, or divorce.

Better yet is setting a default rule in the prenup stipulating that any separate property added to the marital home loses its separate property characterization once contributed. The decision to contribute separate property would be up to the spouse (or the spouse's family) contributing the funds thereby making an implicit choice to blend the separate property into marital property by virtue of the contribution itself.

This is a simple resolution that some people opt for. However, it does come with potential emotional consequences of the more-moneyed spouse appearing (and being) ungenerous if they don't contribute their separate property to the marriage. But if they do, there would be no strings attached, and the property would be fully integrated into the marital assets.

The presumption that separate property loses its characteristics when added to marital property is rarely considered as a replacement for the typical boilerplate, which always keeps it separate. But it has the advantage of making *generosity* the default, thereby supporting core values of marriage. It's likely a good approach for a healthy marriage.

Even if the mediation clients end up deciding to treat any separate property component of the martial home as a proportional ownership in the asset, as typically seen in off-the-shelf prenups, the mediated process offers a key advantage: There will be a thorough discussion of all other possible options before the couple chooses which will apply to them.

This highlights of one of the central benefits of starting with mediation. In a mediated prenup, the clients have an opportunity to fully consider and understand the various choices available to them before making a decision. This client-centered approach ensures that both parties are actively involved in shaping the terms, discovering all possible options, and then in making informed decisions based on their unique needs, circumstances, and preferences. In contrast, the typical attorney-led prenup process generally lacks this level of exploration, with less opportunity for the clients to discuss and choose from a range of possibilities.

Children of Wealthy Families

A common scenario leading to prenuptial agreements is when one future spouse comes from a wealthy family and the other does not. In cases of significant wealth, one or more irrevocable trusts benefiting the wealthier future spouse is often already in place, benefiting that party.

Many affluent families have family offices—organizations that manage the assets of the family and provide financial services and advice to the family members. Recipients of this advice include the beneficiaries of family irrevocable trusts, which include the children and grandchildren of the family members who established the trust. The current terms for these beneficiaries are Gen 2 and Gen 3 (second generation, third generation, etc.), distinguishing them from the generation that originally created the wealth.

Mediation can offer a valuable setting for commencing productive dialogue in such situations; thereby helping the couple explore financial expectations and consider what kinds of arrangements they might want to establish regarding the family money that is expected to flow to one of the future spouses during their marriage.

Wealthy families and their advisors usually offer children guidance emphasizing that the wealth be structured so that the trust fund never becomes part of the marital estate. In addition, the typical advice is that any wealth distributed from the trust remains the protected, sole property of the Gen 2 beneficiaries throughout their lifetimes. Such advisors also recommend to the Gen 2 beneficiaries that the wealth generated by the trust should, as far as possible, be preserved for future generations. Many of these family trusts are structured as dynasty trusts, designed to pass the wealth down through multiple generations, not just to the Gen 2 and Gen 3 beneficiaries.

Additionally, a common aim of the trust structure is to protect the trust assets (termed the "corpus") as well as distributions of income and principal from the trust, from the beneficiary's own improvident financial behavior and claims from creditors. One of the creditors that the trust advisors very much have in mind is the claims of a future soon-to-be former spouse in a divorce. The knowledge that the terms of trust include protection against possible future claims by them can feel quite insulting to the less-moneyed spouse, as it treats the beneficiary's spouse as a potential enemy as to the trust.

While case law does recognize direct claims by former spouses against trust assets, such lawsuits rarely succeed in actually accessing them. These claims (whether litigated or not), however, can influence the division of marital property, sometimes leading to adjustments in asset allocations in favor of the less-advantaged spouse. Trust income, on the other hand, has been deemed available for spousal and child support in certain litigated cases. However, a prenuptial agreement can prevent former spouses from making claims against the family trusts and their distributions—certainly a valid reason to have a prenup in this situation.

Agreements made by the couple regarding anticipated access to wealth during their marriage can and should be carefully considered in their prenup. Many aspects of this impending wealth warrant discussion. First is the proverbial elephant in the room: One future spouse has the expectation of receiving significant wealth during the marriage; the other does not.

The implications of one spouse significantly increasing their separate assets through inherited or gifted money, or via distribution from trust funds during a long-term marriage, without sharing with the other spouse, are extreme. These should be thoroughly discussed and explored in mediation. It can't just be ignored, as many family advisors advocate.

Standard advice from family offices and advisors says that this wealth should always remain under the sole control of the recipient. But does that approach truly serve the marriage—especially when the safeguards of a prenuptial agreement foreclose the rights of the other spouse to breach the trust?

Contrary to the typical advice from family advisors, a marrying couple should carefully consider how income generated by the trust and subsequently distributed to the spouse from the wealthy family, will be handled within the marriage. The same considerations apply to outright distributions of principal from the trust, or by lifetime gifts or inheritance to be received by Gen 2 or Gen 3 individuals outside of an irrevocable trust. Navigation of these particulars are best facilitated by a neutral mediator to ensure that all possibilities are explored.

The following are some key questions for the couple to consider:

- When family wealth is distributed to a spouse, should it always remain separate, or does the couple envision sharing all or a portion of the distribution within the marital estate?
- If wealth distributions are shared, what are possible plans for the sharing?
- Will these plans for sharing be imbedded in the terms of the prenuptial agreement?
- What happens when principal, rather than income, is distributed to a spouse, and what would the plan be for sharing that?
- Who has control over decisions regarding the use and management of these distributions?

There are various approaches beyond the common default rule that says the wealth stays with the benefited spouse, which is the rule contained in most prenuptial agreements. That default rule typically states that trust assets and income, once distributed, remain separate property of that spouse unless the beneficiary spouse chooses to share them.

Gen 2 and Gen 3 individuals entering into prenups should carefully evaluate whether this default rule aligns with their values, priorities, and vision for their upcoming marriage. Gen 2 and Gen 3 beneficiaries in these cases also need to tread carefully between their own preferences versus the potential for alienating their families, family advisors, and the trustees controlling the trust that might result from their choices to share trust benefits within the marriage.

Understanding the distribution provisions of the trust instrument (i.e., the actual text of the trust) is critical for any couple navigating the financial dynamics of family trusts and how they might relate to their marriage.

Key questions to explore include the following:

- Are distributions mandatory at certain ages, or are they made at the discretion of an independent trustee?
- Who is the trustee, and what standards guide their decision-making in distributing money to a beneficiary?
- Do the distribution amounts and their frequency depend on the beneficiary's other assets?
- What happens to the trust assets upon the death of the Gen 2 or Gen 3 beneficiary?

- Is the trust considered a "pot" trust, which means there are other beneficiaries of a single trust fund aside from the mediation client?
- If there are other beneficiaries of the trust fund, how will distributions be allocated among multiple permissible beneficiaries?

A thorough analysis of these provisions helps the couple make informed decisions about what to do regarding this expected access to wealth. Discussions in mediation help ensure clarity and find alignment in their approach to wealth management within the marriage. This type of analysis and educational process should be a joint effort, as both parties are directly affected by the trust's provisions and its impact on the marriage. By providing a structured, neutral setting for open discussions, education, and mutual understanding, mediation is the ideal starting point.

Generally, trust benefits are passed down from generation to generation. When a Gen 2 beneficiary passes away, the trust's benefits are transferred to their children: the Gen 3 beneficiaries. This process continues to subsequent generations, such as Gen 4 and Gen 5—as long as the trust still retains assets.

This default distribution structure can often be modified through a provision known as a "power of appointment," which is included in many (if not most) irrevocable family wealth trusts. A power of appointment allows the current trust beneficiary to designate, typically through their last will, who will receive the benefits they enjoyed during their lifetime upon their death. It gives the current beneficiary some agency over what they want to happen after their death.

However, most trusts that include a power of appointment limit the permissible appointed beneficiaries to the children, grandchildren, and future generations of the beneficiary. If the beneficiary has no children, the power usually can only extend to the children or to further descendants of Gen 1 (i.e., the parents or grandparents), that originally established the trust.

In more modern versions of family irrevocable trusts, some powers of appointment are broader, expanding the scope of possible beneficiaries. Some of these allow for beneficiaries to designate not only their descendants but also their spouses and charities. In certain cases, these trusts allow distributions to be appointed to *anyone* the beneficiary chooses.

This situation provides the beneficiary with agency over who will benefit from the trust upon their death, rather than having that decision solely and irrevocably controlled by the instructions drawn up by the "dead hand" of their, perhaps, now deceased parents or grandparents. Frankly, I find it very satisfying all around when family trusts are drafted with this provision and, happily, I see it more and more in my practice.

Most trust beneficiaries are unaware of the existence and significance of these power of appointment provisions. In mediation sessions, we can review these provisions (and other important features) of the trust in detail with the clients. It's crucial for the engaged clients to understand these provisions, how they work, and how to exercise them in their estate plans. This educational process can occur naturally and smoothly within the context of prenuptial-agreement mediation. I have never seen this important topic (or the idea of reviewing trust instruments) even brought up in an attorney-led process.

There is yet another important impact of family trusts on a couple: The potential impact of passing on substantial unearned wealth to their own children, grandchildren, and future generations through popular dynasty trusts is often concerning. Trusts that ensure that the wealth gets passed down through bloodlines can be troubling for many couples planning for their marriage. They know the effect the trust has on their lives, and they do not necessarily wish to impose that burden on their future children and grandchildren. A mediated discussion of this aspect of family wealth can be very beneficial to the couple embarking on marriage.

A mediator can play a vital role in helping the couple explore options that can address issues raised by family wealth. These options are generally not presented by the family's wealth advisors. Even though the terms of a family irrevocable trust might be limiting, through facilitated discussion, the parties can be made fully aware of their options and be able to make decisions that reflect their shared values and goals for the marriage and for their children. Again, it must be emphasized that these discussions about the implications of family wealth almost never happen in the attorney-led process.

Often the Gen 2 or Gen 3 beneficiary is pressured by their family office or family-of-origin attorneys to have a prenuptial agreement, and to specifically adopt certain provisions in their prenups. These terms are viewed by the advisors as requirements. It takes strength, grace, and some flexibility when a marrying Gen 2 or Gen 3 member and their future spouse attempt to put into effect terms that differ from those that are presented by the advisors.

Many future spouses in this situation do find a way to include terms consistent with their shared ideals pertaining to their own upcoming marriage. This sort of vision can benefit the siblings of the child of wealth when they begin to negotiate their own prenups. I have heard that some siblings, who previously married with restricted prenup terms suggested by family advisors, later reconsider some terms after hearing about alternative possibilities that had been explored by my mediation clients. Some create postnuptial agreements to put such changes into effect.

Most prenup lawyers hold the view that all benefits in the marriage, pertaining to wealth, come from the future spouse of the wealthy family. However, over and over, in my work with couples in this situation, it has become clear to me that the non-wealthy spouse also brings an important (and equal) fundamental value to the marriage.

For the child of wealth, having access to unearned wealth can be both a privilege and a burden. Without the necessity of building their own financial future, many children of wealth struggle to find a meaningful sense of direction in life. For most people, the challenge of finding a purpose-filled life is essential to personal fulfillment. Many children of wealth fail to discover this deeper sense of purpose. This can impact their overall happiness and well-being, and as a result, can affect the upcoming marriage.

Some Gen 2 and Gen 3 individuals manage their inherited wealth gracefully and constructively, leading purposeful lives with rewarding occupations, as measured monetarily or otherwise. However, for others who struggle to find their path and purpose, having a spouse to share the burden—and the benefits—of family wealth, as well as participating in the decision-making involved, provides an invaluable support system. They no longer have to navigate the complexities of this wealth alone.

For all couples in which one party comes from a wealthy family, the shared marital partnership can help them find direction and mutual support, make thoughtful decisions, and lead a more fulfilling life—in terms of personal growth, in society at large, and within their relationship. That is why one party's access to wealth should not be seen as more important than the other party's contributions; that party can provide support regarding the access to wealth. They both contribute equally to the marriage.

Rebalancing the possible extreme conditions regarding access to wealth within a marriage plays an essential role in strengthening the marital bond. These types of discussions and the mutual decisions that arise from them are almost always absent in the attorney-driven model for generating prenuptial agreements, where the focus is typically on protecting assets and access to the wealth of the more moneyed future spouse.

This omission, when a mediator is not involved, represents a significant missed opportunity for the future spouses when planning their lives together, in a more meaningful and aligned way. By addressing these family wealth issues in mediation, couples can build a stronger foundation—not just financially but also emotionally and relationally, ensuring both partners are equally engaged in shaping their futures.

The Challenges and Opportunities of Second Marriage Prenups

One of the most significant areas of my mediation practice involves mediating with couples entering second (or subsequent) marriages. These are often referred to as "gray" marriages. A key aspect of these agreements concerns balancing the financial interests of both partners, especially when one or both individuals have children from a previous marriage or possess significant premarital assets.

Typically, a person entering into a subsequent marriage in middle-age or older results in their having to formulate a prenup that has two competing priorities: how to express in financial terms their love for their new spouse while at the same time making sure the terms also manifest their profound feelings of loyalty and parental protection of their children from the prior marriage. The challenges of second or third marriages (whether there is a prenup or not) revolves around how to sensitively and appropriately balance these two potentially divergent interests.

The prenuptial roadmap for each second (or subsequent) marriage is unique, depending on each situation (e.g., the personalities of the couple, their children, and various other factors). A delicate balance is pivotal to the newly extended family's well-being. Prenups can be useful to correlate these competing goals in a thoughtful and nuanced manner and serve to create peace within the newly extended family.

People entering into second marriage prenups generally face different issues than people entering first marriages at younger ages. First of all, clear-cut distinctions between separate property and marital property are often more reasonable and appropriate in second marriages. But having said this, while it is generally easier to plan a prenup for a second marriage than for a first marriage, second marriage prenups require a careful thought process, especially when financial protection for one of the new spouses is needed.

In a gray marriage, the two individuals might be similarly positioned in terms of wealth and income, but that is not always the case. Sometimes, one spouse needs the financial protection of the more moneyed spouse, both during the marriage and after the death of that spouse, and perhaps even if the second marriage ends in divorce.

The two major issues to plan for in ensuring security for the dependent spouse are protection through assets and spousal support. The mediator's role is to ensure that all options pertaining to these protections are clearly presented, explored, and discussed, so the couple can make their own informed and thoughtful decisions.

In a situation like this, the mediator should be well-versed in estate planning to help provide the appropriate options for the mediation clients, as estate planning options for second marriages can be diverse and complex. There are many ways to satisfy the goal of providing adequate security for a dependent surviving spouse while still preserving assets to maintain a legacy for the children of a prior marriage.

If the first death is that of the wealthier spouse, options for protecting the surviving spouse can include qualified terminable interest property (QTIP) trusts and other types of trusts and life estates in an estate plan. Terms relating to the home in which the couple lives (even if owned by the more moneyed spouse) will be important to decide upon and to plan for as part of this discussion.

If there are enough assets, many spouses decide to leave a legacy for their children immediately upon their death, while also retaining an amount to provide for the security for their new spouse. Sometimes, the security for the surviving spouse will be held in trust, with the children of the deceased spouse as the ultimate beneficiaries. In that case, the children of the more-moneyed spouse would receive additional assets after the death of the surviving spouse.

Or the inheritance for the surviving spouse (or part of it) will sometimes be given outright and not in trust. To the extent the legacy is provided to the surviving spouse in trust, prenup discussions could make it clear that this part of the legacy may eventually go to the children of the less-moneyed spouse upon their death.

These discussions should find their way into the prenuptial agreement in order to ensure that these arrangements are legally binding upon the deaths of the spouses. By incorporating estate planning requirements directly into the prenup, both parties can gain peace of mind, knowing that their financial security and the well-being of their children are addressed according to their wishes—both during the marriage and after their deaths.

The more challenging issue in second marriages often revolves around the possibility of spousal support if the second marriage ends in divorce, especially if the dependent spouse truly needs support.

Many individuals who were providers in first marriages have had lingering alimony obligations that felt burdensome and unfair. Even if there is enough wealth to provide financial security to the other spouse in the event of divorce, some individuals are adamantly opposed to having an alimony obligation, or, alternatively, to providing security by sharing some of their separate assets in the case of divorce. Some of these feelings have come from their having experienced a distressing, litigated divorce in their first marriage or feelings that they were treated unfairly in that divorce.

The problem with the advantaged party advocating for no spousal support (or other support) if the marriage ends in divorce is that it can send a negative message of lack of care, which can damage the future of the upcoming marriage. Having a spousal support provision (when one is foreseeably needed) shows care and concern (you might call it love) for the other spouse.

Sometimes, after the discussion about support if the marriage were to end in divorce, prenup negotiations fail, and the couple breaks up. If the relationship survives with restrictive terms regarding divorce, it still can be irreparably damaged. Occasionally, a compromise path can be found and mutually agreed to by the couple, but not always. This is a situation in which, if the more-wealthy party insists on offering no spousal support or other security in the case of divorce (where it would be needed), it can hinder that party's potential for finding a life partner. I've seen that happen in my practice.

Another factual situation in second marriages that comes up frequently: A financially advantaged future spouse may have recently retired from actively earning income at the end of a successful career, perhaps even at an early age. Or one of the parties may have access to significant family wealth at the time of the second marriage.

Most alimony laws primarily hinge upon earned income from active employment. If there is no earned income on the part of the advantaged spouse, this leads to a timing problem. If spousal security after a divorce is needed by one spouse (and divorce provisions are not adequate to provide that security), that less-advantaged spouse will need to continue to work and earn money to protect themselves in case the marriage ends in divorce. This prevents the new spouses' ability to share a leisurely retirement. When the divorce terms in the prenuptial agreement lack sufficient security for one spouse, they may not be able to share that leisure time together.

In the second marriage situation, a prenup can provide more certainty, reasonable security, and fairness to both spouses, while acknowledging and protecting the legacies of children from prior marriages. Mediation is an excellent route to having open and facilitated discussions as to how best to solve and balance these issues.

Managing a Client-Centered Process with Non-Collaborative Opposing Counsel

Most of my prenup work now consists of mediating prenups for couples engaged in the process of formulating one. I believe this is the optimal method for developing sound and healthy terms of a prenup in most situations because it relies on thorough, facilitated, and client-centered discussions. One might assume that people entering marriage would prefer the most comprehensive and informative approach and avoid adversarial negotiations to the extent possible. (Accepting that both clients agree to engage in the process willingly.)

Unfortunately, most couples aren't even aware that mediation as the first step in the process is possible and available as a process choice. Hopefully this chapter will help familiarize attorneys with this process and the discrete steps involved in creating mediated prenuptial agreements.

Many parties, unaware of the potential of mediation, may have already engaged counsel as a first step. This is often the case for the more financially advantaged party, who is usually the party requesting the prenup. Their attorney may be their business counsel, estate planning attorney, or their former divorce attorney in a prior divorce. Or their attorney may be someone chosen by their family or their family office. That attorney might have even already generated a draft prenup, which (as previously discussed) is generally one-sided and weighted heavily toward the interests of that attorney's own client.

The attorney representing the less-advantaged spouse then must work within that framework to create a more balanced prenuptial agreement. However, it turns out that even within a traditional, lawyer-led paradigm, there are ways to encourage the unfolding of a client-centered process.

First, there are several inherent problems in starting with a fully developed draft agreement. Because prenuptial agreements are so complex, there will be provisions that the attorney deemed normal practice, but were not discussed with their client. Some of these provisions may be an unwelcome surprise to both future spouses and an embarrassing development to the client of the drafting attorney. Usually, that client hadn't anticipated that some offending and unwelcome provisions would be included and would not have agreed to them being in the draft. The other future spouse will surely feel alienated by the terms expressed in that draft, usually assuming that it was their fiancé's decision to include the terms.

This sets up a distressing dynamic between the parties, causing the less-financially advantaged future spouse to be seriously (sometimes irrevocably) offended. That first foray with lawyers has turned the mutual love and care of the couple on its head, as it seems to (and actually does) project an expression of selfishness. This first step in the typical lawyer-led prenup process has, unfortunately, served to corrode the good will (you might call it love) between the parties planning to marry. Sometimes this even causes the breakup of a couple previously headed toward marriage.

However, even when an opposing counsel drafts a one-sided agreement of the type just described, there *is* a way to salvage a client-centered process. The attorney for the less-advantaged spouse can opt to work within this framework to facilitate a more balanced approach.

Here's one technique: When I learn that a draft agreement has already been written by the other side, I often simply ask my client not to read it, even if it had been sent to the other future spouse by their counsel, because it can be quite disturbing.

If the draft agreement has been sent to me as opposing counsel, I might cordially inform the other attorney that I'd prefer to start with a bare-bones term sheet and will not review or respond to the draft agreement at this time. I then ask them to send me a document containing only the proposed terms in a concise manner. That's what a term sheet is. Once I receive that, we can begin the process of negotiating.

Beginning with a term sheet presents a much better negotiation stance than starting with a fully drafted agreement.

It sends a signal that the initial term sheet is just a proposal, that the terms will be a collaboration and can be adjusted. It is less of an uphill battle to respond to a term sheet than to a fully drafted agreement already prepared and circulated by the attorney for the more-moneyed spouse. Ideally, the less-advantaged party would distribute their term sheet first, but that is not always possible. Of course, ideally, the process would begin with mediation including the mediator and the couple.

The initial term sheet (prepared by whichever attorney drafts it) will be then discussed by the parties. I will learn from my client what parts of it are or are not mutually agreed upon. Then the clients will consult with and listen to the advice of their respective lawyers.

Decisions will be made by the parties about what terms and/or changes are acceptable, and which are not. Then the attorneys and the parties can generate new options and share them with each other. When both parties make adjustments that they both agree upon (this latter step is usually omitted in the usual attorney-led process), the drafting can begin.

If working from a term sheet is not possible, after the initial draft agreement is received and my client and I discuss the terms embedded in it; I consult with my client and write up a checklist of changes that my client would like to propose. I ask the client to discuss these terms with their fiancé first, before I present them to the other attorney.

In this way, the two marrying parties can discuss the initial terms with one another. The ensuing conversation can clarify what is possible and what is not possible for each party to agree to. Together, the parties evaluate the various options available to them and communicate with each other directly about any concerns regarding the proposed or contemplated terms. The clients then decide on which terms they will agree to adopt, which ones to modify, and which to omit.

Although this is not mediation, it comes close. At least, with this result, the realm of possibilities is clarified and perhaps even expanded. This goes a long way beyond the initiating attorney's first proposed draft.

During the next stage of the process, each party will again return to their respective attorneys and receive counsel on the terms that they are considering. The parties now have a more complete idea of possibilities to consider. They also are directly aware of each other's questions and receptiveness to (or opposition to) the various proposed terms. It's a more thorough undertaking, which benefits the clients much more than the typical lawyer versus lawyer negotiation with the clients waiting in the wings.

I find that having my client and their future spouse speak directly with each other right after the initial proposal from the attorney for the more-moneyed future spouse (after receiving my counsel) is more productive than immediately presenting counterproposals to the other attorney. It begins to clarify what terms will be possible during the negotiation process.

In my experience, there is great resistance to counterproposals from the attorney for the more advantaged party. The response to any suggestion of a change is often a flat "no." This is particularly true if that attorney is not collaboratively trained, which is usually the case. Having my client first discuss initial terms and counterproposals with their future spouse tends to provide more flexibility as to potential terms and better addresses the parties' needs for agreement on important decisions presented in the prenup.

Staging this discussion over a period of days usually works better than reacting immediately and rapidly making counterproposals. I'm a big believer in taking baby steps when negotiating or mediating. It's productive to have time to think about each term, not only for the clients but also for the attorneys. Because the terms ultimately set will have huge ramifications for the upcoming marriage, the possibilities should be carefully considered by all involved.

Taking it slowly gives the parties time to share their feelings about the terms. This can be a healing process for the couple if the terms were extremely adverse for one of the future spouses at the outset (as they often are). This process, especially within a potentially adversarial situation, can clarify and resolve many aspects of the agreement. It also serves an important function of bonding and unifying the clients. It makes the entire process more peaceful. You might call it a client-centered process, outside of mediation.

Of course, all correspondence I send to the opposing counsel (note the word "opposing"!) should be approved by my client prior to sending. I also ask my client to specifically discuss the terms stated in any correspondence with their future spouse prior to sending. This allows for additional changes and an assessment of the other future spouse's receptivity before the final version is sent. This further streamlines the negotiation process, enabling a more productive and peaceful reception when the approved letter is sent to the other party's attorney. It also puts the other future spouse on record as to their preferences. When discussing changes with their attorney, often the attorney advises them against a term that they had informally already agreed to with their future partner.

Of course, much of the difficulties and challenges inherent in the attorney-led process can be avoided if the other future spouse chooses a collaboratively trained attorney as their counsel. If my client's future spouse is not yet represented, I will send a letter (either to my client, or to their fiancé) explaining the collaborative practice, and the collaborative method of creating a prenuptial agreement. The letter will offer the names of several collaborative attorneys that I recommend.

I am always hopeful that the other party will be open to considering the attorneys on that list and chooses one of them to be their counsel. When a party chooses among a curated choice of attorneys that I have prepared, it often leads to a collaborative negotiation process, which bodes well for the couple.

Mediating Postnuptial Agreements

There are three main reasons people seek postnuptial agreements:

- They didn't quite complete their prenup in time for the wedding and decided to put it off until afterward.
- They signed a prenuptial agreement after a corrosive process. Its terms (and memories of the process) are now causing marital strain.
- Something has come up, which has caused the marriage to become unstable.

Mediation is an ideal process to handle each of these situations. I have worked with postnuptial mediation clients in all three scenarios.

First, in my experience, people who didn't quite complete their prenuptial agreement before the wedding generally *do* return later to complete it. Perhaps they have had children or have built up more mutual trust, now that they're married and have more shared experiences. Perhaps they have a better idea of what terms will suit them for their particular marriage, rather than what resulted from the prior attorney-led process.

If they return to try again to formulate a postnup, but they are unable to agree upon its terms, they may ultimately decide to divorce. However, in such situations, the marriage would most likely not have been a long-term one. Because of its short duration, a divorce would likely not be expected to have significant unintended or adverse financial outcomes for either party.

One of the most interesting and important roles for me as a postnuptial agreement mediator is to work with couples who had a corrosive prenup negotiation experience, signed the agreement anyway, and who now are living (or trying to live) with the results. Often, the prior experience has destroyed marital contentment, and it is literally eating away at them. Divorce looms. Mediation is perfect for this situation.

During our meetings, we slowly, carefully unpack what happened during their prior prenup process. Apologies might be made, and truths might be told, for the first time. Typically, I don't even look at the existing prenup until after a number of meetings, if at all. We start completely anew, with fresh minds, and without rehashing the prior experience. What they want to do *now* is the primary question to be answered. This eliminates retriggering the stress and pain of their prior disturbing experience. As with any prenup mediation, a term sheet is gradually and thoughtfully developed in the postnup process.

For this type of postnuptial agreement, I highly recommend that the clients start with new reviewing attorneys to keep the process fresh. Sometimes the previous attorneys may have done a good job, but the process was so distressing that the parties felt it was poisonous. Something clearly went wrong and it's time to clear the decks.

The couple can now write a new story about the beginning of their marriage to supplant that prior experience. It's time to create a new agreement, in mediation, with new reviewing counsel. The essential thrust of this postnuptial mediation process is to create good experiences to counteract the bad experiences of their previous hurtful effort to develop a prenup. It is the mediator's role, in this postnuptial situation, to foster as many good experiences and successful resolutions for these clients as possible.

The third situation mentioned earlier, leading to postnuptial agreements, occurs when something has come up that destabilizes the marriage. Usually, the couple has been in a long-term marriage, and there might be several factual circumstances that have contributed to the instability. There might have been a business loss or a job loss, an inheritance from parents, or an infidelity. Perhaps they want to solidify and make enforceable their estate planning commitments (often for the benefit of children from prior marriages). Frequently, in this third category of postnups, a strong probability of a divorce looms in the future.

Because of this often-dire situation, a possibility of coercion in negotiating the terms has the potential to exist. For example, one spouse may demand certain important financial concessions as the price for staying married. As a result, courts tend to be very wary about enforcing postnuptial agreements. The theory behind postnuptial agreements is that they are meant to *prevent* divorce—not to be an instrument used to gain an unfair advantage over a spouse. There is also a danger that the purpose of the postnuptial agreement on the part of one spouse is to create a template for an impending divorce, a motive that may not be discerned by the other spouse.

The mediator must carefully navigate these dynamics. They must be wary of hidden intentions and be capable of distinguishing a couple's legitimate mid-marriage concerns—which *can* be settled by a postnuptial agreement—from ones that merely provide an easy and advantageous way out for one client, only to be followed by an imminent divorce.

Because of these potential dynamics, mediating postnups (and mediating or representing postnup clients) in this third fact pattern is very challenging. In my experience, the postnup often fails to achieve its intended purpose: to help the marriage survive the crisis.

Using Collaborative Practice in Prenuptial and Postnuptial Agreement Creation

Couples embarking on prenuptial agreements (especially those entering a first marriage) generally do not want to engage in a lawyer-driven experience at the start of their negotiations. Although the collaborative process is very useful for divorces, the idea of generating a prenup through a formal collaborative practice model, which involves lawyers representing each of them from the beginning and throughout the process, is usually not attractive to most clients. They would rather start by using mediation, for the most part.

A formal collaborative practice process involves multiple four-way meetings with the client couple and their respective attorneys. Modern practice is to include a neutral process coach in all meetings, making these into five-way meetings. The neutral process coach's function is to ensure that the meetings remain collaborative and non-adversarial. Their concern is not only with the behavior of the clients but also the conduct of the lawyers, which sometimes has a tendency to deteriorate into uncivil and aggressive behavior; because lawyers act like, well, lawyers sometimes. In between each group session, lawyers provide advice and counsel to their respective clients, privately.

One of the benefits of the collaborative prenuptial agreement process is that it starts with discussions about the parties' interests, needs, and concerns. It does not begin with a fully drafted agreement presented by one party's lawyer to the other party. Like mediation, the focus then turns to possible terms that would meet the needs of each of future spouse, resulting in the development of a term sheet.

At its best, the group meetings at the core of the process have the feel of mediation (in which the two attorneys function as co-mediators). The mediation feel of the four- or five-way meetings is not surprising, as collaborative lawyers generally have extensive experience as mediators as well. And yet, the collaborative process does include advocacy for the clients, although it is developed during private strategy sessions between the attorney and their own client. It's a good combination of mediation and advocacy that can benefit some couples trying to figure out the financial terms of their marriage.

Another benefit of collaborative law prenups is that, unlike the usual attorney-led process, it creates a safe environment in which the emotions of both future spouses (which are sometimes quite strong and negative when negotiating the terms of a prenup) can be acknowledged, respected, and dealt with openly.

Collaborative practice is appropriate and useful in resolving complex divorce cases, some of which would otherwise result in protracted litigation. The key in the divorce context is the disqualification provision: Collaborative lawyers in a formal process may not represent their clients if the divorce terms are not settled and the matter ends with litigation. This disqualification is not significant in collaborative practice prenups, because getting married is the end point—not a trip to divorce court and a divorce.

Collaborative practice in the divorce context helps the parties maintain respectful post-divorce family relationships, particularly when the parties have children. It is also a helpful process when there are complex business interests or other financial situations that need to be thoroughly considered. In these situations, many collaborative cases include neutral financial experts to help the parties assess these issues.

Though some lawyers practice collaborative law in the prenuptial agreement context, such cases are rare. When they occur, it typically involves ultra-wealthy parties entering into a second or subsequent marriage with financially complex situations.

Because most parties considering prenups do not wish to lawyer-up right at the beginning, the collaborative model is generally less attractive to potential clients than other methods, including mediation—and even a lawyer-to-lawyer process, which doesn't involve multiple face-to-face meetings with the parties and their lawyers.

Having said this, using collaborative practice to negotiate the terms of some mid-marriage postnuptial agreements is often the best way to handle the complexities of arranging marital finances and commitments that may arise during a long-term marriage. In many of these postnuptial agreements divorce terms predominate. Their aim is to *prevent* divorce, but if that goal is not achieved, the divorce terms need to be strong and cohesive. Couples in that situation in mid-marriage would likely find the initial attorney representation within the collaborative divorce model to be more suitable, as well as useful and reassuring.

Mediating Cohabitation Agreements for Unmarried Partners

Some people choose not to get married but wish to live together as committed couples and wish to establish binding contractual rights and obligations pertaining to their assets and finances.

Some of these individuals are seniors concerned about each other's potential financial liability for skilled nursing home costs for their partner if they legally marry. Cohabitation agreements are private contracts. Terms regarding responsibility for medical and nursing home costs cannot override state or federal government rights to recover the cost of benefits from a legal spouse after a disabled spouse depletes their assets and income.

People entering into written cohabitation agreements need to be informed that if they later legally marry without an actual prenuptial agreement, the terms of their existing cohabitation agreement may not be enforceable. That is because prenuptial agreements must be made *in contemplation of* marriage. Cohabitation agreements generally are not. They are basically the opposite; they are in contemplation of *not* marrying.

As a result, if the cohabitating partners enter into a cohabitation agreement and later decide to marry, they need to take the following steps:

- Review their existing cohabitation agreement.
- Obtain legal advice and have an enforceable prenuptial agreement drafted prior to their marriage.

The prenup may contain many of or all of the terms of their prior cohabitation agreement, but it must be created and signed, nonetheless. Their reviewing/drafting attorneys will create a new agreement, enforceable according to their state's laws regarding prenups.

Having said this, mediation is the preferred and most effective way to help a couple think about and define the financial terms of living together. There's a lot to contemplate and resolve, just like in the case of prenuptial agreements. Here are some of the questions to consider:

- What happens to the home they are living in if they terminate their relationship or if one of them dies?
- What happens to their other assets?
- How will they support their living expenses during their cohabitation?
- Will there be any support paid by one to the other if the relationship ends prior to death?
- Do they want to have an enforceable right to inherit from each other?
- What would the provisions relating to an inheritance commitment be?

Even in the non-marital situation, there may be support issues to resolve if their cohabitation relationship ends. Support might be necessary for one of the parties, even though they were not legally married, and even though not legally required under state laws. It is a discussion that needs to take place when discussing the terms of the agreement. All these conversations are best had in the mediation context.

After the mediation is complete—as with a prenup—the parties will consult with their separate attorneys, who will draft the formal cohabitation agreement and provide individualized advice to each of them.

One of the benefits of being married (as opposed to living together) is that once married, couples have a *fiduciary duty* to act in each other's best interests.

That means each party must act in their spouse's best financial interests. Often, it's articulated as requiring one person to put the other's interests ahead of their own. When you think about it, isn't that really what marriage is about?

Unmarried cohabitants do not have this fiduciary duty toward each other. There are provisions in a cohabitation agreement that would be enforceable under state laws, but manifestly unenforceable under the laws relating to enforceability of prenuptial agreements vis-à-vis married couples. Unprotective provisions allowable in a cohabitation agreement would be similarly unenforceable if the couple was legally married *without* a prenup under public policy protections relating to married people.

Because there is no requirement of fiduciary duty, cohabitants are allowed to be less generous and less financially caring toward each other than married couples. The laws relating to fiduciary duty between spouses reflect a state's public policy that supports spouses, families, and marital stability. In general, the law treats unmarried cohabitants like strangers or people creating a business contract at arm's length, without concern for the deeper aspects of their relationship, which may be quite similar to marriage.

Cohabitants must carefully consider whether and to what extent they wish their contractual commitments to replace the protective and caring financial fiduciary obligations present between spouses. Their agreement can go far beyond the "buyer-beware" template the laws might provide; it can include some level of financial kindness, even if not legally required.

Because of lack of fiduciary protection in the laws in a cohabitation relationship, couples who are thinking about entering into non-marital agreements (and their mediators and counsel) should think carefully about how the terms would work out during a long cohabitation so that they (or one of them) are not unduly harmed at the end of the cohabitation, whether due to voluntary dissolution or death.

The Alternate Dispute Resolution (ADR) Clause in Prenuptial Agreements

One of the most important features that can be included in a prenuptial agreement is an Alternate Dispute Resolution (ADR) clause. This clause provides a pecking order or template for dispute resolution if something arises during the life of the agreement or at the time it goes into effect by death or divorce.

My standard ADR provisions consist of a three-tiered process:

1. Mediation
2. Collaborative practice if mediation fails
3. Arbitration (binding in cases where it is permitted; nonbinding if not)

Some parties prefer to skip either the mediation step or the collaborative process and have the final step be arbitration, either binding or nonbinding.

Notwithstanding the ADR clause, prenups always provide that if any matter requires an emergency order or relates to the children of the marriage, the parties can seek an order by filing with the state court with jurisdiction over the matter.

All prenups should contain standard contract language stating that the contract is binding for the parties and their "successors and assigns." That means that if one party has died, there is a process to enforce the provisions of the agreement. In many prenups, the terms "heirs, administrators, trustees and executors" are specifically added to this list, although the term "successors" would seem to include these. Because of this boilerplate provision, when there is an ADR clause, issues arising between a surviving spouse and children of a deceased spouse should be able to be settled by an interest-based consensual form of resolution. And, even if not, it can still serve as an aspirational goal for the marrying couple and their children from prior marriages.

Conciliation is another process that people entering into a prenuptial agreement might find useful to include in their prenups. It sometimes replaces mediation as an option and is another form of ADR. The parties (either the couple upon a divorce, or the heirs/executors of a deceased party and the surviving spouse) would meet with an experienced neutral third party, a conciliator, who would review and suggest resolution of any issues arising out of the prenuptial agreement. It's a voluntary process in which the conciliator is usually an attorney or retired judge.

The conciliator will speak with the parties, listen to their concerns and proposals, and help the parties find workable solutions to their issues. Though it bears similarities to evaluative mediation, it is not considered a type of mediation. Some couples may prefer this over mediation, as an ADR process option.

It is important to recognize that terms relating to child custody and child support are presumptively not enforceable if contained within a prenuptial agreement. Prenups are private contracts; they are subject to the state's overriding supervision under state policy considerations. State supervision of children under the "best interests of the child" doctrine is an important state policy that cannot be waived in a prenup. If the situation is not exigent—needing immediate court intervention—the couple may use the ADR tiered steps, ending in nonbinding arbitration for child-related issues, since binding arbitration will not be available. In this way, agreement might be achieved by means of an interest-based process without going to court.

There are also state policies protecting the well-being of dependent spouses. This means that divorce terms (including spousal support) in an existing prenup might be overridden in a court case. In most states, courts having jurisdiction over divorces are required to approve terms agreed to by the parties. As a result, in certain states, binding arbitration relating to spousal support (as with child support and custody) would not be available. However, a couple who have entered into a prenuptial agreement might agree to the results of non-binding arbitration relating to spousal support or child-related issues, subject to approval by the court in their upcoming divorce action.

Part of the prenup process is to establish a prenup that is enforceable under state law. Having said this, there is great variation among the states as to what terms are enforceable and which are not, with some states taking a very laissez-faire attitude about what can be permissible within the terms of a prenup.

Mediators should be aware of the standards of enforceability in their jurisdiction so that parties aren't led to include unenforceable terms during the mediation process. It's also the job of the attorneys who represent each party to assess the enforceability of the prenuptial agreement being constructed; this assessment is a crucial element in the process. However, having an agreement that is merely "enforceable" can be rather cruel to a less-advantaged spouse and may not be a thoughtful way to start a marriage. It may be highly detrimental to overall marital resilience.

Some practitioners have suggested the possibility of having a bare-bones, limited-purpose prenuptial agreement; one that simply has an ADR clause and leaves everything else to the parties' state's laws for resolution. One might call this a "prenup lite." This could be very useful, especially for couples entering a first marriage who, understandably, do not wish to think intensely about divorce terms immediately before their marriage.

Some people entering new marriages might have experienced a long and protracted litigated divorce in their prior marriage. Some in second marriages have concerns about potential conflict between the children of their first marriage and their surviving spouse if the marriage ends with their death. These are important and legitimate driving motivations for wanting to have a prenup in place before marriage.

For these individuals, and all other types of prenuptial agreement clients, the ADR clause can go a long way to providing comfort to people entering into marriage so that when their marriage ends (because it *will* end one way or another), there will be a relatively peaceful resolution.

Conclusion

Marriage is generous, helpful, affirming, and kind. Married couples share with each other and support each other's aspirations. Negotiating a prenup is often an incongruous way to begin their commitment to a life together. Prenup negotiations at the inception of marriage, for most people (especially in first marriages of relatively young people), are felt as a jarring disconnect from mutual feelings of love and their goals and values for their upcoming marriage.

When a prenuptial agreement is necessary, crafting it judiciously, sensitively, and thoughtfully through a client-centered process will foster continued peace and goodwill within the marriage. This is achievable only when the proposed solutions are perceived to be fair and equitable by both parties (and are so in reality), and when the process itself has been peaceful and collaborative. For this reason, mediation is often the most suitable approach to initiate discussions and facilitate the creation of terms that will establish the financial framework of a successful, resilient, long-term marriage.

Chapter 7
Family Peacemaker as Life Cycle Lawyer

An ounce of prevention is worth a pound of cure.
—Benjamin Franklin

The Role of the Preventive Peacemaker

In the world of family law, lawyers are often seen as problem solvers called in once conflict has erupted—divorce papers filed, custody battles begun, financial disputes entrenched.[1] But what if the lawyer's role could begin long before these disputes arise? What if, instead of merely resolving crises, we helped clients prevent them?

This is the vision of preventive family peacemaking: a practice built not just on advocacy of present (and sometimes past) conflicts, but on foresight, relationship-building, and emotional intelligence with a focus on molding agreements to plan for the future.

Preventive peacemaking invites us to accompany families across the arc of their lives—not just through moments of legal trauma, but throughout a myriad of periodic and ever-present transitions, celebrations, and losses. In doing so, we become trusted guides who understand the ongoing inner and outside conflicts that clients wrestle with and the interpersonal dynamics that shape new and preserved relationships alike. As Heraclius said, "The only thing constant in life is change." And we, as preventive peacemakers, have the opportunity to become soothsayers in the lives of our clients.

By committing to long-term, holistic service, we become able to see beyond the moment. Each case we handle is more than a snapshot in a family's life—it is instead a "file that never closes."[2] Family peacemakers become not only

1. Business and estate planning lawyers practice essentially in the preventive mode. A major goal of the authors is to translate this forward look approach to family law.

2. This concept is attributed to Professor Louis M. Brown, the recognized "Father of Preventive Law." See just a snapshot of his preventive contributions at https://en.wikipedia.org/wiki/Louis_M._Brown; Wolfgang Saxon, *Louis M. Brown, 87, Lawyer Who Emphasized Prevention*, N.Y. Times (Dec. 7, 1996).

legal professionals but also emotional allies, cultural translators, and strategic coaches, and they join other peacemaking professionals such as financial planners, estate lawyers, and the clergy in helping people plan for their futures, not just heal from past or current wounds. This chapter explores how lawyers can fulfill this role with practical guidance for supporting clients through the many stages of life: when children grow, when they reach adulthood, during remarriage, retirement, and ultimately, during end-of-life transitions.

Inner Conflicts and Interpersonal Conflicts of Clients

Preventive peacemaking begins with understanding the dual landscapes of conflict: the inner world of the client and the external web of relationships in which they are embedded. These two dimensions—internal and interpersonal—are often deeply intertwined, and family lawyers working as peacemakers must be attuned to both.

Inner conflicts include a client's unresolved emotions, identity shifts, grief, guilt, fear, and ambivalence. These psychological dynamics often shape how a client perceives events, interprets the actions of others, and makes decisions. A client may outwardly describe a dispute as legal, but beneath the surface lies a tangle of personal wounds, unmet needs, or conflicting values. When left unacknowledged, these internal tensions can sabotage negotiations, fuel reactivity, or derail a collaborative process.[3]

Equally critical are the interpersonal conflicts—those that unfold between spouses, parents and children, extended family members, or even with professionals who have been engaged to help. These conflicts are often rooted in years of accumulated misunderstanding, power imbalances, loyalty binds, or communication breakdowns. Lawyers focused solely on legal outcomes may attempt to contain these disputes, but peacemaking lawyers work to transform them by addressing the human story beneath the legal case.

True prevention happens when we see that legal conflict is often only the visible tip of a much larger emotional and relational iceberg. Peacemaking lawyers do not need to be therapists, but they must possess enough emotional intelligence and insight to recognize when emotional undercurrents are influencing legal choices. They must know how to slow down, ask better questions, and hold space for their clients' deeper fears and hopes.[4]

---

3. *See* Binder, Bergman, Wemblay & Weinstein, Lawyers as Counselors: A Client Centered Approach (4th ed., 2019 West).

4. Actually, gaining mental health training and practicing in an interdisciplinary team approach with therapists as equal teammates may be part of your future. *See* Forrest S. Mosten & Lara Traum, *Interdisciplinary Teamwork in Family Law Practice*, 56(3) Fam. Ct. Rev. 437–60 (July 2018).

Preventive family peacemaking begins, then, not in the courtroom or at the negotiation table, but in the lawyer's ability to see the full and future evolving person in front of them—one who is not just managing a dispute but placing that dispute in the context of their present and future. When lawyers learn to listen for both inner and outer sources of conflict, they begin to offer something rare and essential: legal guidance that honors the complexity of human lives.

Inner Conflicts: The Legal Symptom and the Emotional Root

Most family legal disputes arise not simply from disagreement between family members, but from internal dissonance. Clients may be torn between guilt and anger, fear and desire, or duty and resentment. A mother struggling to leave a marriage may also fear harming her children. A father reluctant to pay support may also worry about losing a meaningful role in his child's life.[5]

Lawyers trained only in legal reasoning may misread or under-read these conflicts. But peacemaking lawyers recognize that legal issues are often symptoms of deeper questions: Who am I in this family? What am I worth? What do I fear losing? Effective family peacemakers must therefore become skilled in active listening, empathy, and reflective questioning—helping clients name and navigate the internal tensions that fuel their external disputes. Rather than treating a client's legal issue as an isolated event, the peacemaking lawyer views it as a chapter in the client's larger life story. Many legal problems are actually symptoms—surface expressions of deeper struggles. Clients may seek out legal help believing they need someone to fix a dispute; often, what they really need is guidance through a personal transformation.

Interpersonal Conflicts: The Family System in Flux

At the same time, clients do not exist in isolation. They are embedded in family systems, shaped by complex roles, expectations, and histories. A legal decision about custody is never just about logistics—it is about legacy, identity, and emotion. Understanding these systems helps lawyers anticipate conflicts and design interventions that respect the client's psychological and relational context.

Preventive insight means knowing that a change in one relationship often ripples through others. A new romantic partner may trigger an ex-spouse's insecurity, which then affects co-parenting or invites a conversation about prenuptial agreements that account for blended family dynamics. A teen reaching adulthood may spark new boundary struggles, disagreements about the

5. See the work of Richard Wollman, Internal Family Systems. Harvard professor and peacemaking practitioner incorporates Internal Family Systems in his practice and training.

purchase of a first car, or concern about international college applications. Lawyers who spot these patterns early can help clients address them proactively—reducing friction and creating room for attempts at peace.

The Life Cycle Lawyer: Being a Family's Lawyer for Life

In traditional legal practice, client relationships are often episodic and transactional. A family comes in for a divorce or a custody modification, and once resolved, we close the file.[6] But in a preventive peacemaking model, lawyers cultivate long-term, evolving relationships with families, serving as ongoing guides through life's many transitions. As Franklin D. Roosevelt knew, "each age has its own special fears, its own special hopes."

Just as a family doctor becomes intimately familiar and plans for a patient's wellness with the health patterns of a patient over time (even over the course of providing healthcare for multiple generations within the same family), a family lawyer can build an equally rich understanding of a client's values, relationships, and history to plan for the future. This knowledge allows for legal advice that is not only accurate but also deeply personalized and wisely anticipatory. Clients benefit from continuity. They don't need to explain the same painful history to a new professional every time a life event arises. And lawyers, in turn, become better advisors—able to spot patterns, offer early interventions, and provide reassurance rooted in history and empathy. In essence, we can help our clients create a record that can be consulted by us and other future professionals throughout our client's life.

The family peacemaker for life becomes a kind of legal and logistical steward—not just intervening when things go wrong but also helping clients think about the long-term implications of their choices. This includes encouraging clients to return for annual asymptomatic legal check-ups, much like annual health exams, to review parenting plans, financial arrangements, deeds and title documents, estate documents, and other important agreements. Another mantra of Professor Louis M. Brown was: "A Client should never leave the lawyer's office without a conversation about when and how the lawyer and client will next be in contact with each other."

---

6. Many lawyers limit future planning and client involvement out of fear of extending statutes of limitations, which limit malpractice exposure. We espouse both: Be vigilant about protection against malpractice and discipline while helping the clients to protect themselves against future conflict and legal liability.

The File Never Closes: Long-Term Client–Lawyer Relationships

The notion that "the file never closes" marks a philosophical shift in family law practice. It reflects the reality that families do not end after court rulings or signed agreements. They evolve and change. They grow. They encounter new challenges. The needs may be continuous, or periodic. As Zora Neale Hurston said, "there are years that ask questions and years that answer."

Relationships are a two-way street, and committed preventive peacemakers do not hesitate to reach out. You can maintain meaningful, long-term relationships with former clients through intentional and thoughtful outreach that extends beyond case closure. This kind of contact not only fosters trust and goodwill but also reinforces the lawyer's role as a steady presence in the life of the family. Simple gestures like sending a birthday card to a client's child, congratulating them on a graduation or milestone, or acknowledging a former spouse's remarriage can be surprisingly powerful. You might also send periodic reminders about reviewing child or spousal support agreements, especially around predictable transition points like when a child turns 18 or graduates from high school. These small acts demonstrate empathy, attentiveness, and continuity.[7]

Annual check-ins can be framed as part of a "family legal health checkup"—similar to a financial or medical review—offering the client an opportunity to revisit estate planning documents, custody arrangements, or beneficiary designations in light of life changes. You can also send curated updates about new laws or court decisions that may impact the client's family circumstances, with a brief note offering to discuss if relevant. For example: "Recent changes in retirement account division rules may affect your divorce settlement—let me know if you'd like to schedule a review." These communications, while professional, are also deeply human. They say, in essence: *"I remember your story. I still care. You are not alone."*

Over time, this practice builds a foundation of trust that can last a lifetime, creating a role for the peacemaker not just as an occasional advocate or conflict resolver, but as a quiet guardian of family peace.

Clients themselves often initiate contact and lean into the relationships during moments of vulnerability: a child going to college, a remarriage, a retirement, or a death in the family. These moments are often emotionally loaded,

7. In bygone eras, such communication generated by a lawyer to a client may have been seen as solicitation of future fee paying work. Just like the quill pen, these attitudes have long been replaced by preventive practice building strategies, often taught and sponsored by the organized bar.

yet legally important. If you are already part of the family's trusted circle, these transitions can be handled with greater care and foresight—and the clients already have your number on speed dial.

Some Life Cycles to Consider

Every family is unique, and the family lawyer should always be prepared to table presumptions and get to know the given family's unique intergenerational players, cultural backdrops, and financial systems. That being said, certain common tropes do recur, and you can anticipate common benchmarks that might warrant preventive intervention and anticipatory peacemaking.

As Children Grow

Children do not remain static, and neither should the legal agreements that structure their lives. From toddlerhood to adolescence, their needs, capacities, and preferences change dramatically. All family lawyers know that a parenting schedule that works for a four-year-old may cause frustration or emotional disruption for a ten-year-old who is developing social independence, school obligations, and a growing voice of their own. Preventive family peacemakers play a crucial role not just in resolving conflicts when they arise but also in helping parents *anticipate and provide for* the changes that growth brings. This proactive legal approach supports stability, reduces the likelihood of future disputes, and keeps the child's well-being at the center of family decision-making.

Let's consider developmentally appropriate planning as a future conflict prevention strategy. Rather than treating parenting plans as immutable contracts, preventively you can guide clients toward creating living, breathing frameworks—ones that adjust with the natural evolution of childhood and adolescence. This begins with an understanding of developmental stages and the kinds of challenges each may bring. For example, you can help parents structure parenting time schedules that are more spacious and predictable for school-age children, while remaining flexible enough to accommodate growing extracurricular commitments, academic workloads, or emerging peer relationships. As children mature, you can support the inclusion of mechanisms that give children age-appropriate ways to express their preferences. For younger children, this might involve scheduled family meetings where parents listen to the child's experience of the schedule. For older teens, it could mean periodic reviews where children's voices are directly consulted (without placing them in the middle of parental conflict). You can also recommend co-parenting strategies that prepare both households for transitions, such as developing consistent routines between homes or offering tools (like shared calendars or transition rituals) to ease handoffs.

In all these ways, peacemaking lawyers act as translators between developmental research and practical parenting. They help clients avoid rigid structures that may become unworkable over time, while encouraging flexibility, communication, and foresight. The result is not only more peaceful co-parenting but also a greater sense of security and agency for the child, who learns that their evolving needs are seen and respected. As Frederick Douglass said, "It is easier to build strong children than to repair broken men."

Of course, there are times when flexibility is in fact the variable that invites conflict, where structure provides boundaries to manage expectations for parents and children alike. As a peacemaking lawyer, you always retain the ability to examine: What does *this* family need? What are the interpersonal pitfalls for *this* family? What might help prevent conflict in the future for *this* family?

As a preventive peacemaker you can serve as informal co-parenting coaches. You can do this as a client's "lawyer of record," neutral mediator, or even as minor's counsel appointed by the court. You might consider seeking additional training as a parenting coordinator and co-parenting specialist to bolster the preventing peacemaking services that you can provide to the families that you serve. By helping parents maintain respectful, child-centered communication—especially around discipline, school involvement, and routines—peacemaking lawyers support emotional stability for children while reducing legal friction.

When Children Reach Majority

"Children begin by loving their parents; as they grow older they judge them; sometimes they forgive them" (Oscar Wilde). Turning 18—or 19, or 21 depending on the jurisdiction—is not only a statutory milestone but also a profound psychological turning point for both children and parents. For some families, this transition can feel anticlimactic; for others, it is jarring. The parent who has long made medical decisions or managed school records may suddenly find themselves legally excluded from matters they once oversaw with daily involvement. Meanwhile, the newly minted adult may feel unprepared to shoulder full autonomy, especially if they are still financially or emotionally dependent on their parents.

This is a critical moment for a preventive family peacemaker to step in—not because conflict has emerged, but to *prevent* confusion and missteps that could lead to emotional rupture or legal complication down the road. By providing education, clear documentation, and space for intentional conversation, you can support families through this tender, sometimes disorienting shift.

The legal implications of a child reaching majority are often misunderstood. You can help clarify these boundaries in a way that is accessible and reassuring. This might involve reviewing the formal end of child support obligations, particularly where state laws or prior agreements define different cutoff points for support based on age, education status, or disability. This might involve explaining how a child's new legal status affects parental access to information. [Laws like the Family Educational Rights and Privacy Act (FERPA) and Health Insurance Portability and Accountability Act (HIPAA) grant adult children control over their educational and medical records.] Many parents are surprised to learn they can no longer call a college registrar or a doctor's office for updates without the student's express permission. You can assist families in preparing advanced healthcare directives, durable powers of attorney, and HIPAA waivers—particularly important if the child has special needs, a chronic illness, or will be living far from home.

These documents don't just protect against emergencies; they offer a reassuring structure in which the young adult's autonomy is respected while keeping trusted family members in the loop when needed.

Legal adulthood also marks an emotional transition that can be challenging to navigate. This is a time when lifelong family roles are quietly renegotiated. The parent is no longer a legal guardian but still a deeply involved and loving presence. The child is now an adult under the law, but rarely feels fully equipped for independence. You can help families reframe this moment, not as an abrupt severing of ties, but as a shift in posture: from authority to advisor, from manager to mentor.

Sometimes, the best legal service is a facilitated conversation. You can help create space for families to talk about new boundaries and expectations—financial, emotional, and practical. Who will pay for health insurance, and for how long? How will decisions be made if the adult child becomes ill? What does independence mean in this household? Framing these questions with clarity and compassion allows families to move forward with mutual understanding, reducing the risk of later conflict or resentment.

In these ways, the preventive family lawyer remains a steady guide—offering insight, language, and structure to moments that otherwise feel ambiguous. By recognizing that legal transitions are deeply human transitions, the lawyer becomes not just a protector of rights, but a partner in growth.

Remarriage

Remarriage can be a hopeful new chapter for one or both parties in their post-divorce lives, but it is also one of the most legally and emotionally intricate transitions in family life. It involves not just the merging of two individuals, but often two extended families, different parenting styles, financial obligations from previous relationships, differently entangled estate plans, and unresolved emotional dynamics. For those who've gone through divorce or widowhood, remarriage can surface complex feelings: vulnerability, guilt, protectiveness over children, or fear of repeating past mistakes. In these moments, you can play an essential role—not simply drafting documents but helping families anticipate challenges and develop the foundation for healthy integration.

Whether the remarriage involves young children, adult children, or no children at all, there are critical questions to be addressed: What responsibilities will stepparents have? How will financial assets be protected or shared? How can this new union avoid legal or emotional landmines that weren't visible the first time around? Do merging families need to re-evaluate life insurance beneficiary designations, talk about relocations and merged household logistics, or hold multiparty blended family co-parenting meetings? Yes, and more.

Legally, remarriage can be complex. You can help clients think through the details before problems arise, guiding them through tools that balance individual protection with collective fairness. One such tool, as extensively discussed in its own designated chapter in this book, is the prenuptial agreement, which serves not as a cynical hedge against failure, but as a respectful negotiation of rights, responsibilities, and boundaries. In the context of remarriage, a prenup might address obligations to children from a previous marriage, spousal support, inheritance expectations, and how future joint assets will be handled.

If children are involved—especially when both spouses bring children from prior relationships into their new one—parenting plans may need to be updated to account for new stepparent roles and a true blended family. Will the stepparent be involved in school decisions or medical care? Will they attend co-parenting meetings? What boundaries are important to protect relationships with the biological parent? Are birthday celebrations now a 100-person affair with a hired chamber ensemble and full circus in attendance? How are those expenses shared? Addressing these questions with legal specificity can prevent misunderstandings and protect everyone involved.

Estate planning also becomes more delicate. Many individuals entering a second or third marriage want to ensure that their children from a previous relationship are not unintentionally disinherited. A preventive peacemaking lawyer can help structure wills, trusts, and beneficiary designations to honor both the new marriage and prior family obligations, avoiding legal disputes and emotional hurt down the road.

How wonderful, right? Well . . . peacemakers know that even the most perfectly drafted legal agreements cannot fully account for the emotional weight that often accompanies remarriage. Children may feel torn between loyalty to a biological parent and openness to a stepparent. Former spouses may become jealous or fearful that a new partner will alter existing custody dynamics or financial agreements. Even the couple themselves may wrestle with old patterns, unspoken fears, or unacknowledged grief from previous relationships.

Preventive family peacemakers become guides through this emotional terrain—not as therapists, but as wise counselors who bring these issues to light in ways that foster empathy and preparation. In some cases, you may encourage parties to consult with family therapists, parenting coaches, or stepfamily educators to help everyone involved enter the remarriage with open eyes and compassionate expectations.

By holding space for both legal clarity and emotional honesty, you can help transform what could be a volatile moment into one of grounded optimism. You can help clients affirm their new commitments while honoring past relationships and future obligations. In doing so, you can protect not only their legal rights—but the fragile, hopeful promise of new beginnings.[8]

Retirement

Retirement marks another major life transition—financially, logistically, emotionally, and in relation to the financial and relationship landscape of a family. After decades of structure, productivity, and identity rooted in work, retirement can bring both relief and disruption to the entire family system. For couples, the shift may mean more time together but also unexpected friction. For co-parents or divorced former spouses, this can mean adjustments to support payments and access to benefits. For adult children, it may signal changes in financial support, caregiving responsibilities, or estate planning. And for blended families, retirement can magnify tensions over inheritance, asset division, or perceived fairness. Just as financial advisors work to ensure economic stability post-retirement, as a preventive peacemaking lawyer, you can further relational and legal stability.

One of the most immediate impacts of retirement is the reduction or reallocation of income. For divorced individuals paying or receiving spousal support from a former spouse, this often raises critical legal questions: Can alimony be modified based on a retiree's new financial situation? Does retirement

8. A personal interlude. Woody met and helped raise Derek from age 9. When Derek was 37, after the death of his bio Dad, both Derek and Woody agreed that the long-term bond and relationship should be transformed to a legal one. They went down to the local courthouse, the judge decreed an adoption, and holding balloons and teddy bears for Derek's children (Woody's grandchildren) they are living the rest of their lives as Dad and Son, not Step-Father and Step-Son. Derek and Woody are not the only ones who find the title "step" to be misleading when love and long-term trust and caring call for a different title for this true family relationship: and Woody is Grandpa to Daniel and Luca without any "Step" to deal with.

count as a material change of circumstances? For some, retirement may bring conflict with a former spouse who relies on support; for others, it may offer an opportunity to renegotiate outdated agreements in a spirit of fairness. You can guide clients through this process early, helping them proactively revisit support obligations as retirement approaches rather than waiting for tensions or nonpayment to spark legal action. For clients still in the workforce but nearing retirement, you can include terms in divorce agreements that anticipate these future changes, adding clarity and preventing emotional escalations later on. Warren Buffett famously opined, "Someone is sitting in the shade today because someone planted a tree a long time ago."

Retirement doesn't just change income—it often shifts the dynamics within a household. For couples, spending more time together may expose unresolved tensions that were previously obscured by work schedules. Preventive peacemakers, especially those who maintain long-term relationships with clients, can serve as trusted advisors during this adjustment period, offering mediation, revisiting co-ownership agreements, or even helping draft postnuptial agreements if needed.

For adult children, a parent's retirement may signal new responsibilities. Will they be expected to provide care as parents age? Will there be a transfer of family business interests? What happens if the retiree moves in with one of their children? You can help families have these conversations in advance, setting out caregiving expectations, cost-sharing agreements, or living arrangements that honor everyone's dignity and protect against resentment.[9]

Retirement is also an ideal time to revisit estate planning. Many people drafted their wills or trusts when their children were young or during an earlier marriage. But families change—remarriage, grandchildren, new step-relatives, estranged siblings—and so should the documents that reflect one's legacy. A comprehensive review of wills, advance directives, powers of attorney, and beneficiary designations is key and can surface important questions: Do you want to leave assets to your stepchildren? Should adult children serve as medical decision-makers? What protections are in place if mental capacity becomes an issue? These are not just legal decisions; they are deeply personal ones.

Retirement can be a time of reconnection, personal growth, and renewed family bonds—but only if the transitions are navigated with foresight. Without planning, this stage of life can become a source of unexpected litigation, family conflict, or emotional distress. Peacemaking is paramount.

---

9. For an in-depth and insightful look at the impact of a divorce on adult children, read *Home Will Never Be the Same Again: A Guide for Adult Children of Gray Divorce* by Carol R. Hughes and Bruce R. Fredenburg.

Death of a Spouse

The death of a spouse is one of life's deepest ruptures. It is both a private, emotional loss and a public, legal event. On paper, it marks the triggering of a will probate or estate administration, the transfer of assets, or the dissolution of a marriage contract by death. In lived experience, it often marks the collapse of an entire world. For families who have maintained long-term relationships with their peacemaking professional—with their "lawyer for life"—this moment can be met with compassionate understanding.

When a peacemaker has been part of the family's story across decades, they may be one of the few professionals in a position to understand not just the legal documents but also the intentions behind them. They remember why a certain trust was structured a certain way, what values the couple prioritized in raising their children, or how they once resolved a conflict over inheritances. This depth of relationship allows the peacemaker to serve not merely as a legal executor, but as a witness to the family's history.

In practical terms, the peacemaking lawyer helps the surviving spouse or family navigate probate or trust administration. This includes interpreting wills, filing the appropriate court documents, ensuring compliance with tax laws, and helping with the distribution of assets. But when you are already known to the family as someone who sat at the kitchen table when the estate plan was first discussed, you can offer far more than technical expertise.

You offer presence.

You can sit quietly with a grieving spouse and say, "You don't have to do this alone." You can make phone calls the family doesn't have the energy to make. You can explain what's coming next in plain language, repeating it as many times as needed. In a time when everything feels unstable, the known and trusted peacemaker becomes a symbol of continuity.

Peacemakers also play a vital role in protecting the relationships that remain. The death of a spouse, especially the second parent, can reignite unresolved tensions among adult siblings. "Why did she leave this to you?" "Who should stay in the house?" "Why weren't we consulted?" In these moments, you may act as a peacemaker and mediator—not just explaining what the documents say but helping interpret what the deceased likely intended. You may convene family meetings to foster understanding. You may reframe accusations as grief in disguise. And you may help family members remember their parents' values—not just through what was written in the estate plan, but through stories and patterns observed over years of representation. In some families, a thoughtful lawyer's involvement during estate settlement can be the difference between a family that stays connected and one that falls apart.

Preventive family peacemaking asks us to look beyond the narrow bounds of an issue-by-issue job and see the fuller arc of human experience. It is a commitment to walking alongside our clients—not just when the storms swirl but also when the waters are calm. It means holding space for both legal clarity and emotional growth.

In a world where conflict often seems inevitable, the preventive family lawyer offers something rare: foresight, steadiness, and hope. When the file never closes, the door never does either. And in that open space, healing, transformation, and peace become not just possible—but enduring.

Practical Tools for Deepening Your Role as a Life-Cycle Lawyer and Preventive Peacemaker

1. Create a Personal Legacy Plan

Just as you encourage clients to prepare for the future, ensure your own legal and emotional affairs are in order. Draft or revisit your:

- Will and healthcare directives
- Letters of instruction to loved ones
- Ethical will: a document sharing your values, lessons, and hopes[10]

Think About: "What would I want my clients or children to learn from how I handled my own life transitions?"

2. Interview a Long-Term Client

Select one or more clients you've worked with for over five to ten years. Conduct a short, reflective conversation:

- What did they value most about your support?
- What did they need that wasn't provided?
- What surprised them about life after divorce, remarriage, or loss?

Think About: "What assumptions do I make about long-term service? What might I do differently in the next ten years?"

10. For more on an ethical will recommended and taught my many caring clergy, see https://www.bing.com/search?q=Ethical+will&form=ANNH01&refig=250cecfbfef34e89874a0ebb5092ee45&pc=DCTS.

3. Host a "Life-Cycle Legal Checkup" Seminar

Offer an annual workshop for former and current clients (and their families)[11] and others either by yourself (even online) or affiliated with a church, senior social agency, or other organization on how legal needs evolve:

- Aging parents, college-bound kids, remarriage, business succession
- Updates in laws affecting child support, retirement, or estate planning
- Invitations to re-engage their lawyer proactively

Think About: Collaborate with financial advisors or mental health professionals for a truly holistic session.

4. Develop a Client Transition Journal

Design a simple workbook or PDF with guided prompts for clients facing major transitions:

- Divorce, remarriage, empty nesting, retirement, or a spouse's death
- Reflection questions like:
  - "What am I most afraid of right now?"
  - "What do I want to protect?"
  - "What legacy do I want to leave?"

5. Create a "Milestone Outreach" Calendar

Build a practice of reconnecting with past clients during personal or legal milestones:

- Children turning 18 (for updates to powers of attorney or college planning)
- Retirement age
- Ten-year anniversaries of divorces or agreements

---

11. Read the story of Angelo DiGangi from Queens, New York, who has been giving these seminars at senior living facilities between lunch and bingo for over 30 years, https://www.hermanyvoices.org/team/angelo-digangi.

Think About: Ways to reach out, such as personal email; short, handwritten note; invitation to a check-in meeting or seminar

6. Write a Letter to a Future Client

Take 20 minutes and write a heartfelt letter to a future client going through divorce, loss, or major change. Share:

- What you wish every client knew
- What transformation you've witnessed in others
- How you will walk beside them, not just through the legal system

Think About: Keep this letter visible in your workspace. Let it ground your approach.

7. Team Reflection on Long-Term Relationships

Gather your legal team or colleagues and discuss:

- Who are the "clients for life" in our practice?
- What systems (or gaps) do we have for staying connected?
- How can we better serve the emotional journey, not just the legal one?

Think About: Follow up by designing one new protocol or communication tool.

8. Ritualize Endings and Transitions

When a legal file closes, especially after divorce or death, consider marking the moment with intentionality:

- Send a closing letter that honors the client's resilience
- Include a brief note with a quote, reflection, or invitation for future contact
- For long-term clients, consider a certificate or note celebrating their "new chapter"

9. Read a Memoir About Family or Aging

Once a year, choose a book that illuminates life's transitions from a personal, human view—memoirs about caregiving, blended families, divorce recovery, or grief.

Think About: "How might I show up differently in a client's life if I held their emotional story alongside their legal file?"

10. Design a Family Timeline Template

Offer clients a "Family Life Timeline" worksheet. It might include:

- Marriage, births, divorces, deaths, major moves
- Financial shifts (inheritance, retirement, job loss)
- Legal milestones (support ending, emancipation, estate planning)

Chapter 8

Family Lawyer as Compassionate Healer

If it is not tempered by compassion and empathy, reason can lead men and women into a moral void.
—Karen Armstrong, *Twelve Steps to a Compassionate Life*[1]

The Calling Beneath the Conflict

There is a moment—sometimes early in a legal career, sometimes years in—when a quiet voice rises inside and asks: *Is this really what I came here to do?*

You may recognize that voice. It arrives after the hundredth affidavit, after another scorched-earth custody fight, after you've won but feel oddly hollow. It shows up when your client is weeping in your office and you realize what they really need isn't a stronger legal strategy but someone who sees them, holds them (figuratively), and helps them begin again.

This chapter is a homecoming for that voice that many of us have but do not think is proper lawyering.

We are not here to shame the work we've done or disown the fierce advocacy that has brought some of us this far. But we are here to deepen it. To expand the vision. To remember that beneath every legal question, there is a human need for the client to be heard, to be safe, to be restored.

To be a family lawyer is, at its core, to be present at the threshold of people's most tender transitions: divorce, parenting disputes, the painful redistribution of a life once shared. The law gives us tools. But compassion gives us the courage to use those tools with grace and make a difference in the lives of our clients. We are not only litigators. Not only drafters of agreements. We are, at our best, witnesses. Translators. Steady voices. Holders of story and sorrow. And yes—healers of client pain and emotional hurt.

1. Karen Armstrong, Twelve Steps to a Compassionate Life 95 (2009). Collected in Armstrong's reflections on the urgent need to bring *heart* into our thinking, this quote reminds us that legal reasoning—even when precise—demands the tempering force of compassion (karma + empathy).

Compassion is not the soft stuff. It is the strong stuff, the sustaining stuff. It is not what you add once the real work is done. It *is* the real work.[2]

The Presence of Presence

There is a kind of listening that changes a room. Not the listening that waits to respond, but the listening that leans in as if the speaker's words are water, and you are parched.

That is the presence of presence.

It doesn't take more time. But it does take more of *you*. More stillness. More courage to let the silence stretch. More willingness to be affected by what you hear. In this kind of presence, clients begin to unfold. Not because you have asked better questions, but because they feel that you are there—not performing concern, but truly with them. In this presence, attorney meetings become something else. Ritual. Encounter. A place where someone begins, maybe for the first time, to believe that their story matters to you and to the next step in their uncomfortable legal journey.

We cannot do this if we are scattered, depleted, or guarded. Compassionate presence begins with resourcing ourselves—not as an act of self-indulgence, but as professional necessity. A lawyer running on fumes cannot hold space for a client's grief. A lawyer too defended cannot recognize their client's unspoken fear. So, we return to ourselves again and again. Through breath, through breaks, through ritual and reflection—we find our still point. From that place, we offer presence like a quiet fire: steady, warming, unflinching. Our internal peace creates space for compassion, and compassion is integral to family healing. Yes, this is real lawyering!

Listening for What Is Not Said

Clients often arrive with their narratives sharpened by pain, distorted by fear, and scripted by what they think they're supposed to say. Their words often wear the armor of legal jargon—protective, impersonal, tightly controlled—because that, they believe, is the language we require. That is the language that will make them credible. Believable. Worthy of defending.

---

2. Neuroscience research has shown that compassion training consistently activates brain regions like the insula and dorsal anterior cingulate cortex—areas linked with empathy, emotional regulation, and higher-order decision-making. Olivia D. Feldman et al., *Neural Correlates of Compassion Training*, 14 Neuropsychol. Rev. 193, 200 (2021).

They come prepared to talk about parenting time and jurisdiction, retirement accounts and real property valuations. But rarely does that language tell the whole truth.

Because beneath the custody dispute, there is often a cry for connection:

Will I still matter to my child when everything changes? Will my family respect me if I compromise with her? Will they still need me?

Beneath the struggle over who gets which assets, there is a wound of betrayal:

How did we end up here, strangers dividing up a life we once built together?

And beneath the silence—perhaps the most painful of all—there could be the heavy presence of shame:

What did I do wrong? Am I the reason it all fell apart?

As compassionate healers, our task as lawyers is not merely to extract the facts but to attune to the full texture of the person sitting before us.[3] We listen not just for the content of the story but for the *pulse beneath the words*—the tremble in the voice when they mention their daughter's name, the catch in their breath when recalling the last holiday before separation, the way their eyes dart away when they speak of their former partner, and the sigh that escapes when they think no one is paying attention. These moments—these micro-revelations—are not distractions from the legal process: *They are the heart of it.*

To listen in this way is to practice a kind of sacred reading. We begin to regard our clients not as case files, not as walking problems to be solved, but as sacred texts—complex, beautiful, torn, and deserving of careful interpretation. We listen as if their words are liturgy, their pauses scripture, their contradictions a kind of poetry still being revised. We lean in not just to gather facts, but to understand *meaning*. And in doing so, we honor our clients' full humanity, make a difference in their lives, and do a better job of helping them.

And then something begins to shift.

When we respond—not with legalese or rehearsed empathy, but with our genuine presence—our clients sense it. Maybe for the first time in months, or even years, they feel seen without being judged. Helped without being fixed.

3. "Compassion arises from recognizing the suffering of others and motivates us to act to relieve that suffering—an essential foundation for moral communities." *See* Jonathan Haidt, The Righteous Mind: Why Good People Are Divided by Politics and Religion 65 (2012).

The lawyer becomes not a distant expert in a suit, but a steady human presence who is unafraid to sit beside them as a true friend in the uncertainty. A witness who doesn't flinch. A guide who doesn't rush.

And the clients? Clients are no longer simply problems to be managed. They are not just parties to a dissolution. They are human beings in the midst of becoming.

They might begin, slowly, to drop the armor. They may start speaking in their own voice again, not the voice shaped by legal fears or social expectations, but the voice of someone who dares to tell the truth to someone who will not judge them. Much like opening up in a confession booth with a priest—only no religious affiliation is needed or expected.

And it is from this place—not the rehearsed performance of a victim or aggressor, but the raw, human center—that real healing, real resolution, real forward motion can begin. Clients do not expect this healing: but will feel it and it will help them get your help!

This is what it means to be a compassionate helper in the legal profession—not just to parse statute and precedent, but to hear the sacred beneath the spoken. To meet people where they are—scared, angry, guarded—and to offer not pity, but presence. Not perfection, but deep regard.

Because needed transformation doesn't begin with solutions. It begins with being seen.

Compassionate Advocacy: Power with, Not Power Over

Compassion does not mean pandering or giving in. It does not mean being meek or retreating from difficult conversations. It means advocating *with* someone, rather than *over* someone. It is power exercised in the service of healing—not dominance. It is clarity without cruelty, firmness without control or hurt. A compassionate family peacemaker knows how to speak directly but not harshly. To say no without shutting a door. To assert a boundary without humiliating the client or the other side.

You have likely seen the lawyer who walks into court with calm authority, who doesn't raise her voice because she does not need to. Who commands attention not through intimidation, but through her presence.

That is compassionate power. It is the power that leads to resolution, not escalation—that refuses to dehumanize even when the stakes are high and the behavior of others is unacceptable. It is power that knows—truly knows—that the children, the parents, and all members of the families involved will live with these outcomes and with the way we approach them for years to come.

So, we speak with care. We write with intention. We reality test positions, and potentially even challenge injustice, without becoming cruel. And we remember: Our job is not to "crush the other side," but to advocate for peace with justice not just for our client, but for everyone in the family.

Rituals of Reconnection: Returning to Your Why

In the rapid machinery of legal work, it is easy to lose sight of why we began. But compassionate helping cannot be sustained on theory. It must be rooted, daily, in practice. Rituals of reconnection are how we return to the center. They tether us to meaning. They make room for mystery and mercy in an otherwise transactional world.

Some of us begin our day with a silent breath before opening the case file. Some write a single sentence of gratitude before leaving the office. Some pause to touch the photo of their children, remembering that every child in every case matters just as much.

These are not luxuries. They are the rituals of professional integrity. They remind us that we are not just technicians—we are human beings bearing witness to some of life's most tender moments.

From that place, we help differently, and we believe: more competently and effectively.

The Quiet Revolutionary Act of Language

Our profession is built on language. Words are our instruments, our shields, our currency. Yet so often, we wield them unconsciously—out of habit, out of tradition, out of the inertia of a system that has long favored confrontation over connection.

We talk of battles and strategies, of "waging" and "winning," as if we are preparing for a war rather than navigating the fragile terrain of human relationships. We speak of "taking the other party to court," of "fighting for custody," of "losing the house," as though families are empires to be conquered.

But what if we started to choose different words?

What if, instead of "taking the other party to court," we said we were "having a neutral experience judge make the decision that we cannot seem to make ourselves"? Instead of "visitation," we spoke of "parenting presence"—an affirmation that love does not vanish with time or distance. Instead of "custody battle," we called it "family reorganization"—a recognition that while the structure is shifting, the family remains, and the relationships within it are still sacred, still worth tending. Instead of "win," we asked, "What brings wholeness?" Instead of "loss," we asked, "What can be preserved while some things change?"

These aren't euphemisms. They are invitations to a new, a compassionate way of lawyering.

Invitations to see our work not as combat but as care. To reimagine the lawyer not as a warrior in a suit, but as a translator, a bridge-builder, a quiet force of steadiness and truth. Language is not cosmetic. It is generative. It doesn't just reflect reality—it creates it. The words we use shape how our clients feel in our presence. They shape how they see themselves—and how we view our professional role. They regulate nervous systems, change the temperature of a room, open or close the door to healing.

A client once said, "When you said, 'family restructuring' instead of 'custody dispute,' my whole body softened. I could finally breathe."

That is not semantics. That is somatic. That is sacred. Because when the energy in the room changes, everything else begins to shift. Options expand. Defensiveness melts. Negotiation becomes more than a transaction—it becomes a form of restoration based on honest sharing and mutual commitment to solve a pressing problem.

To speak differently is not to dilute the legal process. It is to dignify it. To remind ourselves and our clients that words can do more than build arguments. They can build bridges.

And so, we speak with care. We choose our words as if they matter—because they do. We remember that every phrase carries a charge, and that we can choose language that disarms rather than inflames, includes rather than alienates, calms rather than escalates.

This is the work of the compassionate peacemaker:

To speak in ways that heal.

To name what hurts, but also to name what is possible—as well as what is remotely or not possible.

To change the words and, in doing so, begin to change the world of our clients and their families.

Helping as Holding, Not Fixing

Compassionate helping does not require us to have all the answers. "I don't know; I will need to research that question" is not only honest and transparent, but it builds client trust. In truth, it helps us to release that very burden.

We are trained, almost reflexively, to fix. To respond. To solve. To construct airtight arguments, airtight plans. But in the landscape of suffering, that kind of certainty can feel hollow, even violent. When someone is grieving the collapse of their family, or navigating the shame of a mistake, the last thing they often need is a ten-point plan for efficiency. Such a plan may be misleading and creates a false client dependence.

Sometimes, even good news requires quiet presence. A client may come to you after receiving a surprising message from the other party—an offer to reimburse a parenting expense, to split costs more fairly going forward, or even just a kind acknowledgment of shared effort. No judge ordered it. No one demanded it. And still, it happened. Your client is caught off guard—not joyful exactly, but disoriented by the sudden absence of hostility. She's holding her breath, afraid to trust it. You could leap in to analyze, to define next steps, to draft a response that locks it all in. But instead, you pause with her. "It's okay to just take that in," you say. "It doesn't have to mean everything is fixed. But it means something. Let's stay with that for a moment."

Sometimes, our greatest gift is compassionate presence without an answer.

Our job is not to repair our clients like broken machines. It is to walk beside them like fellow travelers. To offer steadiness, not half-baked solutions. And to trust that, often, the simple act of *being with* is far more healing than the swiftest fix.

We heal by just holding space—an overused phrase perhaps, but one that still holds power when understood properly. Holding space means letting silence have dignity. It means not interrupting someone's pain with our discomfort to provide a rescue. It means resisting the urge to push toward answers when the questions themselves are still sacred and vitally important not just to our client, but to the family.

We demonstrate compassion by sitting with our clients' confusion, without rushing to clarity. We heal by allowing their sorrow to unfold at its own pace. We help by acknowledging that legal pain is still human pain, and that some wounds do not want to be bandaged—they want to be witnessed even if they cannot be fixed and are permanent.

This kind of healing, and helping, is profoundly counterintuitive in the legal world. It is not performative. It is not flashy. It will not be rewarded with courtroom applause or LinkedIn accolades. It will not win awards. But it might change people and have us do our lawyering job in a different way.

When a client says, "I felt calmer after our meeting,"—you have helped.

When he says or suggests, "I feel less afraid,"—you have helped.

When they begin to soften their tone when speaking about their co-parent, or pause to consider what their child is feeling before making a demand—you have helped.

When they weep in your office—not because they are falling apart, but because for the first time in weeks, they feel safe enough to feel—you have helped.[4]

This is slow work. Quiet work. Important work.

Compassion requires patience. It requires humility. It requires the kind of courage that is not born from knowing everything, but from being willing to stay present when nothing can be fixed.

You are not here to rescue. You are not here to impress. You are not here to offer answers before the questions are even fully formed.

You are here to accompany. To companion. To bear witness. To remind another human being, by your steady presence: *You are not alone.* To hold space—not as a passive act, but as a radical act of solidarity. And in doing so, you remind yourself: You are enough, even when all you do is listen.

The Neuroscience of Compassion: The Brain's Pathway to Connection

Compassion is not only a moral choice or a learned skill—it is a biological imperative, encoded in the very architecture of our brains. Emerging research in neuroscience reveals that compassion lights up neural pathways that calm our stress responses and deepen our capacity for connection.

Dr. Richard J. Davidson, a pioneer in the neuroscience of emotion, demonstrates that compassionate meditation activates the insula and the anterior cingulate cortex—areas linked to empathy and emotional regulation.[5] These brain regions help us slow down, notice the suffering of another without becoming overwhelmed, and respond with kindness rather than judgment or withdrawal.

Understanding how this science impacts our work can be profoundly empowering for family lawyers. It shows us that compassion is not a finite resource that must be rationed or sacrificed under pressure. Rather, it is a muscle that grows stronger with practice, rewiring our brains to be more resilient, patient, and present.

Moreover, neuroscience confirms what many of us know intuitively: that compassion lowers cortisol—the body's stress hormone—and enhances

4. A longitudinal study found that clients who experienced collaborative or compassion-centered legal processes reported higher satisfaction and lower conflict five years post-resolution. Marc S. Miller et al., *Client Outcomes in Collaborative vs. Adversarial Family Law*, Fam. Court Rev. 58, 215 (2020).

5. Richard J. Davidson et al., *Alterations in Brain and Immune Function Produced by Mindfulness Meditation*, 65(4) Psychosomatic Med. 564–70 (2003).

oxytocin, the "bonding hormone."[6] This biological shift is not just good for our clients, but for us as well. It explains why compassionate presence can lead to calmer meetings, better communication, and more sustainable solutions. How often do family lawyers complain about how our clients drive us crazy. Perhaps a bit of compassion can alter that dynamic?

When we enter a family dispute with this embodied compassion, we create a contagion of calm. The lawyer's regulated nervous system serves as an anchor in turbulent emotional seas. This is not soft idealism—it is hard science, offering a road map for transforming conflict through presence.

In this light, compassion is a practice of neuroscience-informed lawyering; one where awareness, intention, and biology converge to open pathways toward healing and justice.

Reflective Practice and Compassion: The Mirror of the Heart

In the quiet moments between meetings, hearings, and calls, there lies a practice both humble and profound: reflection. Not simply a glance backward at what transpired, but a deep, intentional looking inward—a conversation with the self that reveals our hearts beneath our professional role as lawyer.

Reflective practice is the mirror where compassion is both born and refined. When we pause to consider our own feelings, biases, and reactions, we cultivate a space to respond rather than react. Clients often arrive carrying narratives sharpened by pain and fear, but these narratives echo within us too. Without reflection, we risk carrying their burdens blindly or, worse, hardening ourselves against them. Reflective practice invites us to notice this internal landscape: the moments when frustration flickers, when impatience arises, or when judgment of client behavior or beliefs color our perceptions. By naming these feelings, we reclaim agency, choosing to respond with empathy rather than resistance.

This is not a solitary act. Reflection flourishes when shared—with mentors, colleagues, or through supervision that embraces vulnerability as strength. It is through these shared spaces that we recognize the universality of struggle and the transformative power of compassion. They remind us that to hold another's pain, we must first hold our own without judgment: actually with kindness.

Moreover, reflective practice guards against the erosion of compassion that can come with relentless legal work. It surfaces the subtle signs of fatigue

---

6. Paul J. Zak, *The Neurobiology of Trust*, Scientific Am. (Jan. 2008).

before they become overwhelming. It whispers: "Who are you beneath the role? What do you need to replenish your spirit?"

To engage in this work is to honor the ancient wisdom that healing begins within. As Parker Palmer writes, "Before I tell my life what I intend to do with it, I need to listen to my life telling me who I am."[7] In this listening, we discover the roots of compassionate practice—not as technique, but as truth in the lawyer–client relationship.

In practice, reflection can take many forms. Journaling after a difficult client meeting allows the residue of emotion to surface and settle. Brief mindfulness pauses between cases reset the nervous system and open the heart. Peer reflection groups become sanctuaries where stories are held without judgment, and fresh insight emerges.

When we integrate reflective practice, compassion becomes less an aspiration and more a living presence. It is the wellspring from which patience, creativity, and resilience flow—qualities essential for navigating the complex, tender terrain of family law.

So, as you embrace the role of compassionate healer, remember to turn inward as often as you turn outward. Your presence is a gift—both to yourself and to those you serve. Let reflection be the heartbeat of that presence, steady and sure, guiding you always back to the truth that compassion begins at home: within your own heart.

Training the Heart: The Ongoing Inner Work

To practice law and further peace compassionately is to practice differently. It is not a performance, a mask to don in the courtroom or the conference room. It cannot be faked or outsourced. It must be lived from the inside out, woven into the very fabric of who we are—our thoughts, our breath, our intentions.

This requires inner work. Not once, but constantly. A lifelong cultivation.

Many peacemaking family lawyers find this work through mindfulness practices—not as fleeting trends or corporate buzzwords, but as a discipline of stillness. Practices that invite us to pause and truly *hear* ourselves before reacting. To slow the hurried pulse of a nervous system perpetually primed for battle. To create space between stimulus and response, so that reactivity no longer drives our decisions.

Others seek therapy or professional supervision, for both the solace of support and the accountability of growth. A committed witness to our shadow

---

7. Parker J. Palmer, Let Your Life Speak: Listening for the Voice of Vocation 3 (1999).

sides, our blind spots, and our continual evolution keeps us honest and authentic. Therapists, often helping the same people, customarily (and through state regulation) contract and pay for supervision as a method of professional competence. As lawyers, we can learn from our mental health colleagues!

Some peacemaking family lawyers begin their days with poetry—verses that open the heart rather than sharpen the argument. They let the cadence of language remind them of beauty and complexity, of sorrow and joy entwined. Others take solitary walks in the woods after a tense mediation, breathing deeply the cool air, grounding themselves in the rhythms of nature rather than the chaos of conflict. Some write morning pages—not as a productivity hack, but as an offering of clarity to the soul, a quiet reckoning with their own inner landscape before stepping into the charged world of legal work. You might pick up a copy of Nan Waller Burnett's *Calm in the Face of the Storm.*[8] Three hundred and sixty-two entries: one for every day of the year. Each with a value, followed by a poem, a meditative insight, and application to our client work.

There is no single path, no one-size-fits-all formula. But there is one enduring truth: You must train your heart as diligently as you train your intellect. Your client will not only feel the precision of your legal mind, they will *feel* the presence of your heart. And that presence—the kind that calms, steadies, and holds—is shaped by the work you have done daily, by yourself, in silence. The hours spent far from the mediation zoom or courtroom, when no one is watching, when only your own honesty and courage bear witness.

As a wise voice of spiritual compassion reminds us: You cannot be kind to others if you have not first been kind to yourself. The heart is a muscle. It grows stronger with use. It softens with care. It becomes a compass that guides us when the legal landscape feels cold and fractured. It must be cultivated—nurtured like a sacred garden—through rituals, disciplines, and daily commitments that honor the tender, vulnerable place within.

It is in that quiet, invisible cultivation that the power of compassion begins. Power that does not coerce or dominate, but that invites transformation. Power born not from authority, but from presence. Power that quietly shifts the energy in the room and, over time, how it impacts you and the culture of the entire profession.

8. Nan Waller Burnett, Calm in the Face of the Storm: Spiritual Daily Practice for the Peacemaker (2d ed. 2010) (2007). A reflective daily-practice guide aimed at mediators and peacemakers, Burnett's work centers on the cultivation of calm presence—an inward foundation for outward peacemaking. Awarded the 2008 IPPY Gold Medal for Spirituality/Inspiration, it emphasizes the transformative power of steady, mindful accompaniment in conflict settings.

Compassion as Access to Wisdom

One of the most profound yet often overlooked gifts of compassion is that it opens a portal to wisdom.[9]

When we act out of reactivity—when fear, anger, or frustration drive our words and actions—we may speak with force and certainty, but often our clarity is clouded. Our sharpness can become a blunt instrument; a sword swung without aim. Compassion, contrary to what some might think, does not dull our edge; it refines it. It sharpens our discernment, like a finely honed blade guided by intention rather than impulse.

Compassion creates a space within us—quiet, still, and expansive—where wiser questions can find their way in. Questions that move beyond the immediate to touch the heart of what truly matters:

> What is truly at stake here, beyond the surface claims and demands?
>
> What course of action will serve this family not just today, but in the long arc of their lives?
>
> What is being left unsaid, and why? What fears or hopes hide beneath the silence?

This wisdom is not ethereal or abstract. It is intensely practical. It is the kind of insight that helps us avoid unnecessary battles—those skirmishes that drain energy and deepen wounds without advancing resolution. It equips us to gently de-escalate tensions before conflict spirals out of control. It reminds us when our most powerful tool is not speech but vigilant silence. When restraint, rather than argument, creates space for healing.

In Buddhist psychology, compassion—*karuṇā*—is understood as one of the foundational pillars of insight. It is not mere emotion or sentimental kindness, but a path to deeply understanding the nature of suffering itself. Through this understanding, we find the way out of suffering, not by denial or avoidance, but by radical acceptance and wise action.[10]

For us, as family lawyers, this means our best decisions emerge not in haste or heat, but in the pause when we allow ourselves to truly see and care. When

9. Studies indicate that compassion training not only reduces empathic distress fatigue among legal professionals but also enhances engagement with clients and improves case outcomes. *See* PETER SEAR, EMPATHY FOR LEGAL PROFESSIONALS, PSYCHOLOGY TODAY (Dec. 1, 2023) (highlighting enhanced client trust, communication, advocacy, and system navigation through lawyer empathy).

10. In descriptions of *karuṇā* (compassion), Buddhist thought emphasizes that compassionate insight arises not from emotion alone, but from deep understanding of suffering's nature. PEMA CHÖDRÖN, THE PLACES THAT SCARE YOU 45–46 (2002).

we step back from the adversarial grind and instead look with compassionate clarity.

Wisdom does not arise apart from compassion. It is born from it.

Compassion opens our eyes; wisdom guides our actions and our words.

Together, they become the compass that leads us through the complexity of family conflict toward resolutions that honor both justice and humanity.

Cross-Cultural Compassion and Humility: Meeting the Other in Their Fullness

In family law, the stories we encounter are as diverse as the families themselves. Each narrative is woven not only from personal histories but also from the rich tapestry of culture, tradition, and identity. To practice compassion here demands more than kindness—it requires humility, a willingness to meet the other not as we expect, but as they are in their full complexity. We need to be full-time committed students of diversity and culture.

This humility calls us to recognize our own cultural lenses—the invisible frames through which we interpret words, behaviors, and emotions. Without this awareness, even the most well-intentioned efforts at compassion risk misunderstanding, misreading, or unintentionally imposing our values on those we seek to help.

Anthropologist Milton J. Bennett's *Developmental Model of Intercultural Sensitivity* reminds us that cultural competence is a journey from denial and defense to adaptation and integration.[11] It is a process of expanding our capacity to embrace difference without fear, to listen deeply to stories shaped by unfamiliar rhythms and meanings.

In practical terms, just like changing our mission from providing the right answer, listening deeply also means slowing down the impulse to "fix" or advise, and instead asking open-hearted questions: "What does this mean for you in your family? How do your traditions shape your hopes for resolution?" Such questions are invitations to important dialogue, to relationship-building that honors the client's whole self.

Cross-cultural compassion also demands an active stance against biases—both conscious and unconscious—that seep into decision-making. Implicit bias can cloud judgments, skew negotiations, and deepen divides. Ongoing self-reflection, cultural humility training, and peer conversations become essential tools to guard against this erosion of empathy.

---

11. Milton J. Bennett, Basic Concepts of Intercultural Communication: Selected Readings (1998); *see also* Milton J. Bennett, *Developmental Model of Intercultural Sensitivity*, *in* Handbook of Intercultural Training (D. Landis & R.S. Bhagat eds., 2004).

Importantly, cultural humility doesn't mean relativism or passivity. It is a dynamic dance—holding respect for the other's worldview while also bringing the wisdom of the law and the well-being of the family into compassionate alignment. When we move with this balance, we create spaces where healing and justice can truly flourish.

In this way, our work becomes a bridge between worlds, a sacred meeting ground where differences are not obstacles, but sources of strength and learning.[12]

Stories from the Field: Echoes of Compassion

Sometimes, in the midst of law's complexity and procedure, we need stories more than strategies. Not to replicate them slavishly, but to remember and remind ourselves what truly matters beneath the legal jargon, beneath the motions and briefs.

One lawyer shared a story that still lingers in the way she talks about it. During what appeared to be a routine divorce mediation, she noticed the husband, a man who had worn stoicism like armor, arms crossed tightly, jaw clenched, kept glancing repeatedly toward a photograph resting on the edge of the table. It was a simple snapshot: a sun-dappled beach, two laughing children running ahead of their parents. The tension in the room was palpable, the air heavy with years of unspoken grievances and fractures. Yet something in that small, quiet image called to her.

With gentle care, she paused the meeting and softly asked, "Would you like to talk about that picture?"

What followed was not in the mediation plan. It was not on any agenda or checklist. It was 30 minutes of unplanned, tender conversation in which both parties allowed themselves to step out of their legal roles and back into their shared humanity. They spoke of that vacation long ago, before the cracks appeared, when hope was still a given and laughter flowed easily. They spoke of their children's small triumphs and first words, of dreams once dreamt together.

The room changed. Tears came—surprising, unguarded. The husband's arms unfolded slowly, as if unshackling old grief. The wife's eyes softened,

---

12. *See* David A. Hoffman, *Reducing Unconscious Bias: An Ethical Requirement and Moral Imperative*, Mass. Bar Ass'n, Disp. Resol. Section Rev., Nov.–Dec. 2024, at 1, 1–2, https://www.massbar.org/publications/section-review/section-review-article/section-review-2024-november-december-2024/reducing-unconscious-bias-an-ethical-requirement-and-moral-imperative. Hoffman—mediator, arbitrator, and Harvard Law lecturer—outlines how unconscious associations can compromise ethical duty and fairness in legal practice, urging dispute-resolution professionals to actively identify, understand, and mitigate implicit bias.

the hard edge of anger blurring into something deeper, more vulnerable. They didn't just recall memories. They remembered each other as people, not just adversaries. In that moment, common ground emerged—not from negotiation tactics, but from the restoration of shared humanity. It wasn't magic. It was memory. It was compassion.

Another lawyer spoke of an emotionally frayed mother who arrived in her office filled with a protective defensiveness as thick as armor. The mother faced the imminent loss of parenting time, a fear that had consumed her thoughts for months. But instead of diving straight into legal analysis of what statutes might apply, what arguments might succeed—the lawyer asked something different: "What are you most afraid of losing right now?"

The question cracked open the walls of resistance. The mother's voice broke as she said, "It's not just my daughter. . . . It's the chance to become the mother I wasn't ready to be before." That insight did not weaken the legal strategy. It transformed it. It became smarter, sharper, rooted not in superficial concessions or combative posturing, but in truth—the deep truth of loss, regret, and hope.

When our work reaches the core of human experience, it becomes powerful in a way that no checklist or tactic ever could. Compassion is not a detour from effectiveness. It is the path that leads to it. These stories remind us that compassion is not softness. It is not sentimentalism. It is the quiet, steady force that brings us back to what matters most: people. People whose lives are messy, complicated, painful, and beautiful. People who need to be heard, not just argued against. People who need to be met with presence, not just process. When we listen beyond the case and into the soul, we catch the echoes of compassion—and those echoes change everything.

Compassion Fatigue

Let us name something honestly, without shame or avoidance: Compassion has a cost.

To sit with suffering day after day, to hold the raw edges of human pain with tenderness and steadiness, is an act of courage and grace, but it is not effortless or without a price. It requires energy we cannot always summon on command. It requires vulnerability in a profession often trained to armor itself against vulnerability. Even with the best of intentions, even with rituals that ground us and support systems that sustain us, we are not immune to depletion.[13]

13. Studies show that secondary trauma and burnout are prevalent among family law practitioners, with rates of emotional exhaustion and compassion fatigue significantly higher than in

The term *compassion fatigue* is familiar in clinical fields—therapists, nurses, caregivers—but for lawyers, it often remains elusive, unnamed, slipping quietly beneath the surface like a slow leak in the soul's reservoir. It shows up as a creeping numbness, a subtle thinning of patience, a quiet pull toward cynicism and detachment. There are reasons why so many lawyers succumb to alcohol and substance abuse. You may find yourself rolling your eyes internally at a client's tears—tears that once stirred your empathy now triggering irritation. You dread returning calls that feel like yet another invitation into conflict. You stop believing that resolution, or peace, is even possible.

This is not failure. It is a signal that you should not ignore.

It is your body and soul whispering, and sometimes shouting, that it is time to return to yourself. Because you cannot pour from a well that has run dry.

Recovery begins not with more tasks or self-improvement plans. It begins with recognition—honest, tender acknowledgment—of your exhaustion. It begins with kindness rather than another item on a checklist. It requires a softening toward your own humanity.

Ask yourself, gently:

Have I honored my own needs lately?

Am I trying to carry burdens that are not mine to hold?

Who reminds me of who I am when I forget?

Allow rest to become part of your professional ethics. Let it be as non-negotiable as showing up for negotiation sessions or filing documents. Let joy be a form of resistance against the relentless grind. Let laughter shared with colleagues be a rebalancing of gravity—a reminder that lightness exists even in heaviness.

Compassion fatigue is not a dead end. It is a call to return—not to naïveté or innocence, but to clarity rooted in self-care. When you feel your heart reopening, you will know that the return is happening. You will begin to see with fresh eyes: The client who once felt exhausting becomes a human again. The legal challenges transform from battles to bridges. The work you do is no longer draining but enlivening.

This gentle return is a sacred cycle of renewal. It is a reminder that to be a compassionate helper, you must first be compassionate with yourself. And that may be the deepest wisdom of all.

---

other legal specialties. Anna P. Duffy et al., *Towards Trauma-Informed Legal Practice: A Review*, 18 J. PUB. MENTAL HEALTH 31, 36 (2024). *See also* Michelle Mello et al., *Well-Being in the Legal Profession: Evidence from Lawyers and Judges*, 17 HARV. L. & POL'Y REV. 1, 20 (2019), explaining that "compassion fatigue among lawyers impairs professional effectiveness, underscoring the urgent need for training and institutional support centered on emotional resilience."

Shaping a Practice Culture of Care

As we begin to embody compassion within ourselves, its radiance naturally infuses the professional spaces we inhabit. Compassion is not a solitary virtue but a contagion—a light that spreads quietly, transforming the atmosphere around it.

Imagine, if you will, a law office where the day begins not with the frantic rush of deadlines, but with a collective breath—a moment of stillness. Not as a performance for clients or management, but as a genuine pause to reset nervous systems, to remind everyone present that beneath the roles and responsibilities, we are human beings first, interconnected and vulnerable.

Picture team meetings that open with this shared breath, where the air softens and the usual undercurrent of stress eases, if only for a moment. Where a staff member feels empowered to say, "I need five minutes before I return that client's call," and this is met not with impatience or judgment, but with understanding and respect. Where taking a pause is recognized as strength, not a failure. Where having the office close daily for lunch makes professional and financial sense.

Now imagine onboarding materials that speak as much about the values that animate the practice as about the procedures and policies. Materials that invite new team members into a culture rooted in empathy, presence, and reflection. A culture where mentorship extends beyond case law and technical skills to include emotional intelligence, self-awareness, and the courage to be present with difficulty.

This is not a distant utopia or a mere ideal to aspire to in vague hopes. These cultures are already emerging—in pockets, in practices led by courageous leaders who understand that the law is not just about rules but about people.[14]

When these cultures take root, the impact is palpable. Clients feel it immediately. The tone of communication shifts from transactional and tense to warm and trustworthy. Conflict de-escalates naturally as everyone in the office, from the receptionist to the managing partner, moves with greater care and intentionality. Client retention rises, not just because of excellent legal work, but because people experience something rare: being truly seen and valued. Look at your website: How much of this inner work is made available to prospective clients that just might appreciate your investment of time and emotion to help them?

---

14. The Law Society has formally recommended offering "unplugged" weeks—allowing lawyers to receive billable-hour credit for rest periods—as part of efforts to reduce burnout and support overall well-being. SUPPORTING WELL-BEING IN THE WORKPLACE: GUIDANCE FOR BEST PRACTICE, LAW SOC'Y (Oct. 9, 2019).

Burnout, that silent epidemic within our profession, begins to recede. The relentless pressure eases when we care for each other as much as we care for clients. And perhaps most importantly, those who walk through your doors leave a little more whole than when they arrived. Not just clients, but colleagues too. A little more human. A little more healed.

This is the quiet power of shaping a practice culture of care. It is the radical belief that the way *we do the work* matters as much as the work itself. It is the unfolding of a vision where law is not a battlefield, but a place of healing and transformation. This culture calls us to lead with the softest presence, the clearest intention, and the deepest commitment to humanity.

The Future We Are Building

Family law is undergoing a quiet revolution. Not one sparked by legislation or technological disruption, but by something deeper—by a shift in conscience. A growing number of us are stepping forward to say, with clarity and conviction: *Enough*. Enough dehumanization masked as efficiency. Enough war metaphors masquerading as strategy. Enough treating pain as leverage and suffering as a point to exploit. We are laying down the weapons of adversarial lawyering and picking up the tools of healing: listening, language, presence, courage.

We are building something quieter, yes, but more enduring. A way of practicing that leaves less collateral damage and more space for dignity. A way that honors our clients not as problems to solve or opponents to defeat, but as people—hurting, hoping, afraid, unfinished, just like us. In this emerging future, collaboration is no longer seen as weakness, but as wisdom. It becomes a mark of maturity, of discernment, of strength. In this future, clients are not pawns, and outcomes are not measured solely by judgments or settlements, but by more sacred metrics:

> How many relationships were preserved or strengthened, even in altered form?
>
> How many children were protected not only legally, but emotionally—from the cold draft of bitterness and blame of their "loving" parents?
>
> How many families found a new kind of peace, not because we won for them, but because we walked with them as they found it themselves?

This future does not begin with sweeping reform or grand declarations. It begins with something far more personal: With a change in how we speak. With a shift in how we show up. With the simple courage to pause and say, "There must be another way." And then to live that way, every day, in the small sacred spaces of your practice. It begins in offices like yours—with phone calls returned with patience, with mediations where the temperature drops because someone dared to breathe, with a moment of empathy in the middle of conflict, a kind word where one was least expected. This is how the future arrives—quietly, consistently, through a thousand invisible acts of care.

We are not just lawyers practicing peace or peacemakers practicing law. We are reshaping all of it—through compassionate healing. And in doing so, we are reshaping lives.

A Blessing for the Compassionate Healer

May you be grounded like a mountain, and soft like the light at dusk.

May you speak knowledge with a steady voice,
and listen with the ears of your heart.

May you remember that you are not alone—that
others, too, have chosen this quieter path.

May you be protected from bitterness, and open to beauty, even here.

And when you are tired, may rest find you before despair does.

May you know that your work matters, even
when the outcome is imperfect.

And may your helping help you remember who you are.

Chapter 9
Peacemaking from the Bench

Judge Elizabeth Potter Scully

This book recognizes that every space can benefit from the touch of a peacemaker. While it emphasizes the advantages of mediation, collaborative family law, and other non-adversarial dispute resolution methods offered in the private sector, we must also acknowledge a practical reality: Despite the best efforts of settlement-focused attorneys and parties wanting an out of court settlement, many family law cases inevitably find their way into the courtroom. When you step into that courtroom, how do you maintain your commitment to peacemaking? Should you automatically view the judicial officer hearing the case as an adversary stranger to peacemaking, or is there still some opportunity for collaboration? Is there any room at all for peacemaking values and approaches within the litigation process? In this chapter, I share my perspective as a family law judicial officer and former family law mediator, collaborative attorney, litigator, and court-appointed minor's counsel who believes that not only is there *room* for peacemaking in the family law courtroom but, in fact, legal and ethical authority *mandates* it.[1]

On a personal note, the idea of integrating mediation and collaborative skills and concepts into the family law courtroom was my fundamental "why" in deciding to apply for a judicial appointment. Representing family law litigants as well as their children over the years, I had spent countless hours in family law and probate courtrooms observing hearings and fielding the powerful responses of participants (myself included), both positive and negative. I often found myself observing court proceedings through a mediation-tinted lens, noticing how judicial officers, lawyers, and litigants were communicating

1. Many core ideas in this chapter arise from a presentation Judge Gary Roberts and I shared with colleagues on the Los Angeles Superior Court Family Law Bench in 2023. I am indebted to him for his wisdom, ongoing collaboration, and thoughtful engagement on peacemaking and dispute resolution topics. The views expressed in this chapter are my own and not official statements of colleagues or the Los Angeles Superior Court.

and wondering what might be said or done differently. When hearings went south, resulting in tension, dissatisfaction, or lack of progress, miscommunication was frequently the culprit. It was heartbreaking to experience a hearing as tense or unproductive in cases where I knew that the parties, the judge, and the other lawyers were all smart, well-intentioned, and genuinely focused on the best interests of the children. It was joyful and transformative to participate in court hearings where litigants felt heard; all participants engaged one another with sincerity and respect; and the outcome included satisfaction, healing, and closure. One common denominator I noticed in the successful hearings was behavior on the part of the judicial officer that I recognized from my mediation training—clearly explaining the agenda, using lay language instead of legalese, engaging in active listening techniques, confirming meaning and inviting clarification, making time and space for feelings and questions, exploring and acknowledging interests and concerns and circling back to those when explaining rulings, treating participants with respect and courtesy, creatively tailoring solutions, fostering accountability, acknowledging experiences and contributions, empathizing, modeling constructive communication, encouraging settlement, and the list goes on. I think of these, collectively, as "peacemaking skills." Although my background in family law and dispute resolution was nontraditional for a judicial applicant at the time,[2] I came to believe that peacemaking training was not ancillary or incidental but instead my most salient qualification. I am fortunate and grateful to have been given the chance to put this theory into practice. As I engage in the lifelong process of developing my voice in this new role as judicial officer, it is reconfirmed for me daily that peacemaking skills and values are very much at home in family law court.

Let me pause here with a strong caveat so there can be no confusion about what I am and am not saying. I am not suggesting that judges are mediators or that adjudication is mediation or that mediation and adjudication are one and the same. They are not. As a judicial officer, understanding the differences between litigation and non-litigation processes is essential to maintaining legal and ethical boundaries and staying in my proper lane.[3] Moreover, the fundamental orientation of the judicial officer often differs from that of the mediator. For example, mediators routinely try to suggest and anticipate future issues that may arise in an effort to preemptively avoid them. In contrast, judges must take care not to raise or decide issues without proper due process notice and are bound by the limited framework established by the parties. Judges must

2. We are all pleased to witness the increasing appointments of family law judges who understand and practiced the art of peacemaking in their pre-judicial careers and relied on those perspectives and skills once on the bench.

3. My focus in this chapter is not Mandatory Settlement Conferences or other processes in which judicial officers who are not the ultimate triers of fact are explicitly engaging with parties in a settlement capacity.

avoid raising new issues that turn out to favor one side or the other in a way that tips the scale or compromises actual or perceived neutrality. The list of differences between mediation and adjudication is long (the black robe is one prominent tipoff, the Court of Appeal another—not to mention the Evidence Code). I am not saying there is no difference between a judicial officer and a mediator. What I am suggesting, instead, is that mindfully and appropriately incorporating peacemaking skills and values into the family law courtroom can promote judicial, litigant, and public policy goals in profound and meaningful ways.

Similarly, I don't want my comments to be interpreted as gratuitously bashing the court system or saying litigation is never an appropriate option for families. Before I took the bench, I was one of the few attorneys I knew of who mediated, handled collaborative cases, and also went to court, and I know from personal experience there can be an unfortunately polarized "us vs them" mentality between family law attorneys who go to court and those who don't. I believe the availability of court redress as an option for parties is a crucial and non-negotiable building block of our democracy.[4] I also believe strongly in our judicial institutions and their capacity to render just decisions and provide lasting resolution for family law litigants. Every day the commitment to public service, thoughtful and disciplined engagement, work ethic, professionalism, humility, and dedication I see in the court administration, staff, and my judicial colleagues awes and humbles me. All this notwithstanding, it is amply documented and essentially beyond dispute that the adversarial system as it exists today poses some serious challenges for families in general and self-represented litigants in particular. These challenges include, without limitation, polarization and entrenchment; lack of privacy; inaccessibility; cost and delay; disempowerment; cultural, linguistic, and other barriers; unacknowledged feelings; lack of resources; and even litigation abuse as a form of coercive control.[5] Among

4. In an open forum during discussions of the Uniform Collaborative Act at which Woody was present, collaborative professionals were asked to vote on a simple binary question: Which do you find more important if you could only have one of these two systems: 1. collaborative law or 2. the Rule of Law. The collaborative practitioners at that forum voted overwhelmingly for the Rule of Law. The reason as revealed by a post-vote discussion: While there are many benefits to collaborative practice, The Law is society's ultimate guarantee of fairness and citizen empowerment.

5. There is extensive and heated debate in the mediation literature regarding whether and how mediation can play a role in domestic violence cases, which goes far beyond the scope of this chapter. Suffice it to say that judicial officers must work to ensure that judicial processes are handled in a safe and appropriate way in the domestic violence context. California Family Code section 6309 was amended in 2024 to recognize misuse of court processes as a form of coercive control and call out judicial officers and court staff to increase awareness: "Domestic violence survivors who enter the family or civil court systems seeking protection often face ongoing abuse in the form of litigation abuse. Litigation abuse is the use of legal or bureaucratic procedures by abusive partners to continue to attack, harass, intimidate, coercively control, or maintain

many other interventions being researched and implemented, and pending wholesale structural reform, incorporating peacemaking values and skills in the courtroom can mitigate some of the shortcomings inherent in adversarial court processes.

The concept of bringing peacemaking skills and values into the courtroom took shape in my mind over time as a function of my own training and experience, but I did not originate it. Many other scholars, commentators, judges, attorneys, and dispute resolution professionals have had the same idea. This concept appears in blogs, books, and articles and is sometimes referred to as "facilitative judging." For example, "Facilitative judging refers to the conscious integration of communication and facilitation skills into judicial adjudication. Facilitative techniques such as active listening can help calm down anxious witnesses or parties and can increase their perception of procedural justice. Emotional intelligence and communication skills can help judges convey their decisions in a sensitive and appropriate manner, which, in turn, may increase the acceptance of, and compliance with, their decisions by the parties[6]

Although the concept of facilitative judging may sound kooky or radical, it is by no means out on a limb. In California, where my courtroom is located, there is unambiguous, well-established, and extensive legal and policy support for promoting settlement within the court process and otherwise incorporating peacemaking skills and values in the courthouse—from the initial court pleading to the notice of appeal.

For example, California's public policy[7] as reflected in both statutory and case law is to promote settlement of litigation, and the legislature has expressly charged the Judicial Branch with implementing this policy. Code of Civil Procedure Section 1775 could not be clearer: "The *peaceful* resolution of disputes in a fair, timely, appropriate, and cost-effective manner is an essential function of the judicial branch of state government under Article VI of the California Constitution." In the family law context specifically, Family Code 271

---

contact with their former partners through the litigation system by exerting power over them, forcing them to have contact, financially burdening them with excessive discovery and litigation, degrading and insulting them in legal papers, unduly delaying the court process and final resolution of important issues, or dissuading them from pursuing legal protection. Studies show that litigation abuse causes severe consequences for survivors, including economic hardship and psychological harm, and foregoing legal relief in part or in whole. Research also shows that judicial officers and court evaluators often misunderstand or overlook litigation abuse and its effects on survivors."

6. Nadja Marie Alexander, Judges Mediate and Do Other Things—Whether We Like It or Not (Dec. 9, 2011). *See also* T.M. Sourdin, *Facilitative Judging: Science, Sense and Sensibility*, *in* The Multi-Tasking Judge: Comparative Judicial Dispute Resolution 231–47 (T. Sourdin & A. Zariski eds., 2013).

7. I cite California authority because it is the jurisdiction in which I sit and know best. Other jurisdictions approach peacemaking in different ways, and we recommend that you take a deep dive to learn about and work to expand peacemaking in your own jurisdiction.

provides: ". . . the *policy of the law to promote settlement of litigation* and, where possible, to reduce the cost of litigation by encouraging *cooperation between the parties and attorneys*" (emphasis added). Family Code 2450(a) states: "The purpose of *family centered* case resolution is to benefit the parties by providing judicial assistance and management to the parties in actions for dissolution of marriage for the purpose of expediting the processing of the case, reducing the expense of litigation, and *focusing on early resolution by settlement*. Family centered case resolution is a tool to allow the courts to better assist families. . ." (emphasis added). Per the local rules in my jurisdiction, LASC Local Rule 5.12: "It is the intent of the court to provide judicial assistance and management to the parties in family law cases in order to focus on *early resolution of cases through settlement*, expedite the processing of cases, and reduce the costs of litigation.[8]

The canons of judicial ethics in California are also consistent with peacemaking values such as respect and dignity for litigants, free expression of interests and concerns, a full and fair hearing, and fair and workable outcome, and with implementation of appropriate tools and techniques to operationalize those values. For example, California Judicial Ethics Canons require that judges shall be "patient, dignified, and courteous to litigants, jurors, witnesses, lawyers, and others with whom the judge deals in an official capacity. . . ." Judges shall "accord to every person who has a legal interest in a proceeding, or that person's lawyer, the full right to be heard according to law." Judges "shall dispose of all judicial matters fairly, promptly, and efficiently." Finally, the Judicial Canons specifically authorize judicial officers to participate in *settlement efforts where there is informed consent*, neutrality is maintained, and the judicial officer's conduct is not coercive: "A judge may participate in settlement conferences or in other efforts to resolve matters in dispute, including matters pending before the judge. A judge may, with the express consent of the parties or their lawyers, confer separately with the parties and/or their lawyers during such resolution efforts. At all times during such resolution efforts, a judge shall remain impartial and shall not engage in conduct that may reasonably be perceived as coercive."

While judicial officers are tasked with promoting, encouraging, and supporting cooperation and resolution, we aren't the only ones. The law independently obligates family law lawyers and parties to meet and confer. For example, California Rule of Court 5.98(a) provides: "All parties and all attorneys are required to meet and confer in person, by telephone, or as ordered by the court, before the date of the hearing relating to a Request for Order (FL-300). During this time, parties must discuss and make a good faith attempt to settle all issues, even if a complete settlement is not possible and only

8. *See* Cal. Fam. Code § 2450 (emphasis added).

conditional agreements are made. The requirement to meet and confer does not apply to cases involving domestic violence."[9] Local Rules provide authority as well; for example, Appendix 3.A(k) to the Los Angeles County Local Rules of Court (Guidelines for Civility in Litigation) provides, in part, "Except where there are strong and overriding issues of principle, an attorney should raise and explore the issue of settlement in every case as soon as enough is known about the case to make settlement discussions meaningful. . . . In every case, counsel should consider and discuss with the client whether the client's interest could be adequately served and the controversy more expeditiously and economically disposed of by arbitration, mediation or other forms of alternative dispute resolution . . . Counsel are encouraged to discuss the various ADR processes with their clients and explain the confidentiality and non-binding nature of the selected process."[10] The California State Bar identifies many other similar local rules and resources in its online Civility Toolbox.[11]

Having spent some time on the issues of whether and why we might incorporate peacemaking skills and values into the courtroom, let's think about when and how judicial officers might do this. Throughout the course of a hearing or case there are points at which a peacemaking skill or technique might come into play. For example, at the moment of commencing a court hearing, the judicial officer might engage in what mediators would call "agenda setting," that is, explaining clearly what issues are before the court and asking counsel and their clients to build on the judicial officer's explanation by adding or deleting issues or offering linkage of issues. By breaking down the problem into the various components, phrased neutrally, the decision-maker ensures that all issues are addressed. The judicial officer can also inquire about any agreements the parties have reached at the outset and find out whether additional time to meet and confer might be useful to lead to further mini-agreements or a full settlement of all the issues. During family law hearings, judicial officers frequently engage in fact-gathering. By invoking peacemaking techniques such as active listening, reflection, open-ended questioning, reframing, acknowledging emotions, normalizing experiences, curiosity, and expressing empathy, the

---

9. We are aware that many lawyers treat "meet and confer" as a "pro forma" requirement. However, any conversation and document exchange is better than none. It is our hope that books like ours will encourage more meaningful "meet and confers" that are actually productive conversations leading to better understanding, if not settlement itself.

10. Mediation scholars and practitioners have worked for decades to codify such informed consent conversations between clients and their lawyers.

11. *See* California State Bar, Attorney Civility and Professionalism, https://www.calbar.ca.gov/Attorneys/Conduct-Discipline/Ethics/Attorney-Civility-and-Professionalism (last visited July 22, 2025). The California State Bar's *Civility Toolbox* includes resources such as sample local civility guidelines; codes of conduct adopted by California courts and bar associations; checklists for civil behavior; model oaths; training materials; and videos aimed at promoting professionalism, respect, and courtesy in legal practice.

judicial officer can gather necessary information in an effective, respectful, and trust-building way. If the fact-gathering process uncovers common interests and concerns or other information suggesting a pathway to settlement, a judicial officer can again restate these common issues and concerns and offer to pause or reschedule the hearing so everyone can meet and discuss. At the end of the hearing, in announcing judicial decisions, peacemaking techniques like explaining things in lay terms, acknowledging interests and concerns and pointing out how those may be reflected in the court's orders, and acknowledging positives about the litigants' or counsel's participation in the hearing can increase confidence that rulings were thoughtful and all parties fully heard. Such judicial explanations can prevent unnecessary relitigating, appeals, or continued anger and conflict between the parties.

One area where I have found peacemaking skills especially valuable is in referring a case to another judicial officer for a settlement conference. This happens frequently since there are ethical problems with acting both as a settlement neutral and the trier of fact absent the express waiver and informed consent of the parties. Anecdotally, when I engage in behavior that a mediator might call "priming" or "conditioning" parties for settlement (i.e., by communicating optimism and positivity about settlement processes), normalizing settlement, appealing to party self-interest, emphasizing benefits of self-determination, and identifying shared interests (such as minimizing fees, maximizing privacy, speed of resolution, maintaining control, and/or minimizing adverse effects of conflict on children) it sets cases up for settlement success. Judicial officers must remain mindful of the ethical prohibition against being or even appearing coercive. Parties should understand that the courthouse door is always open to them. I might therefore conclude a matter by saying something like, "A settlement can only take place if both of you agree to it and feel comfortable. You are not required to settle. If you remain stuck on some or all of these issues, you can always come back to court; we will set a trial at which the court will hear evidence and argument from both sides and decide any open issues for you."

When a judicial officer clearly communicates that the court expects and encourages good faith settlement efforts, it reassures parties and counsel who might otherwise fear appearing weak or feel nervous about pursuing settlement. Hearing the judicial officer acknowledge how stuck they feel and express positivity and optimism about the possibility of a resolution can also be eye-opening and powerful. When I address myself directly to the parties and say things like, "You may be feeling really stuck in this conflict, and maybe pessimistic about whether a settlement conference will help," the response is often the great big emphatic nod of acknowledgment (what Woody, a dyed in the wool Dodgers (now Padres) fan, sometimes refers to as "The Bobblehead"—the neck going up and down in agreement with the Judicial Officer) that mediators recognize as the hallmark of an active listening success. Validation of feelings by the judicial officer can resonate deeply. I might then say things like, "Even if you are feeling that way, I urge you to keep an open mind. It can make a real difference having a neutral third party involved in the discussion, especially someone like Judge Colleague who is experienced and knowledgeable about the issues involved in your case. Our settlement conference process is highly effective; the vast majority of cases I refer out settle completely, and the ones that don't are often able to limit and focus the remaining issues.[12] Based on my review of your file it looks to me like yours is a settleable case. Even if you aren't feeling it right now, I will be optimistic enough about the settlement process for both of you!"[13] Colleagues who conduct judicial settlement conferences share that they see a marked difference in outcomes depending on *how* a case is referred for settlement. This is consistent with mediation research suggesting that inducing positive emotions (feeling happy or optimistic) and reducing negative ones (feeling anger or distress) correlates with improved negotiating conduct and improved outcomes.[14]

Another common kind of court hearing that benefits from use of peacemaking skills is an initial request for court orders seeking a parenting plan where the parties are self-represented. A judicial officer may have all kinds of possible goals for this kind of hearing, depending on the situation, the amount of time available, and how much (or how little) information is in the pleadings. To end up with a clear, workable, and appropriate short-term parenting plan so there is predictability and certainty for the family while things are being worked out, the judicial officer needs to gather basic information about what has been happening in terms of timeshare, schedules, living arrangements, transportation, schooling, any special needs, et cetera. In conducting these hearings, I hope to create a calm, respectful space in which the parties, who are probably highly anxious and intimidated, can say what they need to say and feel like they have been heard. I want to explain process and set clear expectations about what steps the parties need to take in order to complete their case. I want to reduce tension and hostility and protect the children from exposure to parental conflict to the greatest possible extent. I want to make sure the parties understand process options and direct them to available resources through the court. I want them to trust the court and the process and feel like things are being handled fairly.

---

12. These are the same words that trained mediators use with their clients. Mediation literature refers to these kinds of words and actions as "interventions."

13. This is a reference to the concept that the mediator may be a "beacon of hope," the only one in the room with some optimism for resolution.

14. *See* BECK & SALES, FAMILY MEDIATION: FACTS, MYTHS, AND FUTURE PROSPECTS (Am. Psych. Ass'n, 2001).

Peacemaking skills are central to how I pursue and achieve these strategic goals—and active listening is my main tool. For example, conveying that I am attentive and receptive by making eye contact with parties, leaning forward and communicating engagement and focus via my body language. I often narrate what I am doing physically to ensure parties know they have my attention; for example, if I need to find something in their file while they are talking, I don't just turn to the bench computer monitor and start scrolling. I might say something like, "I want you to know I am listening to you even though I am turned towards the computer; I am pulling up a copy of your request so I can refer to it," or else ask them to pause so that I can pull up the document. I tend to take a lot of notes, which can be perceived as focusing more on my paper than on the speaker, and so to anticipate and prevent that I might say something like, "your words are important, and I am writing them down to help me understand and remember what you are saying. I may not be looking at you, but I promise I am still listening."

Additional peacemaking techniques I use include reflective listening—paraphrasing the speaker's core message, emotions, or underlying interests—and inviting clarification or confirmation with phrases such as "Am I understanding you correctly?" or "Have I got that right?" Understanding that litigants may not feel comfortable correcting a judicial officer for fear of appearing disrespectful or for cultural reasons, I go a step further by saying something like, "My goal is to make sure I understand the important things you are communicating." When I ask whether I am understanding correctly, that's a real question. It's appropriate to correct me if I am not understanding you—I invite you to—and if you do, I will not interpret that as disrespectful. It's important to me that you have a chance to say what you need to say and feel confident that I have understood you."

Productive reframing of the litigants' statements from positional ones to interest-based ones or from complaints about the past to shared statements about the future is also key. For example, in response to "I need sole legal custody. [Other Parent] ghosts me all the time or else yells at me when I try to handle something and I can't deal with them," I might say, "It sounds like you have a concern about having an appropriate line of communication open and some ground rules in place about responding to one another so that decisions about your child can get made in a timely way. Have I got that right?"

Respectful and attentive listening is in and of itself trust building, and I find it to be essential to creating in litigants a sense of confidence in how the court is handling their case. Again, this conclusion is not unique to me; it is an established part of our judicial training in California. For example, the 2019 Benchguide: Handling Cases with Self-Represented Litigants, at pages 2–3 and 2–4, states: "When self-represented litigants are stumbling in their stories, or the evidentiary foundational requirements of some forms of evidence confuse and confound them, they are unable to get relevant facts before the court, rendering them 'voiceless.' California judges have long been asking questions of the litigants themselves, following up when those questions are answered inadequately, summarizing the law when that is helpful to move the case forward, and answering the parties' questions about the proceedings when such answers are helpful in promoting understanding and compliance. All of which is both appropriate and encouraged in the law." At page 2–5, the Benchguide notes, "Litigants pay close attention to their perceptions of each individual judge's motivation toward them and toward others in the courtroom. If participants believe that the judge was trying to be fair, they tend to view the entire procedure as a fair one. Similarly, if the judge treats people politely, and exhibits a clear concern for their rights, litigants are likely to view the entire process as fair." At page 2–7, it states, "Taking the time to listen to the positions of both sides and to communicate clearly the basis of the ultimate decision can result in a feeling of calm reassurance and stability that is almost palpable in the courtroom." Chapter 10 of that Benchguide deals with communication and includes sections on "Active Listening: Capturing and Confirming the Message," "Potential External Barriers to Communication," and "Tools for Dealing with Cross-Cultural Communication Issues."

A final example of how to bring peacemaking into the courtroom is through the issuance of detailed pretrial orders. In addition to setting deadlines and discussing the mechanics of how exhibits are to be numbered, my pretrial orders address civility, include specific meet and confer requirements, and strongly encourage counsel to discuss consensual dispute (CDR) options like mediation and collaborative practice with the parties and refer them to CDR resources to make sure parties have given informed consent to whatever processes (including litigation) are pursued. Some sample language might include the following:

- "Civility Guidelines: Counsel and Self-Represented Litigants shall behave in a civil and courteous manner with one another, with witnesses, and with court personnel in all oral and written communications regarding this case."[15]
- "Meet and Confer Regarding Factual and Procedural Stipulations: It is the policy of the law to promote settlement of family law litigation and, where possible, to reduce the cost of litigation by encouraging cooperation between the parties and attorneys.[16] To that end, counsel and the parties are ordered to meet and confer in detail at least seven

15. *See* Los Angeles County Superior Court Local Rules, app. 3.A, Guidelines for Civility in Litigation.

16. *See* Cal. Fam. Code § 271.

calendar days prior to the Trial Readiness Conference regarding factual and procedural stipulations that might streamline the presentation of evidence at trial/long cause evidentiary hearing. Such stipulations might include, without limitation, recitation of undisputed facts, identification of issues that have been resolved, agreements to admit declarations as direct testimony subject to cross-examination, agreements as to the order in which evidence or issues shall be presented, and agreements as to the authenticity and/or admissibility of exhibits."

- "Consensual Dispute Resolution/ADR Processes: The Legislature has determined that 'The peaceful resolution of disputes in a fair, timely, appropriate, and cost-effective manner is an essential function of the judicial branch of state government under Article VI of the California Constitution.'[17] 'In the case of many disputes, litigation culminating in a trial is costly, time consuming, and stressful for the parties involved. Many disputes can be resolved in a fair and equitable manner through less formal processes.'[18] The court strongly encourages Counsel to consider and discuss with clients whether the client's interests could be adequately served, and the controversy expeditiously and economically disposed of, by mediation, arbitration, neutral evaluation, settlement conference, collaborative family law process, or any other available form of consensual dispute resolution. The court strongly encourages Counsel to provide clients with a detailed explanation of each available consensual dispute resolution/ADR process, including without limitation the extent to which each process is confidential and the extent to which each is non-binding."[19]

When I set a matter for trial, I explain to the parties and counsel that my pretrial orders are designed to promote communication and mutual understanding about interests and concerns and to facilitate early exchange of information and resolution of issues. I encourage counsel to share a copy of the pretrial orders with the parties right away and prompt the parties to read them carefully, go over them with counsel, and ask lots of questions. While I can't interfere with the attorney–client relationship or order parties to mediate (other than required Family Court Services mediation about parenting issues), I can make orders that support counsel's settlement efforts, articulate the law and policy favoring settlement, and alert the parties and counsel to

17. Cal. Civ. Proc. Code § 1775(a).

18. *Id.* § 1775(b).

19. *See* Los Angeles County Superior Court Local Rules, app. 3.A(k), Guidelines for Civility in Litigation. Some basic information about types of non-litigation dispute resolution is available through the Judicial Branch of California, https://www.courts.ca.gov/programs-adr.htm.

CDR resources.[20] Most of all, I can facilitate parties' informed consent to dispute resolution processes by prompting them to ask their attorneys about all available process options and explore with the advice of counsel whether any non-litigation options might meet their needs and goals even more effectively.

While at first blush the inside of a courtroom might seem like the last place to expect to find peacemaking, there are profound and concrete ways that peacemaking in the courtroom can mitigate challenges of litigation. And I don't mean grudgingly giving lip service to peacemaking by plaintively asking parties to meet and confer. I mean robust, intentional, impactful conduct on the part of judicial officers that is not just fully consistent with their roles but essential for carrying out legal and ethical mandates designed to promote fairness and justice.

Hon. Elizabeth Scully sits in a family law assignment on the Los Angeles Superior Court, primarily handling long cause trials and settlement conferences. She received her AB in Classics (Latin) magna cum laude from Harvard in 1993 and her JD from the University of California Hastings College of the Law in 1996. Prior to taking the bench in December 2020, she was a certified Family Law Specialist (California State Bar Board of Legal Specialization) in private practice and a founding partner of Jacobson Scully LLP, providing mediation, collaborative and minor's counsel services, in addition to traditional litigation representation. As an attorney, she was also Vice President of the Board of Directors of LevittQuinn, a nonprofit law firm serving the working poor, and a member of A Better Divorce, a collaborative practice group in Los Angeles's South Bay. She has taught experiential courses in mediation and in negotiation theory and practice at UCLA School of Law and has co-authored numerous books and articles (with Woody and others) on topics relating to consensual dispute resolution in the family law context. She was co-recipient of the Association of Family and Conciliation Court's 2016 Meyer Elkin Essay Award, honoring the best article in Family Court Review. In 2024, she received LevittQuinn's Outstanding Community Service Award.

20. For many years, Woody has urged court reform to provide procedural and financial incentives to work on settlement. For example, a party that proposes mediation (that is rejected) might be rewarded with a contribution of attorney fees from the refusing party. Or parties that attempt mediation or collaborative law voluntarily before trial might be given priority on the court's calendar. Woody is hopeful that courts will adopt such reforms in the future.

Chapter 10

Justice with a Human Face: Family Peacemakers, Systemic Change, and the Heart of Access to Justice

How wonderful it is that nobody need wait a single moment before starting to improve the world.
—Anne Frank

For most people, the first place they experience law is not in a courtroom—it is in the silence of a family dinner turned tense, in a slammed door, in the voice of a child caught in the crossfire. Justice, for so many, does not begin with rights or remedies, but with confusion, fear, and the overwhelming sense that their private lives have become public problems.

In these moments, what families need most isn't a courtroom victory. They need to be heard. They need support. They need someone who sees their dignity beneath the conflict, who can guide them not just through a legal process but also through a human transition.

This is the quiet, powerful work of the family peacemaker.

More than just lawyers, we are conflict navigators, trust rebuilders, and system reformers. We are redefining what it means to practice law—not as gatekeepers to a rigid legal structure, but as bridge-builders, standing at the intersection of law, community, and care.

Our work is reshaping the justice system from the inside out—not with grand pronouncements, but with everyday courage. And at the heart of it all is a radical idea: that justice must be human-centered, culturally respectful, and community-anchored—or it is not justice at all.

Reimagining the Family Court: Healing in a Hall of Justice

Family and matrimonial courts were never meant to carry so much. Today, they are inundated with the consequences of poverty, trauma, addiction, bigotry, and violence. They are expected to resolve not just legal disputes but also the legacies of systemic failure. And too often, the system itself, despite the efforts of well-intentioned judges and well-trained court personnel, adds to that harm.

Courtrooms can be cold, adversarial places—intimidating even for the most well-resourced, sophisticated litigant. For a parent navigating divorce while working two jobs, or an immigrant mother unsure of her rights, or a father struggling with substance abuse while desperately yearning to connect with his child, the legal system may feel like an impossible labyrinth of languages they cannot speak, processes they cannot navigate, and decisions they cannot trust.

Family peacemakers know this. They see how systemic choreography can retraumatize rather than heal. That is why peacemaking lawyers promote a different kind of justice system—one founded on listening, collaboration, and repair—one that partners with practitioners who are not burdened by bureaucratic expectations and have the luxury to offer more time, more attention, and more tailor-made process options.

Peacemakers help redesign how families experience justice—advocating for trauma-informed courtrooms, child-sensitive procedures, and culturally competent dispute resolution modalities. They work alongside judges to make processes less adversarial and more relational. They push for triage systems that divert families away from court and toward community-centered solutions, when appropriate. Because, many times, the greatest act of justice is keeping a family out of the courtroom altogether.

Family Justice Is Interdisciplinary and Multicultural by Necessity: Law and the Whole Person

Families don't live in isolated silos of "custody disputes," "alimony," or "parental rights." They live in stories, in histories, and in communities that are far more complex than any set of legal definitions can capture. Behind every legal case, there are layers of lived experiences.

Family peacemakers understand this deeply. They know that to truly serve families, law cannot stand alone. It must be responsive to the fabric of people's lives, needs, cultures, and struggles. Without integration, the law risks becoming sterile and disconnected—a tool that serves justice only in the abstract, ignoring the humanity at its core.

Take, for example, a father fighting to keep custody of his children. On the surface, the case may seem straightforward—a legal battle between two parents—but this father is also battling untreated PTSD from his military service, which influences every bone of his being and every moment of his life, including his parenting, his emotions, and his relationships. His trauma is not visible in legal briefs, but it is there—an invisible burden that the court cannot fully grasp unless it listens for it. And it simply does not have the gift of time in order to listen deeply enough. A simple ruling on this father's parental fitness is not enough; this father needs the support of a mental health counselor, the understanding of a judge familiar with the effects of trauma, and the compassion of a peacemaking team that sees him as a whole person in search of peace on many levels—not just a defendant.

Consider the teenage parent caught in a custody dispute. Digging deeper exposes the fact that this teenager is struggling to finish high school, to find stable housing, and to create a support network that can help them raise their child. They might be caught in the relentless cycle of poverty and school dropout, their potential crushed by systemic barriers, and their mental health compromised by stress and isolation. This isn't just a "custody battle"; it is a cry for help, for guidance, for resources. A legal decision about their future doesn't just hinge on a set of arguments; it requires understanding the underlying socio-economic challenges, the psychological strain, and the community context in which this young parent is living.

Then there's the grandmother seeking guardianship of her grandchildren. Perhaps the children's parents are absent due to substance abuse or incarceration, and this grandmother, in her late years, is navigating a system that does not speak her language—literally and figuratively. She may not only be struggling to raise her grandchildren in her retirement years, but she may also be facing a language barrier as a non-English speaker, trying to navigate a system that is inherently not designed for her. She may not even trust the court, as it represents a system that has historically overlooked her cultural values, and she may feel the added weight of being overlooked by both family members and the legal system. For her, this case is not just about a legal document; it is about preserving the family unit, protecting the grandchildren she loves, and doing so in a way that is both legally sound and culturally congruent.

None of these deeply human experiences can be untangled by legal arguments alone. The law is necessary, but it is insufficient on its own to heal, support, and guide families through such complex terrain. It is not, on its own, inherently just.

This is why family peacemakers are so much more than lawyers: They are advocates, connectors, and healers. They are professionals who understand that real justice requires more than a verdict; it requires understanding, healing, and the capacity to incorporate the myriad of resources needed to address the full scope of a family's challenges.

Interdisciplinary teams of peacemaking professionals foster access to true justice. Peacemaking family lawyers consistently work alongside social workers, mental health professionals, financial planners, educators, community organizers, and cultural advisors. Together, they meet families not as "cases" to be processed, but as whole human beings. They understand that seemingly small decisions about one family member's future impacts the emotional, psychological, and financial well-being of the entire family. Truly just solutions are not exclusively legal in nature; they come from a collective, compassionate effort to restore and repair the underlying issues that caused the conflict in the first place while envisioning a practical, peaceful, holistic future.

Interdisciplinary peacemaking is not a system of noblesse oblige or benevolent "fixing." It is simply justice done right. When family peacemakers educate courts and community organizations about the benefit of building interdisciplinary teams, they are furthering frameworks for sustainable, long-term healing—justice that nurtures and restores instead of punishing or separating.

In districts that are linguistically and culturally diverse, family peacemakers often additionally bridge the gap between the law and language. In many immigrant and refugee communities, the legal system is seen not as a source of justice, but as a foreign and inaccessible institution. Families may primarily speak a language other than English, may not authentically be able to express themselves in English, or may not speak English at all, and may feel disconnected from the mainstream legal process because it does not reflect their values, beliefs, or even their way of life. For them, access to justice is not simply about "understanding the law," it is about feeling understood, feeling heard, and feeling like the system is working in their best interest. In an equitable society, access to justice must include access to understanding, dignity, and belonging. For a parent who speaks little English or an elderly grandmother from a marginalized community, justice is not merely a matter of translating words on a page. It is about creating the conditions for true participation, where families feel safe and empowered to tell their stories, to express their needs, and to trust that the law will serve them, not alienate them.

Family peacemakers advocate for language access through interpreter services or the retention of bilingual attorneys, mediators, therapists, and other members of the peacemaking team. Peacemakers strive to secure culturally competent legal assessments for families, ensure access to multilingual resources, and often include culturally relevant stakeholders in the mediation room such as community leaders, integral intergenerational decision-makers, and members of the clergy. At times, peacemakers sit back and listen—knowing that it might be meaningful for a family to amplify the voices of invited community elders, spiritual leaders, and grassroots organizers. These truly culturally competent peacemakers are redefining what access to justice truly means. Because access to justice should also be access to dignity, access to respect, and access to true, whole-person and whole-family understanding.

Peacemaking and ADR: A Community's Path to Justice

Alternative Dispute Resolution (ADR) is no longer a niche or an optional detour. For many families, ADR is not alternative at all. It's the only pathway to justice that feels safe, respectful, and real.

In mediation, collaborative law, and restorative dialogue, families can speak in their own voices. They can center the needs of children, honor the bonds that still exist, and craft solutions that reflect their values. They aren't told what to do by a stranger in a robe; they are empowered to co-create their future. This is especially vital in multicultural communities where state institutions might not be trusted and where family structures may not fit American legal molds.

For multicultural and immigrant families, ADR is often the only mode of resolution that aligns with their values. In many of these communities, going to court feels foreign, intimidating, or even hostile—not simply because of language barriers, but because the very structure of adversarial law conflicts with collectivist, interdependent, or kinship-based understandings of family. In Latino communities, for example, it is common for extended families to help raise children and make decisions together. Mediation and family-group conferencing allow these voices—abuelos, tías, padrinos—to be part of the conversation, something traditional courtrooms often exclude. In Somali refugee communities, elders and clan leaders may be consulted informally for family disputes long before any government body is approached. When ADR models are adapted to respect these practices—including offering services in native languages and acknowledging religious or customary norms—families are far more likely to engage and follow through. In these contexts, ADR becomes not just efficient, it becomes culturally congruent, community-driven justice.

Peacemaking lawyers are the stewards of this process. They bring humility and skill, but also something more radical: the belief that people, when given support and structure, can resolve their conflicts without violence, shame, or vengeance. We see this in Indigenous peacemaking circles, in Chinese communities embracing family-focused mediation, in refugee groups crafting kinship solutions that reflect both tradition and survival, and beyond. Peacemakers meet people in those spaces and, in doing so, help bring the law into harmony with the lives it claims to serve.

Embedding the Ethic of Peacemaking into Law and Policy

The work of family peacemakers is not limited to mediation rooms or collaborative law offices. Increasingly, their ethos is pushing its way into the very structure of the legal system itself. This is not incidental. It is the result of decades of advocacy, research, and community-led efforts to make justice not just accessible but also equitable, humane, and culturally responsive.

In some jurisdictions, courts are beginning to shift from adversarial postures to problem-solving models. Family courts in places like Los Angeles, Minneapolis, and Brooklyn have piloted trauma-informed courtrooms, where judges, clerks, and attorneys partner with community justice organization and are trained to recognize signs of domestic violence, intergenerational trauma, and cultural nuance in family systems. These spaces are beginning to move away from punitive assumptions and toward compassionate accountability.

Some judges have begun to mandate mediation or restorative practices before litigation can proceed—not as an afterthought, but as a first step in addressing family breakdown. These practices are rooted in a belief that conflict resolution must not simply end with legal closure, but open a path toward relational repair. The rise of restorative justice legislation, such as Colorado's House Bill 1254 and New York's restorative practices initiatives, underscores a growing recognition: families need space to speak, to be heard, and to build forward—not just to be sorted and judged.

Across the country, we are seeing a push for codifying language access and cultural competence in court services. In Washington State, interpreters are mandated in many court proceedings and are increasingly being incorporated into mediation services through court-connected programs. This recognizes that meaningful participation requires more than just physical presence; it requires linguistic and cultural inclusion. In Illinois, family court forms and parenting plans are being translated into a growing number of languages, including Arabic, Tagalog, and Somali—a nod to the richly diverse communities these courts serve. But laws and courtrooms are only part of the puzzle. True systemic change requires reimagining the very culture of law—moving away from "win/lose" paradigms toward shared problem solving. Multistate legislation that has recognized collaborative divorce processes and budget lines allocating state funding for community mediation centers underscore an attempt to legally institutionalize peace-building—to make it not just a philosophy, but a system-supported practice.

When community-based dispute resolution centers are funded and recognized by the court system—as they are in New Mexico, Hawaii, and Vermont—we begin to see law not as a distant authority, but as something embedded in and accountable to the community. This reflects the vision described by Rabbi Abraham Joshua Heschel, who said, "In a free society . . . all are responsible." These models honor that collective responsibility by involving not just professionals but also elders, spiritual leaders, interpreters, youth workers, school counselors, and other community stakeholders in family resolution processes.

Additionally, the interdisciplinary integration of mental health professionals, domestic violence advocates, and financial planners into legal proceedings is becoming increasingly common—and necessary. Laws supporting wrap-around family services, such as those under the Families First Prevention Services Act (FFPSA), reinforce the understanding that legal conflict is often the surface symptom of deeper social wounds. The grandmother seeking guardianship might be grieving a child lost to addiction; the father fighting for visitation might be working three jobs and sleeping in his car. Peacemakers and the legislation that backs them refuse to treat these stories as irrelevant to the legal question. They recognize that justice cannot be severed from context.

The integration of peacemaking into law is deeply resonant with enduring ethical traditions, such as those found in Jewish thought. The teaching from *Pirkei Avot*, that "you are not obligated to complete the work, but neither are you free to abandon it," becomes more than moral poetry; it becomes a call to legal visionaries to design systems that honor partial, participatory, and community-driven forms of justice. Rabbi Jonathan Sacks' framing of peace as the presence of mutual dignity mirrors exactly what restorative family law strives to create: not merely agreements, but understandings. Across law schools and judicial training centers, there is a rising movement to teach relational lawyering, cultural humility, and restorative ethics. Programs like those at the Cardozo School of Law's Kukin Program for Conflict Resolution, or Pepperdine's Straus Institute, or CUNY Law's Mediation Clinic offer a new generation of legal professionals the tools to listen deeper, re-humanize, and expect more of their future advocating, adjudicating, and legislating colleagues.

One example of utilizing court reform to enhance peacemaking is a movement to develop and accept joint petitions to initiate a family law proceeding. Rather than labeling spouses and parents as Petitioner/Plaintiff and Respondent/Defendant (which label is less pejorative?), some states invite divorcing parties to submit one shared petition (unless an adversarial contest develops down the road—which is quite a low percentage of all filings).

Following the lead of Massachusetts and Wisconsin, each featuring different types of joint petitions, in California, the governor signed into law a new family code (section 2342.5) on January 1, 2025, and the forms/rules will go into effect on January 1, 2026.[1] Led by Jeffrey Jacobson and Jennifer Winestone, this new process creates the option of a joint petition where spouses who are committed to resolving their divorce without judicial intervention can begin the process in a manner consistent with that goal. They do not need to take legal positions (which they often do not understand) at the outset of the matter. They can begin a process on equal footing without the labels of "petitioner" and "respondent." They can both concurrently appear in a matter upon filing a joint petition without getting unexpectedly served. In other

1. *See* Appendix for related materials.

words, the joint petition offers a streamlined process for spouses to begin a divorce on equal footing and facilitate the ultimate goal of a negotiated agreement in order to get closure.

The new Uncontested Joint Divorce process in New York—where spouses collaboratively complete and file for divorce—marks a notable shift toward a more cooperative model, yet it still retains some traditional legal structures.[2] From a peacemaking perspective, the process offers clear benefits: It allows both spouses to initiate the divorce together, avoiding the adversarial posturing that typically comes with assigning blame or litigating terms. This joint approach promotes mutual respect, lowers emotional and financial costs, and can ease the transition for families, especially when children are involved. However, despite the collaborative intent, the template paperwork still retains the option of assigning one spouse as the "plaintiff" and the other as the "defendant"—a legal convention that subtly reinforces a binary dynamic even when the filing is entirely mutual. For peacemakers, this creates a tension; while the overall process supports shared decision-making, the persistence of adversarial labels may evoke old patterns of conflict or inequality. Ultimately, while the reform is a step in the right direction—toward more respectful, self-determined divorces—it's not fully divorced from the system's adversarial roots. But that is the beauty of peacemaking—there is always something to work on. Baby steps.

The various joint petition processes typically continue to provide the same protections for spouses as currently exist through the mandatory process to begin a divorce. The automatic temporary restraining orders will apply in a joint petition process. Spouses can even propound formal discovery while in a joint petition process. If either spouse elects to seek judicial intervention (e.g., filing a request for order or request for trial setting), there is an easy off ramp at any time through the filing of an amended petition or amended response, after which the matter will proceed like any litigated divorce. In California, the automatic temporary restraining orders remain in effect, and the six-month jurisdictional clock continues from the date on which the joint petition was filed.[3]

None of this is easy. Systemic change is slow, and resistance is real. But the shift from adjudication to accompaniment, from verdicts to voice, is quietly and steadily reshaping the very bones of family law. To root justice in healing is to change the legal imagination itself.

---

2. *See* Appendix for related materials.

3. *See* Letter from Jeffrey Jacobson to California Senate Judiciary Committee (Mar. 24, 2024). Jeff Jacobson and Jennifer Winestone are full-time peacemakers who have used the insight and experience of helping families achieve peace within their families to help all families in California benefit from their commitment to peacemaking.

Social Responsibility: Law as Love in Action

The peacemaker's work flows from a profound sense of social duty. You know that your service is not just a profession—not even just a personal calling—it is a promise. A promise that no matter who the client might be, that person will be treated with fairness, respect, and humanity.

Peacemakers do not accept the systemic ways in which these promises are often broken for members of the LGBTQ+ community, for immigrants, for people of color, for people living in poverty, for people with disabilities, for members of religious communities, and for so many others. Peacemakers push back, not just in court or outside of court, but in every aspect of how they structure their practices, speak in public, and mentor the next generation. They create sliding-scale clinics. They design materials in multiple languages. They meet clients in synagogues, in community centers, on Zoom calls from rural kitchens. They listen deeply—not just for facts, but for fears, for hopes, for dreams. And they act.

This is law as love in action. And when done right, it does more than resolve conflict—it heals communities and rebuilds faith in justice as a shared human project.

Justice with a Human Face

You, as a family peacemaker, are not a passive observer or distant reformer watching from the sidelines. You are an architect of a movement that challenges the very foundations of how we define and experience justice. Each peacemaker understands that justice is not a one-size-fits-all decree handed down from on high, but rather something that is co-created—a process built through relationships, trust, and a shared sense of humanity.

Your decision to become a peacemaking lawyer is a decision to reclaim the heart of justice—to re-humanize a system that has too often turned the intimate, messy, and beautiful complexity of families into impersonal files and abstract processes. Your work, rooted in empathy, furthers the understanding that real justice is not something that can be imposed from the outside, but something that must emerge from within.

As our communities become more diverse, our challenges more complex, and our institutions more fragile, the work of family peacemakers becomes ever more urgent, vital, and indispensable. We are navigating a landscape of cultural multiplicity, where traditional legal frameworks may fail to truly meet the needs of all. We are confronting systemic failures with a profound commitment to change, understanding that the rules of engagement are never as simple as right and wrong, black and white. In this context, our role is to fundamentally reshape how we imagine justice itself—to redefine justice as something collaborative, restorative, and inherently human.

In every quiet mediation room where children's futures are decided not by a court but by the parents themselves, you are creating something far greater than a legal agreement. In every child-centered parenting plan that takes into account not just schedules but emotional and developmental needs, you are helping families rebuild what was once broken. In every tearful, yet healing conversation that you facilitate, you are offering something beyond words: a chance for families to be heard, to express pain, and to share hope.

Resolution is not the end of our work. It is the beginning. We are weaving something far beyond individual cases—we are weaving hope. Hope that families can be restructured peacefully, that children can grow up in homes where love, not fear, is the foundation. Hope that communities can be healed, not through the weight of laws, but through the strength of shared understanding and mutual care. Hope that the law can be something that serves people, not the other way around.

In the quiet moments of our peacemaking work, we, together with you, are making a lasting impact, one family, one conversation, one act of care at a time. Our collective efforts ripple out into the broader fabric of society, creating the conditions for true peace, equity, and justice to flourish. We are nurturing the possibility of transformation within individuals, within families, and within the institutions that serve them. We serve to remind our world that justice is not a transaction, but a relationship built on understanding, care, and a shared commitment to everyone's right to thrive.

Chapter 11
Commitment to Peacemaking

Peace is not something you wish for; it's something you make, something you do, something you are, and something you give away.
—John Lennon

A Summit Reflection: Inhaling the Journey

We arrive now at the summit of our shared odyssey.

We are now at our last chapter of our effort to share our passion for peacemaking. Throughout this book, we have leaned on our colleagues in the field for their brilliance and insight. Here, we would like to leave you with our own thoughts, dreams, and heart messages.

In our opening pages, we stepped into the calling of the Family Lawyer as Peacemaker, recognizing law not merely as an adversarial mechanism but as a vessel for healing and forward movement—supported by history, by culture, and by the enduring rhythms of the human condition—well outside the contours of traditional family lawyering. We challenged assumptions and began the slow turning—an inward and outward shift from the reactive terrain of adversarial negotiation and litigation into the proactive, transformative field of peacemaking. We affirmed what once felt radical: that lawyers—especially family lawyers—*can* be open agents for peace.

We explored how to maximize help by sharpening the quiet tools: listening, empathy, presence, discernment. We built toward a more human-centered model of service. Along the way, we added offerings to our practices, tools to our toolboxes, and widened our vision to embrace the full arc of the family life cycle.

We stepped into the delicate and hopeful terrain of collaborative and mediated prenups, postnups, and preventive peacemaking—learning how proactive legal planning with a peace paradigm can foster not fear, but clarity, security, and care. We discovered it is, in fact, possible to build strong and durable bridges before conflict arrives.

We leaned fully into the humanity of this role, seeing the lawyer not only as advocate but as compassionate healer—a steady companion through seasons of grief, fear, and transition. We considered the role of the bench, discovering how judges and court personnel, too, can serve as facilitators of peace when they step into their roles not simply as arbiters but as guardians of family well-being.[1]

And we faced the most urgent moral imperative: access to justice. We came to see that peacemaking cannot remain a privilege. It must be made accessible; equitably imagined; and courageously extended across class, language, geography, and circumstance.

From these chapters—these vistas and valleys, roaring oceans and still waters—we emerge.

And we breathe.

What opens now is not conclusion, but covenant.

Not a final word, but your first vow in your peacemaking lawyering journey.

The Peacemaker's Pledge: A Vow Made Sacred

At the heart of this chapter lies a pledge—a personal and professional commitment of enduring weight. Originally crafted by Professor Louis M. Brown[2] and later refined by Woody Mosten, the Peacemaker's Pledge stands not as a slogan but as an ethical and spiritual commitment, inviting us to realign our role as lawyers into a higher calling. It asks us to bring our best selves—trained, tested, and tender—into the room where resolution happens. Not as warriors. As witnesses. As weavers.

---

1. Brady Johnson, *Justice in a Circle: How a Peacemaking Court Works*, JUDGING (NAT'L JUDICIAL COLLEGE) (Nov. 20, 2016), https://www.judges.org/news-and-info/justice-in-a-circle/ (describing peacemaking protocols in tribal courts, including round-table seating, de-robes judges, opening rituals, and consensus building to foster healing).

2. LOUIS D. BROWN PEACE INSTITUTE, PLEDGE FOR PEACE, https://ldbpeaceinstitute.org/pledgeforpeace/ (last visited July 2025) (on file with author) ("[T]he Seven Principles of Peace: Love, Unity, Faith, Hope, Courage, Justice and Forgiveness."); *id.* (noting that its curriculum and programs "instill[] the value of peace" by encouraging individuals to "practice love . . . foster unity . . . uphold faith . . . embrace hope . . . be courageous . . . persist for a more just world . . . give and receive forgiveness"); Professor Louis M. Brown (1909–1996), "father of preventive law," quietly shaped mediation and conflict-resolution, culminating in his 1990s Peacemaker's Pledge. *See* Forrest Mosten, *The Peacemaker Pledge,* MEDIATE.COM (Feb. 4, 1025), https://mediate.com/the-peacemaker-pledge (recounting Prof. Brown's collaboration with Rabbi Jeffrey Marx and framing it as a "Pursuer of Peace" or *rodef shalom*).

A version of the Peacemaker's Pledge reads:

I will think about peace—why peace is important and how it works.

I will bring my peacemaking efforts to resolve and prevent conflict:

- *In my legal office—with colleagues and staff*
- *With clients, their families, friends, and allied professionals*
- *In mediation, collaborative practice, and preventive peacemaking*
- *In my community and profession, striving to share peace more broadly*

This is a personal commitment to be a peacemaker for the next twelve months. I will date and sign a written pledge, seal it, and revisit it in twelve months to assess, renew, or recommit.

__________________________ ______________________

Signature *Date*

This is your invitation now. To sign this page and commit to the spirit of this work. Not simply as a professional aspiration, but as a sacred discipline. There is no certification required. Only sincerity.

The Seven Principles of the Peaceful Lawyer: Living the Legacy

Peace, like law, requires a framework. And so, we look to the *Seven Principles of Peace*—Love, Unity, Faith, Hope, Courage, Justice, Forgiveness—and see in them a mirrored ethic for the family lawyer. These are not virtues reserved for saints or philosophers. They are daily practices, quietly transformative for lawyers committed to helping people during their difficult days.

To practice *love* in law is to choose empathy where judgment might be easier. It is to pause in the intake meeting and see not a "case," but a complex human being—scared, angry, overwhelmed—and to offer steadiness without sacrificing clarity. In our firms, love can be shown in how we treat staff, how we listen to disagreement, and how we hold space for the inner lives of our colleagues.

Unity comes in how we assemble teams, and how we treat the other side—not as opponents but as fellow travelers. Unity invites us to open dialogue at the start of a case with opposing counsel, to name a shared intention: "Let's help this family land safely." That changes the air.

To live by *faith* is to trust the process of peace itself. We believe, even amid high-conflict emotion, and in a volatile and disappointing world, that resolution is possible. We believe in the capacity of our clients to choose growth, to co-parent with dignity, to reimagine their futures. Even when they do not yet believe it themselves, we hold the light for them.

Hope is not naïveté. Hope is strategy. Hope is designing services that acknowledge trauma and skill-build emotional literacy. Hope is creating client pathways that begin not with litigation but with visioning, goal setting, and coaching. Hope is the architect of resilience. Often in the mediation room, the mediator is the beacon of hope for those who do not know the next step.

Then there is *courage*. It takes courage to leave the comfort of default legal models and say, "What if we did this differently?" It takes courage to bring up reconciliation to clients who feel scorched. It takes courage to tell a client the truth about the cost—emotional, financial, generational—of war.

Justice, our long-held north star, remains. But we widen its definition well beyond the courtroom or negotiation. Justice is ensuring a parenting plan is trauma informed. Justice is translating documents for nonnative speakers. Justice is helping two ex-partners share a child's birthday in the same room with grace.

And finally, *forgiveness*. In clients, it may take the form of letting go of betrayals in service of a child's future. In ourselves, forgiveness may mean accepting when we didn't get it all right—when we could have listened longer, reacted softer, or stayed more curious.

Together, these principles create the heartbeat of the peacemaker.

A Poetic Invocation—Litany for the Legal Healer

May the words you draft be more than legalese—
may they be seeds of healing.

May every conference room become a place of transformation.

May every parent—wounded, fearful, still loving—
see, in your presence, a path beyond "win/lose."

May each child breathe more freely when peace is the frame.

May the hush after agreement be louder than any courtroom applause.

Let this be your prayer. A silent one, if needed. Whispered before entering a mediation. Murmured before writing an affidavit. This invocation is not for others to hear—it is for your own soul to remember.

The law is sacred when spoken from the heart. When practiced with presence, it has the power to heal. When married to courage, it can restore. When held in the hands of a peacemaker, it can become the poetry that provide comfort and insight to our clients.

A Visionary Commitment: Peace in Motion

There is a difference between believing in peace and building it. Belief, though vital, lives in the realm of abstract ideas. Building lives in the world—imperfect, messy, unpredictable. And yet this is the great invitation: to become not merely believers in peace, but artisans of it. To make peace not an intention, but a practice.

The Peacemaker's Pledge is not an abstract document. It is a mirror. By writing it in your own hand, by dating it, sealing it, and placing it somewhere sacred (your desk drawer, a client file, the inside of a family law statute book) you begin the practice of remembering. When you revisit it one year later, not to measure perfection, but to trace growth, you will find that even the small steps mattered. Saying no to a litigated escalation. Saying yes to a new collaborative partner. Listening longer than is strictly necessary. Taking a breath before an email reply. These are not dramatic moments. They are revolutionary, nonetheless.

That inward movement can become outward transformation for those who trust us. Every practice has a culture, whether intended or accidental. Peacemaking begins to shape that culture at its roots. In some offices, the culture is set by billing goals or firm hierarchy; in ours, it can be set by the quality of presence. Begin with the small things. Invite your team—paralegals, assistants, receptionists, fellow lawyers—to explore what peace might look like in the way you greet each other, in the tone of your communications, in how you handle pressure. Staff meetings can begin with one-minute pauses or check-ins. A weekly story of grace from the field. A roundtable where even the most junior voice is heard without interruption. These rituals may seem minor, but over time they fertilize the soil in which all grows.

Clients feel this change. They may not have words for it, but we believe that they feel it. And this client feeling gives rise to the next commitment: to consciously expand what you offer. If the only tools you hold are adversarial, then every client might wander into a war. But if you offer useful and tested alternatives—guided consults, pathways to mediation, collaborative frameworks, emotional coaching, holistic planning—then clients walk into that possibility. Imagine a client coming to you not only for legal advice but also for a co-created parenting vision. Imagine a couple exploring a prenuptial agreement not as a fearful shield for a marriage that might fray but as a tool for relational health and future clarity . . . to make a stronger more enduring marriage. Imagine offering couples a road map for respectful separation to restructure their family, one that centers children, preserves emotional dignity, and respects cultural context.[3]

---

3. Laurie Israel, *Is Mediating Prenups a Form of Marital Mediation?*, MEDIATE.COM (Sept. 19, 2014), https://mediate.com/is-mediating-prenups-a-form-of-marital-mediation

This work is not done alone. It thrives in constellation. Begin gathering partners across disciplines—mental health professionals, financial planners, clergy, elder care consultants, divorce coaches, and community elders. Let your practice be a hub of wisdom, a node in a larger network of care. Peacemaking work is rarely solitary. We are strongest when we see ourselves as part of a family-oriented web.

The courthouse, too, is not beyond transformation. In fact, it hungers for it. We often forget that judges—especially those on the family bench—witness immense emotional pain every day.[4] They carry the weight of broken relationships, frightened children, financial despair. When you walk into a courtroom not just as an advocate for your client but as an emissary of peace, you have an opportunity to be seen as more than an advocate. And when you offer judges a way out of reflexive adversarialism—when you coach a client to settle, or bring a restorative idea to a status hearing, or help create and forge an alternative path—you create ripples that go well beyond your docket.

The stories of transformation are many. In one courthouse, a family lawyer began convening lunchtime "peace circles" with other counsel and a few open-minded judges. What began as quiet conversation turned into a proposal for a local rule allowing peacemaking protocols in custody disputes. In another town, a family lawyer created a volunteer settlement program where trained senior attorneys help self-represented litigants reach agreement without lawyers—saving the court hours and saving the families months of heartache. These innovations don't begin with mandates. They begin with a peacemaking mindset. With showing up differently. With choosing courage over convention.[5]

(describing how prenuptial agreements negotiated through mediation tend to foster generosity, clarity, and relational trust rather than adversarial division); Diana Shepherd, *The Benefits of Prenuptial Agreement Mediation*, FAM. LAW. MAG. (Nov. 5, 2019), https://familylawyermagazine.com/articles/the-benefits-of-prenuptial-agreement-mediation/ (noting that mediated prenups provide a safe environment for less-advantaged spouses to voice concerns and be treated fairly); Teris Deitsch, *Crafting Prenuptial Agreements Using the Collaborative Divorce Model*, ARTEMIS FAM. LAW, https://artemisfamilylaw.com/crafting-prenuptial-agreements-using-the-collaborative-law-model/ (last updated June 7, 2025) (highlighting that collaborative prenups decrease adversarial dynamics, encourage creative, personalized agreements, and preserve relationship dignity).

4. *See* Thomas Trent Lewis, *Helping Families by Maintaining a Strong Well-Funded Family Court That Encourages Consensual Peacemaking: A Judicial Perspective*, 53 FAM. CT. REV. 371, 374–75 (2015) (describing how structured, consensual processes—such as court-ordered counseling and alternative mediation—promote child-centered resolutions and reduce adversarial conflict). *See also* Mary Elizabeth Lund, *The Place for Custody Evaluations in Family Peacemaking*, 53 FAM. CT. REV. 407, 409–10 (2015) (arguing that well-designed custody evaluations can encourage settlement, reduce children's exposure to conflict, and support therapeutic jurisprudence goals).

5. *See* Johnson, *supra* note 1 (detailing how peacemaking courts—often in tribal jurisdictions—employ round tables, non-robed facilitators, and ritual openings to foster consensus and community healing).

But even the most beautiful practice vision is hollow if it is not available to most. Access to justice should also mean access to peacemaking. So we must ask: Who is being left out? Who is not aware of the benefits of mediation or cannot afford to pay full fees for it? Who cannot attend during work hours? Who lacks transportation to the courthouse or language support to understand the impact of what is going on? In one firm, the answer might come in a new offering: Saturday peace clinics staffed by rotating volunteers, with sessions in Spanish, Korean, and Arabic, and Sunday peace clinics staffed by rotating volunteers, with sessions in Hebrew and Yiddish. Another peacemaking lawyer may begin providing low-cost or free "peace consults" via phone for parents in conflict, drawing on a simple question script rooted in shared values and child-centered care. In both cases, justice would no longer be aspirational. It would be operational—a family change agent.

As you move through these commitments—from inner pledge to team culture, from client service to community presence, from advocacy to access—you begin to notice something: Your work feels different. Less draining. More grounded. You begin to remember why you came to law in the first place.

Stories from the Field: The Practice of Peace in Motion

Stories ground theory in the soil of real life. In every peacemaking practice, there are stories—some dramatic, some quietly luminous—that remind us of what's possible.

There will be Maria and Paolo, a young couple on the brink of marriage, both carrying scars from their parents' divorces. When they approach you about a prenuptial agreement, they will be hesitant. They will have heard that prenups are cold, transactional, a hedge against betrayal—a plan for divorce. But you can offer them something different: a process grounded in curiosity, mutuality, and clarity. Over several meetings, with a therapist present as a communication coach and a financial professional to help them understand and plan, they will co-create not only an agreement but a set of relational values to improve their marriage. Their contract will do more than just outline assets—it will map their vision of partnership, their hopes for children, their plan for navigating hard seasons. Years later, they might write to you: not because they need to enforce the agreement, but because the process itself will have deepened their trust.

Then there will be Lila and DeShawn, siblings locked in a brutal fight over their late mother's estate. Their dispute will be about more than just property—it will be about decades of resentment, miscommunication, and grief. In traditional litigation, their relationship might shatter completely. But with peacemaking, they will be given a chance to speak for themselves and truly see each other—not just as parties, but as siblings. With your careful facilitation, each will be able to express what the house, the belongings, the photos mean. What will emerge will be more than just an agreement to divide up "stuff"; it will be an agreement to co-host a family memorial that neither would have been able to plan alone.

There will be Judge Eliana, a seasoned jurist presiding over family court in a busy metropolitan district. After observing your use of a "values conversation" at the beginning of a high-conflict custody hearing, she might call you into chambers and ask you to explain what she had seen. You might share the framework, the guiding questions, the intention behind it. Months later, she may launch an initiative within the court to pilot "peace protocols"—voluntary, pre-motion settlement sessions using peacemaking language, facilitated by trained attorneys. She might later call it one of the most meaningful innovations of her judicial career.

These stories will not be miracles. They will simply be what happens when you shift the lens from winning to healing, from adversarial to restorative, from fear to dignity. They will be reminders that transformation was always possible.

The Ethical Horizon: From Profit to Purpose

To be a lawyer is to live within a dense forest of obligations—ethical rules, fiduciary duties, codes of conduct. But peacemaking invites us to look beyond compliance and into conscience. It asks: What kind of service do we offer, and what kind of world does that service create?

The answer lies in the stories we choose to tell ourselves about our role. The traditional legal narrative exalts the lawyer as defender, strategist, tactician. And rightly so—we are trained to guard our client's interests. But in family law, the stakes are more intimate . . . beyond protection, the wounds are more personal, and the costs of combat more destructive and enduring. When a family lawyer shifts from adversary to ally, from technician to listener, a quiet ethical evolution begins to unfold. This evolution doesn't replace the old role—it transcends it.

The measure of a peacemaking practice is not found in hours billed or battles won. It is found in the sighs of relief, the softening of voices, the eye contact that returns after months of estrangement. It is found in the way a child's name is spoken gently during a mediation, or in the way a client says, "Thank you for helping me see a way forward."

Our financial sustainability matters. But peacemakers can expand the ledger. They begin tracking other metrics: the number of cases that de-escalated without litigation; the number of clients who co-parented better than they expected, and for longer (even when new partners enter the family photo); the number of agreements that are crafted and upheld by the parties themselves, not just legally but relationally. We can notice that staff turnover drops, that team morale rises, that clients become sources of not just income but inspiration.

This is legacy work. It is not only about the reputation we build or the referrals we receive, but about the imprint you leave on families, on systems, and on your own soul. In ten or 20 years, what will your practice have cultivated? A resumé, or a refuge? A reputation, or a movement? One of our co-authors will be 79 when this book is released, with his timesheets covering over 54 years. Even though his trunk is covered with the rungs of a full career, he still cannot wait to get up in the morning to bring peace to his clients.

To choose peacemaking is to choose to be remembered not only as a legal expert but as someone who changed the tone of the room. As someone who made it safer for others to speak, to cry, to hope.

Closing Affirmation: A Benediction of Peace

And so now we arrive—not at the end, but at a threshold. A liminal moment. A quiet hush before the next beginning.

Let the Peacemaker's Pledge be more than a token. Let it be a practice. Place it where your eyes land each morning. Let its words be your touchstone when a client's fear rises, when a colleague lashes out, when a judge questions your method. Come back to it when you are tired. Come back when you feel proud. Come back when you wonder if it's working. It is.

Let these words guide you—not just today but every day you stand in a room where tension threatens to overtake truth.

I commit to be more than advocate—I commit to be Peacemaker.

I pledge love within conflict, unity across disagreement, courage toward fair solutions, and hope beyond despair.

With justice as my compass and forgiveness as my pathway, I will serve clients, families, and communities in the highest calling: peace.

These are not small promises. They are vows that echo beyond the file folder, beyond the courtroom steps, beyond even your client's final goodbye. They are the quiet revolution by which the family law profession heals itself.

The world may not yet understand what you do. Many may still associate family lawyers with strife, with scorched-earth battles, with drawn-out custody wars. But you know better. You are building something different. Every peaceful prenup, every collaborative divorce, every mediated elder care plan, every circle process—each one sends a signal that peace is possible.

The work is not easy. But it is sacred.

You will stumble. You will doubt. You will lose your footing at times. But you will also help someone sleep again. You will help a child live with fewer scars. You will help parents stop seeing each other as enemies. You will help people live the rest of their lives with more dignity than they imagined.

And in the quiet hours, you will feel it: the hum of integrity, the glow of purpose, the fierce, soft knowing that you have chosen a higher road.

Invitation to the Journey Ahead

Hold this book in your hands. Let its weight be a reminder: Peace has substance. Peace has presence. You carry that now, and it carries you.

This book does not end here. It continues every time you walk into a mediation with calm resolve. Every time you invite your team into a deeper way of working. Every time you decline to escalate. Every time you remind a frightened parent, "You are not alone. We can do this differently."

You may be one person. But the peacemaker's work is exponential. Your one act of dignity ripples across households, classrooms, courtrooms, generations. Peace doesn't end with an agreement—it begins there.

So go forward with your Pledge. Say it aloud. Say it silently. Say it with your work. And when you are asked, as you surely will be, "What kind of family lawyer are you?"—may you smile with grounded clarity and say:

"I am a peacemaker."

Abridged Bibliography of Additional Resources

Armstrong, Karen. (2010). *Twelve Steps to a Compassionate Life*. Anchor Books. A study in compassion that can be your guide to be an effective peacemaker.

Bowling, D., and Hoffman, D.A., eds. (2001). *Bringing Peace into the Room: The Personal Qualities of the Mediator*. Jossey–Bass. An anthology of some of the world's greatest peacemakers, including Ken Cloke.

Burnett, N.W. (2005). *Calm in the Face of the Storm: A Guide to Managing Conflict in the Workplace*. New Harbinger Publications. Three-hundred-sixty-five values, one for each day of the year: with meditation and practice idea for each.

Coleman, P.T., and Deutsch, M., eds. (2000). *The Handbook of Conflict Resolution: Theory and Practice* (2d ed.). Jossey–Bass. A resource for a social science approach to peacemaking.

Deutsch, R.M. (2024). "Apologies in Relational Repair." In *The Psychology of Mediation* (Chapter 7). Cambridge University Press. Based on a career of research and careful thinking, this book is foundational for use of apology in your work.

Diamond, L. (2003). *The Peace Book: Healing for the Community Through Spiritual Practices*. Wisdom of the World Press. Covering the dynamics of peace in easy to read bite-sized pieces for you and your clients.

Doherty, W.J., Harris, S.M., and Wilde, J.L. "Discernment Counseling for 'Mixed–Agenda' Couples." *Journal of Marital and Family Therapy*, 40, no. 1 (2014): 18–35. Introduces a structured protocol helping couples on the brink of divorce reach clarity about their next step - as most families in transition have one party leaning into the relationship while the other is leaning out.

Doherty, W.J. (2017). *Helping Couples on the Brink of Divorce: Discernment Counseling for Troubled Relationships*. Center for Healthy Relationships. An expanded guide offering detailed sessions and rationale. Some couples need one last opportunity to save their relationship; Bill Doherty of the University of Minnesota lays out the rationale and protocol for discernment counseling that can lead to further training.

Eddy, B. (2021). *Calming Upset People with EAR: How Statements Showing Empathy, Attention & Respect Can Change Conversations*. High Conflict Institute Press. Provides practical EAR tools for de-escalation in high-conflict scenarios. Both a social worker and lawyer, Bill Eddy is perhaps the most accomplished author and trainer for professionals to work with a high conflict population.

Fahey, J.J., and Armstrong, R., eds. (1992). *A Peace Reader: Essential Readings on War, Justice, Non-Violence, and World Order* (rev. ed.). Paulist Press. An anthology of peace readings to provide a conceptual and academic overview of peace.

Galton, E., and Love, L.P. (2000). *Stories Mediators Tell*. American Bar Association. Pepperdine Dispute Resolution Journal. Mediators go step by step from meeting the clients to possible resolution.

Hoffman, D.A., and Wolman, R.N. (2011). "Mediation as a Spiritual Practice." In *Bringing Peace into the Room: The Personal Qualities of the Mediator*, edited by D. Bowling and D. Hoffman. JosseyBass. Explores how mediation can be pursued mindfully and spiritually.

Lang, M., and Arms, R.A. (2019). "Why Case Consultation Reflective Practice Groups Matter to Mediators." *Dispute Resolution Magazine*. Argues for peer-based reflection to enhance mediator effectiveness and maintain professional competence. A co-trainer with Forrest Mosten, this article provides a guide to learning from colleagues through proving questions rather than didactic advice.

Lang, M., and Taylor, A. (2000). *The Making of a Mediator: Developing Artistry in Practice*. Jossey–Bass. Adapting the groundbreaking work of Donald Schön, every peacemaker should make this book a must read.

Lechman, J., Avery, J., and Coleman, P. (2008). *Pathways to Peace: Building Conflict Resolution Skills in Children*. National Association for Community Mediation. This well-researched book transports scholarly peace literature into helping children cope.

Lucas, A. (2025). "Stages of Healthy Divorce." In *The Divorce Conflict Scale and Well-Being in Separation*. Former president of the International Academy of Conflict Professionals, Anne Lucas shares her lifetime of practice through an interdisciplinary team approach.

Mosten, F., and Hoffman, D.A. (2003). *25 Wild and Crazy Ideas for Breaking Impasse*. Presented at the 12th Annual International Academy of Collaborative Professionals Forum. Co-authored practical innovations for overcoming mediation impasse that are used by both authors in their respective practice work.

Nolan-Haley, J. "Informed Consent in Mediation." *Journal of Law & Mediation Ethics*, 15 no. 4) (2022): 210–225. Discusses essential elements and strategies to ensure participant understanding and voluntary engagement. A pioneering piece on focusing conflict resolution and prevention work onto the clients.

Retsinas, Z., and Zumparo, A. "Comments on Interdisciplinary Teams in Mediation and Child Welfare." *Child & Family Mediation Quarterly*, 7 no. 2 (2023): 56–68. Reflects on collaboration between counselors, lawyers, and social workers in family mediation contexts. This lawyer-therapist team provides best practices for building and monitoring teamwork.

Rosenberg, M.B. (2003). *Nonviolent Communication: A Language of Life* (2d ed.). PuddleDancer Press. Marshall Rosenberg is the Ghandi of peaceful dialogue. This is just one of many important books to form your peacemaking foundation.

Sarat, A., and Felstiner, W. (1995). *Divorce Lawyers and Their Clients: Power and Meaning in the Legal Process*. Oxford University Press. You are permitted behind the mirror to watch what lawyers do and fail to do in working with families restructuring their lives.

Schön, D.A. (1983). *The Reflective Practitioner: How Professionals Think in Action*. Basic Books. Like Rosenberg, Schön from MIT is a giant in this field.

Wright, J.K. (2010). *Lawyers as Peacemakers: Practicing Holistic, Problem-Solving Law*. American Bar Association. One of the early books in peacemaking focusing on a problem-solving approach.

Index